VOICES OF THE SACRED FEMININE

A wonderful book by a wonderful woman, sounding a sacred roar that rises from the rich compendium of voices within – all recovering and transmitting age-old knowledge of the Sacred Feminine – knowledge that has been hidden and denied us for far too long.

Anne Baring, beloved foremother, co-author of *The Myth of the Goddess* and author of *The Dream of the Cosmos: A Quest for the Soul*

Join Wisdom's feast...with this four-part anthology, featuring many entries by women and men covering topics on ritual and healing, archetype and ideal, sacred activism, and social change. *Voices of the Sacred Feminine* is sure to inspire, challenge, and enlighten all who are interested in exploring greater balance, justice and understanding in our world today, from the traditional to the cutting edge. Each contribution may be seen as its own unique 'beat' of the frame drum, including a chapter in memory of the late Layne Redmond's musical legacy, whose story is featured in this volume's final section. Providing a rich banquet for our contemporary times, this volume is highly recommended.

Karen Ralls, PhD, Oxford UK-based historian, and author of *Medieval Mysteries: History, Places and Symbolism; Music and the Otherworld* and *The Templars and the Grail*

This is a vital work to bring the indispensable feminine co-creator into the field of Conscious Evolution.

Barbara Marx Hubbard, author, visionary, Foundation for Conscious Evolution

Voices of the
Sacred Feminine

Conversations to Re-Shape Our World

Karen Tate

To Kate my dear Sister!
Blessings of the Goddess
in all Her forms to you!
I love you & cherish
the treasure you are
Amalya
Dec 2014

Voices of the Sacred Feminine

Conversations to Re-Shape Our World

Edited by Rev. Dr. Karen Tate

CHANGE
MAKERS
BOOKS

Winchester, UK
Washington, USA

First published by Changemakers Books, 2014
Changemakers Books is an imprint of John Hunt Publishing Ltd., Laurel House, Station Approach,
Alresford, Hants, SO24 9JH, UK
office1@jhpbooks.net
www.johnhuntpublishing.com
www.changemakers-books.com

For distributor details and how to order please visit the 'Ordering' section on our website.

ISBN: 978 1 78279 510 0

Design: Lee Nash

Printed and bound in the USA by Edwards Brothers Malloy

We operate a distinctive and ethical publishing philosophy in all
areas of our business, from our global network of authors to
production and worldwide distribution.

CONTENTS

Dedicated to
Metis
The Muses
and
The Cognitive Minority...

Brave, dedicated and tenaciously shifting the paradigm
past that all-important tipping point.

Titles by this author

Goddess Calling: Inspirational Messages and Meditations of Sacred Feminine Liberation Thealogy

Walking an Ancient Path: Rebirthing Goddess on Planet Earth

Sacred Places of Goddess: 108 Destinations

Anthology contributions

Waters of Life

Jesus through Pagan Eyes

Heart of a Woman in Business

The Goddess Guide to Business Bliss

Acknowledgments

My sincere thanks to the folks at WSMB Radio in New Orleans who taught me to love talk radio and to Lillian Cauldwell of Passionate Internet Voices Radio for getting me back in the saddle as host of my own show. Blog Talk Radio deserves kudos for providing an affordable platform that enabled this to happen without big bucks or show sponsorship.

I am über grateful to the hundreds of guests who came on Voices of the Sacred Feminine Radio over a decade, sharing their ideas, wisdom and vision with listeners across the globe. You taught me and my followers so very much and left us inspired, uplifted and hopeful. My fans, you know you are the gas in my tank that kept me going year in and year out. Thank you for your listener loyalty, for your suggestions regarding show ideas, your dedication to your own continued education and your heartfelt messages that warmed my heart and helped me know I was really making a difference each week.

To the contributors of this anthology, you deserve double thanks for your time on-air and for your contribution to this labor of love, this collection of conversations, so we might document in print our many ideas to change the world.

Thanks and acknowledgment goes to Dharma, for expertise and generosity in cover selection, to Gina who keeps my website and archives coordinated, and to Liz who aided in the acquisition phase. Kudos to Flash Silvermoon for sharing her Astroflash, keeping us informed about what the cosmos was cookin' up for us, and to Samantha for her co-creation of *ritual on the radio*. Cindy, your help with social media and patience transcribing radio show interviews was a huge help!

To the John Hunt Publishing staff…Tim, Mollie, John, Maria, Dominic, Catherine, and all the rest, thank you for helping me birth these conversations into the world in print!

And finally, to my husband Roy, you're the best! I so appreciated all those dinners you cooked on show nights, and for your continued encouragement and support. You gave up lots of hours we might have spent together because you knew how important the show was to me and the people it touched!

Foreword
by Rev. Dr. Karen Tate

Sex, religion, power, and politics. In the Bible Belt, the southern and most conservative part of the United States, those were all the topics I was taught nice girls did not talk about, especially at the dinner table. These were the topics of discussion for men. It was more socially acceptable for women to keep their interests geared toward recipes, having babies and keeping the house clean. I can still see that dreaded list of chores Mother put on the refrigerator every week.

My parents lamented not being able to afford the costs to keep me in Catholic school, so off I went to public school, and gradually I managed to stop going to Sunday School. Just as well, because the young Irish priest with his thick Irish brogue who taught the class didn't much like my questions. Books on ancient cultures and faraway places, especially Egypt, filled the waking hours of my early years, but no one I knew shared these interests. Neither did anyone share my questions, and I instinctively knew not to discuss these things, even in whispers. Eventually I forgot the questions – at least for a time.

I went on to do what so many women in New Orleans seemed to care most about: getting married, buying a house and car and getting a job. Only those things never quite managed to satisfy me so I kept searching. I learned to garden and cultivate spider plants. I must have had dozens in all stages of growth. For a time, I loved transplanting the baby spiders in their own little pots before they were clipped from their parent. I learned to do ceramics. I felt I had to equal my mother-in-law's skill and learn to cook tasty meals. Fortunately, I resisted having a baby. Yes, I was childless by choice, but I told inquiring minds I believed I died in childbirth in a past life so becoming a mother was not for me this time around. That extraordinary excuse usually put a prompt end to the discussion. It was pointless explaining I did not feel the attraction most women had for children and I did not want to be valued by the output of my womb. Looking back, I thank my mother for allowing me to be true to myself and not push that "baby" envelope. I truly believe, whether she was conscious of it or not, she would not have had children given a choice. Like many women of her generation, I suspect she was fulfilling her role in society and there was no Roe v. Wade constitutional protection then to help her with an unwanted pregnancy.

Just before marrying my high-school sweetheart, I got a job at WSMB Radio. The station was in the penthouse of the Maison Blanche building in what we called Uptown. Very classy indeed! Maison Blanche was the department store famous for miles around for filling its storefront window with animated holiday decorations for Easter, Thanksgiving and Christmas. As a child, I remember pressing my nose on the glass every holiday, particularly marveling at Santa's Toy Shop, and now as an adult, I was going to work in this very building! I'd been hired as the Public Service Director when the station owner's daughter left her position to have a baby. Imagine my excitement starting this new adventure!

What a change of pace from my previous jobs! No more impersonal cubicles in a formal corporate environment with others breathing down my neck. The station felt casual and relaxed and the work space was more like a large personal home office where we could hear piped-in music and the banter of the radio personalities in the background throughout the day. Free tickets to local events and visiting celebrities were the norm. I enjoyed watching the producers record commercials and every month the Office Manager, Rosalie, would take the girls out to lunch at New Orleans' most famous and award-winning restaurants. In no time, I was learning the business, especially the power of talk radio, and with all the fun and perks, I thought I could easily get used to this!

I remember how receptive visitors to the station were to the media talent. I would see them arrive in the lobby and press their nose against the glass of the control room and watch the stars of WSMB, like Keith Rush, as he regaled the public daily. A popular and recurring guest of Keith's show came on and talked about astrology and horoscopes. Her name was Star Child and she made a point to seek me out and talk to me one day. She asked my birthday and went on to say something I've never forgotten in all these years because of the awkwardness of the conversation. She said she saw I was going to be married twice. Imagine a soon-to-be newlywed hearing that prophecy! She quickly covered the awkward moment by whispering something that felt obviously contrived. Apparently, I shouldn't worry because according to the Laws of the Universe, people who were intimate were considered married, so if my fiancé and I had indulged in any of that before we were legally married, she was sure that was what she was seeing in the stars. Little did I know just how prophetic this job at WSMB Radio would actually be and how it would prepare me for my own show years later!

In time, I left WSMB Radio and went to work at the local Chamber of Commerce and then a major hotel chain. Turns out Star Child was right. Soon I met my second husband, Roy, and when we compared notes, the Universe had been working overtime conspiring to have us meet for years. Apparently Roy and I went to lunch at the same restaurant every Friday. We worked across the street from each other when I was employed at the Chamber of Commerce and we went to gyms in the same shopping center. Finally, at the hotel, our paths crossed, and the rest is history.

We moved to California, where Roy had enjoyed living as a youth for a brief time. I discovered the rich potency of the Sacred Feminine and I never had to fill my time raising spider plants or painting ceramics again. Instead my husband was helping me lead tours to sacred sites of Goddess across five continents and supporting my work as a spiritual and social justice activist for the last thirty years – which circles back to radio.

I've often said to my friends that sometimes I have to be hit between the eyes with a *clue-by-four* before I hear the Universe, or Goddess, calling and lighting my path. I get so busy and sometimes fail to see her lantern shining down an avenue, showing me the way. Radio was no different. I was doing a lot of radio interviews promoting my first two books, *Sacred Places of Goddess: 108 Destinations*, then again with *Walking an Ancient Path: Rebirthing Goddess on Planet Earth*. I kept hearing over and over from show producers I was a natural. I should be the host of my own show. They often offered me my own show, but it wasn't registering. I was not seeing the path I was being shown. I just enjoyed the positive feedback and went on to the next interview or speaking gig – until Lillian Cauldwell at Passionate Internet Voices Radio wouldn't take no for an answer.

I thank Lillian for helping me see Hecate's lantern lighting my way back to radio, otherwise Voices of the Sacred Feminine Radio might never have come to exist. It was the beginning of a solution to a problem so many of us discussed. We wanted to replace patriarchal oppression but there was no clear roadmap. We had no platform or megaphone to share ideas. We had clues from the past and we had new ideas for the future but these new concepts and practices were not yet in the mainstream world. We believed if we could vision it, we could manifest it and Voices of the Sacred Feminine Radio could help with that. The show started there at Passionate Internet Voices Radio with a weekly half-hour show until listeners started saying they wanted more. They did not want such rich topics discussed in a mere 30 minutes, leaving so many interesting and relevant topics unexplored.

The solution was moving Voices of the Sacred Feminine Radio to Blog Talk internet radio where guests and I could really delve deeply into topics. I had to say goodbye and thanks to Lillian, but I knew there was so much to say and had to be said about the

Sacred Feminine as deity, archetype and ideal. After all, I spent the first thirty years of my life unaware of so many issues of sex, religion, power and politics as I lay unactivated and unaware, my authentic self dormant, in that bubble in New Orleans. My life totally changed as I came to understand more about herstory and the world around me, and I wished the same for others. If my eyes could open, I believed others could be shown as well, so I set about doing my small part trying to facilitate that awakening.

Along the way I was named one of the Top Thirteen Most Influential Women in Goddess Spirituality and a Wisdom Keeper of the Goddess Spirituality Movement in *Sagewomen Magazine*, as I wrote about and discussed global and personal issues with a broad spectrum of advocates, visionaries and forward thinkers from a Divine Feminine, right-brain point of view. Some call it the Feminine Consciousness or the shift away from patriarchal values. These are issues that could raise one's consciousness or save the world! It's all the stuff Mom taught me to NEVER discuss at the dinner table – sex, religion, power and politics.

With the logo of a woman reaching out for an apple, a metaphor for Eve reaching for the Tree of Knowledge, my weekly show challenged listeners to fear not and taste the forbidden fruit! To rethink, reclaim and embrace the age-old knowledge that's been denied us for too long. To unlock our intuition and the innate wisdom I call our Sacred Feminine tool kit, and empower ourselves as we learn long-hidden truths from our home altar to the voting booth. I wanted my listeners to understand what denying the feminine face of god, whether the Great She be deity, archetype or ideal, has cost humanity – particularly women! I wanted them to know how the world might change if these ideals were once again a part of our culture and psyches.

Listeners would regularly hear my What's the Buzz segment where I would share with them the bees buzzing 'round in my bonnet, the headlines in the news, at home and across the globe, where Sacred Feminine ideals were either under assault or making progress. Flash Silvermoon, an astrologer, came on from time to time, advising listeners what the cosmos had cooked up for them in the coming month. There was storytelling and poetry. For a time I did ritual on the radio, called Sacred Salons, sometimes with Samantha Sage, for those who had no community and wanted inspirational messages. I hoped to help them develop a spiritual connection with the Sacred Feminine. Somewhat regularly I would remind them of the show's mission statement:

> Adversaries of the Sacred Feminine tried to sweep away awareness and knowledge of her for all time, and with that sweeping away, when the Great She was made to disappear because of the religion of patriarchy and selfish and disconnected men and their war gods, women and their power, their leadership, their spiritual authority was thwarted, repressed, diminished, disrespected and their sexuality became taboo. That's why here on the show we are dedicated to recovering the Great She, whether she be deity, archetype or ideal. Yes, we intend to defy tradition, to taste the forbidden fruit, to be powerful and uppity women and men, to throw off the shackles, look under every rock, behind every locked door, peer into the abyss of the past so we know why things are the way they are. We want to shed light on how beliefs have become turned on their head and so unnatural, and we're going about setting things right. Why? Well, if we want to save ourselves and Mother Earth, our beloved Gaia, then we have no other choice. If we want to live in a world of balance, harmony, wholeness, sanity, equality, fairness and partnership, it is women and our like-minded brothers, armed with ideals of the Sacred Feminine, who will set things back on course.

And I would share a few of the show mottos:

All truth passes through three stages. First, it is ridiculed. Second, it is violently opposed. Third, it is accepted as being self-evident.

– Arthur Schopenhauer, nineteenth-century German philosopher

First they ignore you. Then they laugh at you. Then they fight you. Then you win.

– Mahatma Gandhi, Indian philosopher, non-violent social justice activist

I chose these two mottos because I believe we are currently living through the phases of a paradigm shift these wise men so aptly described. We are in the cognitive minority in this moment of time, just as scientists once were as they tried in vain to have people understand the world was not flat and the Earth revolved around the sun. Eventually we will see that shift in consciousness. We *will* shift the morphic field and that "100th monkey" will make our worldview a reality.

As dozens of listeners turned into hundreds of thousands of downloads over the years, I was filled with hope we were blazing a trail with our pink-handled machetes and clearing a path of understanding as we reclaimed old beliefs and they were being embraced as new again. We were showing how the Sacred Feminine ideals offered hope for a sustainable future, and the acceptance of these ideas was reflected in listener feedback.

Some listeners have called Voices of the Sacred Feminine Radio their lifeline in places where no one dares talk about these subjects. Other listeners say Voices of the Sacred Feminine Radio and my conversations with these wonderful people, some of which are in this book, are changing their lives. Sex, power, religion and politics – we cover it all with no restraints imposed upon us by patriarchy or conservative society. From Vandana Shiva to Noam Chomsky and female orgasms to the sexism and misogyny of Abrahamic religions, to abortion rights and reconciling one's spirituality with their politics, no subject is taboo. Everything needs to be re-evaluated and discussed everywhere, including at the dinner table, by not just men, but by women, too. We have to understand the source of how things have come to be so turned upside down so we can go about setting things right as we strive to achieve partnership and justice for every species inhabiting Gaia.

Yes, for the last nine years, I have encouraged my listeners to be informed, empowered and uppity women and men. I encourage them to challenge what we accept as normal and find the new normal and, in doing so, find their Sacred Roar! After all, when we manage to shift the paradigm we had better be ready to fill the gap with evolutionary change and fresh ideas that work for the most of us. And my wonderful listeners help me to know what I am doing is exactly right for now and the interviews I've enjoyed on Voices of the Sacred Feminine Radio are truly conversations that are helping re-shape the world. I hope you will tune in soon!

Introduction
by Rev. Dr. Karen Tate

We know our mythology shapes our society and culture. If people across the globe revere a male god and sweep the female face of god beneath the sands of time, the result is what we have today – patriarchy, rule of the fathers or a male-dominated society, where divinity is only recognized in the male form. That leaves Goddess, women, Mother Earth and every species on the planet subject to male authority. That authoritarian father archetype and patriarchy has infiltrated every facet of life, with some falsely believing it has been no other way. The worship of a Divine Mother and Daughter, Persephone and Demeter, for thousands of years, is shrugged off with a wave of the hand. Amaterasu of the Shinto people in Japan, Guadalupe in Mexico, White Buffalo Woman of the Native Americans, Kwan Yin in Asia, and all the other faces of Goddess, some as old as 36,000 years old, older than male gods, are ignored or their importance goes unknown to countless humans on the planet and so do their energies, archetypes and ideals. Yet, Goddess Advocates believe the Divine Feminine is the great equalizer, a thealogy of liberation and balance that rights the wrongs of patriarchy and tempers the authoritarian father.

To more fully understand you must know patriarchy stands on four legs of a stool: racism, sexism, environmental and cultural exploitation. The result is an imbalance everywhere we look that manifests as inequality, abuse, poverty, suffering and exploitation from female genital mutilation to income inequality despite women being the majority gender on the planet. In the United States, women are 52% of the population but there is less than 20% female leadership in politics, academia, corporate boardrooms and religious institutions, denying society and culture women's unique and innate abilities and perspectives.

9

Patriarchy is also propped up by religion. As Egyptian feminist Nawal El Saadawi rightly said on Free Speech television, "Patriarchy needs god to justify injustice." If god orders it, or by association authoritarian male dogma demands it, we can justify anything. Patriarchy dominates our bodies and overwhelms our psyches. White male privilege runs amok. Driven by the need for power over or cheap labor, people stop using critical thinking, act against their own best interests, seem devoid of empathy and accept this state of affairs as normal. It is no wonder the moral imperative of our time is the empowerment of women! And fortunately we have courageous leaders, just one of which is former President Jimmy Carter who set an example for this imperative by leaving his church, citing as his reason the sin of sexism that robs women of their potential. It is becoming clear to more and more evolved minds that, until we have equality for all cultures, women and species across the planet, there will be no sustainability and peace.

So how does a society go about changing course or making a correction to beliefs that permeate every level of society from womb to tomb, boardroom to bedroom, from the voting booth to our places of worship?

We start by taking responsibility for our own educations. We find the courage to throw off the shackles imposed on us by family, political parties or the pulpit. The like-minded must ignore wedge issues that divide us, and women must learn to stand in solidarity for the sake of what's at stake. We must counteract the greed, oppression and exploitation that comes along with this imbalance, using our wisdom, scholarship, common sense, intuition, sense of justice and body knowing to find a new way. We must be courageous, creative, and caring. We must remember. We must rethink. We must be willing to recover that which was swept beneath the rug. We must re-vision how society and culture might be re-shaped and only then can we actually manifest it!

In the nine years Voices of the Sacred Feminine Radio aired, and continues to be aired, hundreds of wayshowers and foremothers, men and women, who dedicate their lives to re-visioning our world shared their insight and knowledge with listeners. They all have kernels of truth, seeds that can be sown to help society and culture evolve and grow into a world we and our children all deserve. This book is just a small cross-section of those vital voices helping re-shape our world, presented as essays that reflect our on-air interview or in actual transcript format. I invite you to avail yourself of this wisdom. See if their voices sound like a better way. Tune in to the many other conversations still available in the internet archives of Voices of the Sacred Feminine Radio on Blog Talk Radio. Some interviews can also be accessed from my own website at www.karentate.com.

Recognize our interdependence. Find your Sacred Roar. Become part of the evolution toward a new paradigm shift of caring, sharing, balance, equality and justice. We can each be a beautiful thread in a wondrous tapestry that is a healthy, peaceful and loving humanity! And please, let me hear from you.

Rev. Dr. Karen Tate
ancientcultures@ca.rr.com

Part I

Sacred Feminine
Deity, Archetype and Ideal

Another world is not only possible, she is on her way. On a quiet day,
I can hear her breathing.

– Arundhati Roy

Chapter I

What Is the Sacred Feminine?

by Amy Peck, MA (aka Amalya)

The Sacred Feminine is a paradigm of Universal Motherhood. It is a principle that embraces concepts of the Holy Mother, the Goddesses of ancient mythologies, the angelic realms, the Divine Self within, Mother Earth doctrines and lore of indigenous peoples. It is a spiritual model that weaves concepts of wisdom, compassion and unconditional love, plus other metaphysical, shamanic, pagan and magical practices. And it is a principle that returns the lost knowledge from prehistoric matrifocal societies around the world to contemporary application and appreciation. The Sacred Feminine paradigm restores the balance of the spiritual, cultural, and pragmatic relationship between Feminine/ Masculine, Mother/Father, Women/Men and Earth/Spirit ideals.

The Sacred Feminine is a concept that recognizes that "God" ultimately is neither anthropomorphically male or female but a Divine Essence (Goddessence) beyond form and duality – an essence that is in balance and unification of masculine and feminine principles – a dynamic interdependent "Immanence" that pervades all life. The Asian Yin Yang icon is a good representation of this idea.

However, seeing the divine as an abstract concept of omnipresent consciousness, or immanence, is a challenge for most humans. We all have a basic human need to put the inexplicable into a tangible form in order to explore our relationship to it. Thus we tend to anthropomorphize or attribute human characteristics to the unknowable. In other words, we name and assign form to an abstract concept in order to relate to it at our level of ability. So the Divine Essence or Absolute has become a "Father" God figure that we were taught to visualize, pray to and imagine having a personal relationship with. Unfortunately, seeing the vast, infinite, absolute and indescribable Goddessence only in the form of masculine metaphor and symbol has severely limited our human spiritual potential and greatly hindered our ability to live in peace and balance on this earth.

For the last several thousand years the dominant religious belief systems of our world have been patriarchal which sanctioned societal ethics that elevated God the Father over Mother Earth, and man over woman.

But it hasn't always been this way! It is vital to remember that for eons before patriarchy, throughout the Paleolithic and Neolithic ages of pre "his-story," there were worldwide "Mother/ Female and Earth" honoring societies that lived in a more egalitarian, sustainable and peaceful culture that thrived without war for thousands of years. It is urgent to rediscover and exhume the lost memory of those cultures to inform us and inspire us to construct a more stable foundation for society's future. Remembering these lost matrifocal civilizations authenticates and validates the significance of the Sacred Feminine and the importance of women and female values as we rebuild a healthier global unity.

It is time to balance the masculine and feminine principles within our belief systems, our religious doctrines, our cultural ethos, and within ourselves. To gain this equilibrium, we must shift our focus for a while to the idea of Universal Motherhood – we need to explore the metaphor of the Mother, the symbol of the Goddess and the model of Priestess. We need to bring to light the archaeological evidence of ancient Goddesses and their stories. We need to emphasize "Motherly" love, wisdom, compassion and creativity as well as respect sexuality as natural and sacred. We must empower women and celebrate their contribution to spirituality, culture and society. And we must awaken ourselves, teach our children and educate our men.

Awareness of the Sacred Feminine will aid us to appreciate the feminine nature in women *and* men. Awareness of a Universal Motherhood will help us to respect the earth and Mother Nature. Awareness of the Feminine Principle will help us honor women's bio-physical and emotional passages through life, and to help all people (women particularly) to attain healthy self-esteem. And this awareness will encourage all persons to find inner balance and peace, thereby increasing respect and tolerance of each other – which ultimately will promote greater world harmony.

It is time to honor the Sacred Feminine. "Honoring the Sacred Feminine", in the spiritual sense, means valuing the feminine principle, along with the masculine principle, as equal and fundamental aspects of the Divine. From a planetary level, it means respecting and healing our Mother Earth. From a cultural standpoint, it means revivifying the archetype of the Goddess through entertainment and the arts and using language that gives equal emphasis to the pronouns "she" and "her". In the societal sense, it means re-creating the role of Priestess, and respecting the contribution of women in business, science, art and politics, as well as the home and community. In a religious view, it means offering ceremony and service that reaffirms our connection to the divine, the Goddess, the earth and each other. In the human sense, honoring the Sacred Feminine means especially valuing the innate worth of woman's mind, body and soul, as well as appreciating the "feminine" qualities in the male character.

As the "Hugging" Motherly Saint, Ammachi (Mata Amritanandamayi Devi) declared in her address given at A Global Peace Initiative of Women and Religious and Spiritual Leaders Conference, Palais des Nations, United Nations, Geneva, Switzerland on October 7, 2002:

Women are the power and the very foundation of our existence in the world. When women lose touch with their real selves, the harmony of the world ceases to exist, and destruction sets in. It is therefore crucial that women everywhere make every effort to rediscover their fundamental nature, for only then can we save this world. What today's world really needs is cooperation between men and women, based on a firm sense of unity in the family and society. Wars and conflicts, all the suffering and lack of peace in the present-day world, will certainly lessen to a great extent if women and men begin to cooperate and support each other. Unless harmony is restored between the masculine and the feminine, between men and women, peace will continue to be no more than a distant dream.

Ultimately, what we should advocate is not that a concept of the Goddess replace that of God, but that we hold each spiritual principle with equal reverence. Then in the human dynamics, we can strive not so much to make woman equal in strength to man – but to regard her *strengths* as equal. In so doing, perhaps then our interpersonal and inter-cultural relationships can achieve a healthier balance and unity. It is time to honor the Sacred Feminine – to re*member* and reclaim our *Heri*tage – in order to restore wholeness within our religions, ourselves, our communities, and our earth.

* * *

Defining the Sacred Feminine, like defining "God," is an impossible task. However, to begin to nurture our awareness of this concept, I offer the following collection of ideals, values and attributes that describe "Sacred Feminine" which I have summarized from the comments and writings of many people:

The "Sacred Feminine" paradigm...

- is the nurturing, welcoming, accessible, kind, gentle (yet firm or fierce when necessary), compassionate, accepting, affectionate, forgiving, patient and wise attitude of the Loving Mother Essence.
- affirms and values the "Divine Mother" or Goddess as birthgiver and creatrix – as the aspect that brings life into the world. Regards consciousness and love as the dynamic powers of Life and Creation.
- cherishes nature and all the earth's beings – affirms life and appreciates all its beauty, bounty, diversity and mystery as well as respecting its ferocity. Acknowledges the multi-dimensionality of Being. Sees the human body, and soul or spirit as inherently good and worthy of esteem.
- sees the Divine as the intelligent consciousness and life force essence within all life and immanently accessible within each being, versus the Divine as only an external "God" or "prophet" or only accessible through "chosen" or "ordained" individuals or unchallengeable scriptures.
- fosters peace, moderation, and balance. Promotes respect, acceptance and tolerance of others – "Do unto others as you would have others do unto you" and "Do what you will, but harm no one."
- believes in "Magic" as events (currently scientifically inexplicable) of positive synchronicity, serendipity, "coincidences" to which an individual contributes in the creation of by one's intention through visualization, affirmation and action, and recognizes by intuition.
- encourages a holistic approach to healing of mind, body and spirit and fosters positive self-esteem, inner growth, Self-awareness, Self-realization, and Self-actualization. Values the cultivation of one's inner wisdom, intuition, inner truth, inner divinity.
- is especially respecting, empowering, and encouraging to women (to balance the centuries of suppression of the

feminine nature), yet without elevating one gender over another. And particularly validates and celebrates woman's passages of menarche, menstruation, birth-giving, and menopause.

- values the reclaiming, rediscovering, remembering and restoring of the lost ancient evidences of matrifocal societies and cultures, Goddess archetypes and lore, and the history (herstory) of empowered women – leaders, priestesses, healers, mothers, artists, saints and activists.
- cherishes devotional, creative or artistic expression (dance, drumming, music, poetry, etc.) as a valuable, sacred experience.
- respects egalitarian, partnership and democratic models of community and societal structure, and promotes non-hierarchical, non-authoritative, non-dogmatic style of leadership.
- honors *cycles* of life, nature, of the body and the individual. Respects the process of death as a natural (and sometimes potentially benevolent) cycle of nature and respects an individual's freedom of choice in death.
- respects a woman's freedom of choices in family planning, birth control and birth-giving.
- regards the dark side of nature and human consciousness not as evil but as a manifestation of the "winter" and destructive cycle of nature and thus part of the eternal process of life and learning.
- encourages us to be present in the moment; appreciates inner reflection and meditation.
- encourages us to hold the intention of compassion, love and patience in all actions and thoughts no matter how significant or mundane.
- appreciates the inventing, adapting, and sharing of ceremony and ritual to assist one and another through life's cycles, individual changes, passages and yearly seasons.

- regards sexuality as a natural and intrinsically good and sacred experience between loving, consenting partners whether for pleasure or procreation and values timely and tactful sex education of our youth.
- promotes personal integrity. Encourages us to live life honorably for the experience of the blessing it is now – not for some reward in "heaven" or out of fear of punishment in "hell." And since all life is seen as interconnected, we are also encouraged to be accountable and responsible for our intentions and actions, knowing "What you sow, you reap."
- honors the language of the Heart as well as the reason of the mind.
- recognizes that there is a male and female aspect to each personality and encourages both men and women to cultivate the balance of their own inner masculine and feminine aspects.

About Amy Peck ...

Amy Peck, MA (aka Amalya) is the founder/creatrix of the Goddess Studio in Escondido, near San Diego, California, which celebrated its tenth year in 2013 of offering Sacred Space for the Sacred Feminine. After completing her Masters in Art & Consciousness in 1996 at John F. Kennedy University, Amalya's purpose and passions came into focus, eventually inspiring her to build the Goddess Studio in 2003. The studio is a beautiful, private, dance and "temple" space where she presents and hosts a variety of events, meetups, rituals and retreats for women.

Amalya is a Priestess of the Goddess, a ceremonialist, belly dance instructor and workshop presenter. She is an accomplished artist and photographer, and she creates original photo-digital Goddess art and commissioned, personalized Glorious Goddess Portraits of women. She is also a graphic artist and produces visionary images for books, CD/DVD covers and website pages.

She has produced and facilitated hundreds of ceremonies, classes, performances and events, and has appeared on local TV and internet radio – all with the intent to empower women and mainstream the paradigm of the Sacred Feminine.

Amalya's life mission is to empower women to love and accept themselves, embrace the Sacred Feminine, and live in balance.

Email: AmalyaGoddess@aol.com

Website: http://www.Goddess-Studio.com

Facebook: Goddess Studio Fan Page:

https://www.facebook.com/GoddessStudio

Chapter 2

Lady Liberty: Goddess of Freedom

by Selena Fox

The honoring of the Goddess of Freedom began more than 2,000 years ago among the ancient Romans. They called her *Libertas*, the Latin word for Freedom. Libertas signified freedom of action, freedom from restraint, independence, rights, and related forms of personal and social liberty.

The Roman religion had a large and complex pantheon with a great assortment of Goddesses, Gods, and other sacred forms. Ancient Romans revered and deified certain values, known as Virtues, and Libertas was one of the most important of these. A few of the more than two dozen other private and public Virtues were Hope (*Spes*), Justice (*Justica*), Piety (*Pietas*), and Courage (*Virtus*). According to their religion, Roman citizens were to uphold Virtues in their personal lives as well as in the culture as a whole.

Libertas as a deity usually took the form of a Goddess. A temple to her on the Aventine Hill in Rome was dedicated around 238 BCE. Sometimes she merged with the chief Roman God Jupiter, in the form of Jupiter Libertas, whose feast was celebrated each year on April 13.

Libertas also was closely associated with the Goddess Feronia, and some viewed them as aspects of the same Goddess, including the Roman scholar Varro, a contemporary of Cicero. Feronia is thought to have been originally an ancient agricultural and fire Goddess among the Etruscan and/or Sabine peoples. During the Roman Republic, Feronia's Feast Day was November 13.

Libertas/Feronia were honored in central Italy as the Goddess of freedwomen and freedmen, and She was associated with the granting of freedom to slaves. Part of the passage from slavery into freedom in Roman society involved having the head ritually shaved, being ceremonially tapped by a magistrate with a rod, called a *vindicta*, and then wearing a cap, known as a *pilleus*, to symbolize freed status.

Some of the Roman depictions of Libertas have survived to this day on coins and other artifacts. Libertas usually is pictured as a matron in flowing classical dress. She often is shown holding both the Liberty Pole (*vindicta*) and Liberty Cap (*pilleus*). In some depictions Libertas wears the Liberty Cap or a crown of laurel leaves. Sometimes she carries a spear instead of the Liberty Pole. Sometimes the Goddess of Freedom is shown with a cat at her feet.

Although the Roman empire is no more, the Goddess of Freedom continues to be in the world. Over the centuries and across cultures, she has continued to signify freedom in her appearances in paintings, sculptures, songs, stories, poems, and other literature. In recent centuries, the form the Goddess of Freedom has taken most often is that of Lady Liberty.

Libertas as Lady Liberty began emerging in America during the colonial era as part of the American quest for political independence from Britain. American patriot Paul Revere may have been the first to depict Lady Liberty in that context. In 1766, on the obelisk he created in celebration of the repeal of the Stamp Act, he used the image of Liberty with a Liberty Pole surmounted by a Liberty Cap. Another patriot leader, Thomas Paine, included her in his song/poem, the "Liberty Tree," referring to her as "The Goddess of Liberty."

Freedom Goddess depictions not only emerged in America during its Revolution, but a few years later in France during its own Revolution, with the female symbol of the French Republic, the Marianne, depicted wearing the Liberty Cap, and often accompanied by Liberty's cat.

As the United States of America developed as an independent

nation, Lady Liberty became part of the official symbology of some of its newly formed states. Holding her Liberty Cap atop the Liberty Pole, Lady Liberty appears along with the Goddess of Justice on the New York state flag. On the obverse of the Great Seal of the Commonwealth of Virginia, created in 1776, Liberty holds the Liberty Cap atop a pole in her right hand and She is flanked on her left side by the Roman Goddess of Eternity (Aeternitas) and on her right by the Goddess of Fruitfulness (Ceres). In addition, the Goddess Liberty, also with a Liberty Pole and Cap, appears with Ceres on the front of the Great Seal of New Jersey, adopted in 1777.

As more states were formed in the USA in the 19th and 20th centuries, some of them also chose to include Liberty imagery as part of their iconography. In addition, Lady Liberty images appeared on coins, paintings, stamps, and in sculptures throughout the land.

Atop the US Capitol building in Washington, DC is the Statue of Freedom, a colossal bronze Americanized form of Libertas created by American sculptor Thomas Crawford. It was commissioned in 1855 and was placed on top of the dome in 1863. In 1993, the statue was removed for several months as it was refurbished and then returned to the top of the Capitol with much fanfare. The full-size plaster model used in creating the statue is now the centerpiece of Emancipation Hall in the US Capitol Visitor Center, opened in 2008.

It is interesting to note that during America's Civil War era, both sides claimed Liberty and sought to use her images to promote their own causes. Among Abolitionists, Liberty was depicted freeing slaves, while States Rights advocates used her image to signify independence from the "tyranny" of centralized government. Today, Liberty images are used in connection with a wide range of political parties, candidates, and positions on various issues.

The most famous of the American depictions of the Goddess

of Freedom is the Statue of Liberty. This Lady Liberty statue was a gift from France to the United States in honor of America's 100th birthday. Originally called "Liberty Enlightening the World," the Statue of Liberty was designed by French Freemason and sculptor Frederic-Auguste Bartholdi with the assistance of engineer Alexandre Gustave Eiffel.

The head of Lady Liberty's statue wears a crown with solar rays, similar to the crown on the Colossus of Rhodes, a magnificent monument to the Sun God Helios that once stood astride a Greek harbor and was considered one of the seven wonders of the ancient world. The seven rays on Liberty's crown represent the seven continents and seven seas. The torch Liberty holds in her right upstretched hand is the Flame of Freedom, and underneath her feet are broken chains representing overcoming tyranny and enslavement. The tablet Liberty holds in her left hand is inscribed with July 4, the date of the signing of the Declaration of Independence and the birth of the USA as a nation. Her flowing gown is similar in design to depictions of Libertas in ancient Rome.

More than 100,000 people in France contributed money to the creation of the 151 foot (46 meters) high copper-clad Statue of Liberty. In the USA, in a grass-roots effort spearheaded by newspaper magnate Joseph Pulitzer, thousands of Americans contributed money for the creation of the 65 foot high granite pedestal to serve as the statue's base. The statue was completed in Paris in May of 1884 and shipped in pieces to the USA where it was reassembled. Work on pedestal construction began in August 1884 following the laying of the cornerstone by Masons of the Grand Lodge of New York in a traditional Masonic ritual.

The Statue of Liberty was erected on top of her pedestal in New York Harbor on Bedloe Island, which was renamed Liberty Island in her honor seventy years later. Thousands of people attended the dedication ceremony held on October 28, 1886, including Suffragettes, who, while circling the island in a boat, loudly proclaimed through a megaphone their freedom demand that women have the right to vote.

In 1903, a plaque was added to an interior wall of the pedestal containing "The New Colossus," the poem written by Emma Lazarus in 1883 as a tribute to the statue and to immigrants coming to America for freedom. In the twentieth century, in preparation for the 100th birthday of the Statue of Liberty, an extensive renovation project was undertaken from 1984 to 1986. On the weekend of July 4, 1986, a great centennial celebration was held and the newly restored statue was re-opened to visitors.

The Statue of Liberty continues to be one of the most beloved of America's civic shrines. It was declared a national monument in 1924. The United Nations designated it as a World Heritage site in 1984. The Statue of Liberty receives over 5 million visitors each year.

Goddess of Freedom images can be found not only throughout America, but elsewhere in the world. She sometimes makes appearances at political rallies, usually in her iconic Statue of Liberty form. Such was the case in May, 1989, when she gained worldwide attention as she emerged as the Goddess of Democracy in student demonstrations in Beijing, China. Pro-democracy demonstrators fashioned and erected a 33 foot styrofoam and plaster Liberty Goddess statue in Tiananmen Square, and this became a powerful rallying symbol of their quest for freedom. Although, a short time later, tanks moved in and crushed this statue and ended the demonstrations, the quest for democracy and greater freedom has continued within and outside of China since that time.

Images of Lady Liberty now abound in American popular culture. In addition to the variety of Statue of Liberty replicas, postcards, T-shirts, and other souvenirs at tourist shops in New York City and elsewhere, Lady Liberty imagery can be found in movies and on television, on websites and social media, on postage stamps and posters, in books and newspapers, in art museums and theaters, in poems and songs, in cartoons and advertisements, in public squares and private homes, in pageants and costume parties, plus in many other contexts.

Lady Liberty's biggest Feast Day in the USA is Independence Day, July 4. She is honored by some on other occasions as well and often appears on floats in nationally and globally televised parades such as the annual Macy's Thanksgiving Day Parade in New York City and the Rose Parade in Pasadena, California.

To many contemporary Pagans and practitioners of related forms of Nature religion, Lady Liberty is more than a symbol in popular culture and history. She is a powerful and ancient Goddess who can guide, inspire, protect, and comfort. Pagans invoke her in rituals for personal liberation and for social justice in the world. Some Pagans include her image on personal and group altars, and some create and keep Goddess of Freedom shrines.

Because of her ancient Pagan origins, Lady Liberty is an excellent Goddess to work with in support of Pagan religious freedom.

In 1988, I renamed Circle Sanctuary's Pagan religious freedom and civil rights network "the Lady Liberty League" in her honor because of the help she had given us in defeating federal anti-Wiccan legislation (1985) and in winning Circle Sanctuary's zoning battle for the right to use our land for spiritual activities (1988). Those affiliated with the Lady Liberty League invoke her not only in workings on specific cases, but each year as part of our annual meeting, held in June during the Pagan Spirit Gathering.

I have created a variety of Goddess of Freedom rituals and meditations. Here are some of them:

- Personal Liberation Meditation: Call to mind a habit you wish to break or a restrictive situation you seek release from. Imagine it taking the form of a chain binding you.

For a few moments, experience its restrictions and the problems it causes. Then, invoke the Goddess of Liberty to come to your aid. Imagine her wearing a Liberty Cap and carrying a Liberty Pole. Imagine your chains falling away as she touches them with the Liberty Pole. Imagine her placing her Liberty Cap on your head. As you experience yourself wearing her Cap, allow guidance to come to you about specific things you can do in your daily life to break the habit or change the situation and take on healthier behaviors. When this guidance comes to you, imagine the Goddess giving you her Liberty Pole as well. Give thanks to her. Write down the guidance you received and other impressions. Select an action that can help your situation and do it.

- Lady Liberty Feast Day Celebration: Begin the day with a Lady Liberty meditation. Call to mind one of her images and imagine her in that form standing before you. Invoke her by at least one of her names: Liberty, Libertas, Lady Liberty, Goddess of Liberty, and/or Goddess of Freedom. Then name and give thanks for each of the freedoms that you experience in your own life. If you are an American, do your meditation on July 4 and work with her Statue of Liberty form. If you are from another country, select the date and image that you feel is most appropriate.

- Religious Freedom Support Ritual: Do this ritual to send spiritual support to Pagans and others involved in religious freedom cases. Obtain an image of Lady Liberty, such as a sculpture, illustration, or photograph. Set it on a central altar and position the image so that it faces the direction where the person and/or group needing help is located. Place a piece of paper with the names of those needing help before the image. Around this, place and light white votive candles, one in each of the compass points, plus a fifth on top of the paper naming those needing help. Invoke the Liberty Goddess by repeatedly chanting her ancient name, Libertas. Peak the energy and then be silent for a time. Imagine She is in your midst, holding her Flame of Freedom high, and facing in the same direction as her physical representation on the altar. Welcome her and then ask her to guide, protect, and support those in need. Then chant the names of those in need and as you do, imagine Lady Liberty being with them. As the chant peaks, imagine those in need glowing with Lady Liberty's Light and receiving strength, healing, protection, guidance, and support from her and from you and others taking part in the ritual. Then give thanks to Lady Liberty and ask her to continue to work her magic on the situation. Use the Lady Liberty physical representation again in additional rituals or, if you feel it is appropriate, give it to those in need as a reminder of the support they are receiving from Lady Liberty and those who took part in the ritual.

About Selena Fox ...

Selena Fox is a priestess, environmentalist, religious freedom activist, writer, teacher, and psychotherapist. Selena is author of the online guide *Celebrating the Seasons*, the research study *When Goddess Is God*, and other works. She hosts a weekly internet radio show and her writings, chants, rituals, and photographs have been widely published in print and online. Selena has a M.S. in counseling from the University of Wisconsin-Madison and does counseling, readings, and life coaching through telephone consultations with clients from across the USA. Selena travels widely, presenting workshops and facilitating ceremonies on campuses, at conferences, festivals, and other venues. Also known as Rev. Selena Fox, she is senior minister of Circle Sanctuary, a shamanic Wiccan church which has been serving Pagans, Goddess worshippers, and Nature religion practitioners worldwide since 1974. In addition, Selena is founder of Circle Sanctuary Nature Preserve, a 200-acre Nature sanctuary located near Barneveld, Wisconsin, and is director of Circle Cemetery, a national Pagan cemetery which also is one of the first Green cemeteries in the USA. Selena is Executive Director of the Lady Liberty League, a global Pagan civil rights network. In addition, she is active in international interfaith endeavors and does diversity consulting and training for federal and state agencies.

Website: www.selenafox.com

Facebook: www.facebook.com/SelenaFoxUpdates

Twitter: @Selena_Fox

Audio and written resources at:

http://circlepodcasts.org

www.circlesanctuary.org

Chapter 3

Persephone Returns: Worshipping the Divine Mother and Daughter

by Rev. Shirley Ann Ranck, PhD

One of the most exhilarating experiences I can think of is diving under a huge ocean wave which is about to come crashing down on your head. You dive deep into the quieter water. You barely feel the wave go over. You surface, and there you are facing another one. Down you go again, outwitting the powerful monster by going under it, by making use of the quiet depths. This image of diving is often used as a metaphor for exploring the depths of the personal unconscious, the deep longings and the emotional shipwrecks that lie beneath the conscious selves we present to the world. And that journey inward with all its fears and with all its rewarding insights about who I am and what meaning my life may have is seen by many of us today as analogous to the great mythic journeys of the deities and heroes of the past.

But the great mythic journeys were more than personal adventures and they carried more than personal meanings. They involved the acquisition of some treasure or understanding that would be brought home to the community for its well-being. So too with our spiritual journey. Diving is only part of the adventure. We also have to surface, to face the next wave, and eventually to ride one of those waves to shore, bringing with us the hard-won treasures to share with our community.

As a psychologist I was especially interested in the personal spiritual journey which can yield insights that make life meaningful. Like many women I was drawn to the myth of Demeter and her daughter Persephone. The Homeric Hymn to

Demeter, assigned to the seventh century BCE, is a story written to explain the Eleusinian Mysteries, which honored Demeter. The tale became famous as "The Rape of Persephone," who was carried off to the underworld and forced to become the bride of Hades. However, according to classical scholar Charlene Spretnak, there was no mention of rape in the ancient religion of Demeter and her daughter prior to the Olympian version of the myth. Evidence indicates that this twist to the story was not part of the original mythology. In Spretnak's re-telling of the pre-Hellenic version of the myth, Persephone makes her own decision to explore the depths of the underworld and visit the spirits of the dead.[1] She returns each spring to her mother as all of nature celebrates.

It is difficult to describe the intense shock of recognition and anger that I felt as a woman at the moment when I realized that in contrast to Christians, who worship a divine father and son, the pilgrims who made their way to Eleusis for 2,000 or more years worshipped a divine mother and daughter. The medium is indeed the message. All the teachings of love and justice in the world could not erase or make up for the stark and overwhelming absence of the divine female in my Protestant Christian upbringing.

Try to grasp the immensity of the fact that the chief divine actors in this drama were a mother and her daughter. Persephone decides she must leave her mother and embark on her own spiritual journey. This journey has its antecedents in the spiritual quest of the Sumerian Goddess Innana, who also descended to the underworld. Demeter fears for her daughter, grieves at her absence, is angry and forbids new life to grow, but knows that the journey is necessary. Ultimately Persephone returns to her mother, transformed into an adult by her journey, and they rejoice in a new kind of relationship.

In the later patriarchal version of the myth, Persephone is captured and carried off by force; she does not make her own decision, and Demeter is more angry than aggrieved. The daughter is never allowed to grow into her true self, and her relationship with her mother is strained and arbitrary.

As women raised in a patriarchal society we often have terrible problems in our mother–daughter relationships. As tiny children both girls and boys in Western cultures must separate from their mothers and go into what has traditionally been perceived as the world of their fathers – even though most mothers have always worked outside the home. Mothers are still our primary caretakers and in order to separate we reject them. In addition, psychology and sociology often have blamed mothers for every problem imaginable. Both young men and young women are taught to blame and reject their mothers far more than they do their fathers. But women often have an added reason for resenting their mothers: by accepting society's stereo-types of women, some mothers have inadvertently collaborated in the stunting of their daughters' growth. As women we are all daughters, and only by becoming fully adult can we return to our mothers and establish an adult-to-adult relationship.

When adults enter psychotherapy it is often the case that their problems stem from unresolved conflicts with their parents. The first big step in therapy is often the total rejection of a parent, really telling your mother or father off. Not only is it painful for everyone, it is only the first step. At some point a new relationship must come into being, one in which parent and child face each other as adults. Very often we think our problem is with the father because we have rejected mother much earlier in life. But when we dig deeper we may discover that it is our old longing for that rejected mother that needs to be resolved. What has to happen then is that we face that mother, in real life if she's still alive or within ourselves if she's not, and reclaim her love, not as the mother of an infant but as a wise woman we might like to have for a friend. Just as Persephone returned each year to be with her mother Demeter, we need to reclaim the Goddess as a symbol of our earliest religious history, but more importantly as a loving power within ourselves.

Another reason some women may fail to grow up is that only young women are considered desirable or valued in our society. Older women often try to look young because they know they are not wanted if they are old. This attitude was not part of the ancient Goddess religions. These myths and metaphors celebrated not only the Maiden and the Mother but also the Crone or wise old woman who had much to teach.

Let us then begin the journey into our authentic selves, into the energies which will free us from the stereotypes and the hatreds which bind us. From the dark, cold, difficult places on our journey, let us return like Persephone with new insights, new hopes, new life.

About Shirley Ann Ranck ...

Rev. Shirley Ann Ranck, PhD is a Crone of wisdom and power who has touched the lives of many women with her feminist thealogy curriculum and book *Cakes for the Queen of Heaven*. She is an ordained Unitarian Universalist minister and has also been a licensed psychologist in California. The Unitarian Universalist Women's Federation gave her their Ministry to Women Award a few years ago, and in March of 2012, to commemorate Women's History Month, the Harvard Square Library honored her for her curriculum. Her new book *The Grandmother Galaxy* tells the story of her journey into feminist spirituality.

Shirley is now retired and lives in Santa Rosa, California. She has two sons and two daughters, five grandchildren and three great-grandchildren. She loves to fly and celebrated her 80th birthday with a ride in an open-air 1942 Boeing Stearman biplane.

Chapter 4

Kali-Ma: Goddess of Social Justice and Change

by Rev. Sandra Spencer

When I was a child I cannot remember not knowing how to read. I was a voracious reader and consumed everything I looked at, from the cereal box on the breakfast table to the classics insisted upon by my parents. Thanks to the persistent spirit of children, in grade school I was introduced to comics. I reveled in the irony and silliness of *Mad Magazine*, was fascinated by Dick Tracy and Flash Gordon. That is until I discovered Wonder Woman, Paradise Island, her mother Queen Hippolyta and all the other Amazon women warriors. They stood for justice, equality and truth. All commendable aspects of heroes and heroines.

If you pay attention to today's news stories where a woman has acted in a heroic manner, she is called a hero not a heroine. Is this a slip of tongue or editing or a more subtle way of saying that a heroic figure cannot be recognized as female? When women actresses are given awards they are called actors, instead of actresses – why is that? Again is this a subtle way of minimizing women and their skills in their chosen career of acting? Why do women not speak out when their restaurant server, usually a woman, calls them "guys" when she hands them their bill? When women in a group are referred to as "girls" almost no one speaks up. Perhaps it is because we have such complete conditioning that most women do not even notice something demeaning has been said.

It is my opinion that, like so many injustices and inequalities perpetrated on the female population of the earth, this is just one more way to enforce the repressive state of patriarchy we all live in. All my adult life, I've been active with the National Organization for Women, working for many years for reproductive rights and equality, only to see women take one step forward and two steps backward in their efforts. Why? The "good old boy network" in government, religious institutions and private industry unfortunately still persists in the 21st century. We have made inroads in politics but it is still not enough for full acceptance and equality, even in the United States, known throughout the world as an example of freedom and democracy.

I have been called a "Femi-Nazi," a stinking feminist and all sorts of nasty names. "Sticks and stones can break my bones but words will never hurt me." Perhaps you may remember that from your childhood. They are comforting words, but words can actually hurt and can damage the psyche of young forming minds. Possibly this is why so many women seek professional medical help from psychiatrists and psychologists, as they unconsciously resist our culture's insidious ways it demeans women who want and deserve justice, equality and truth.

One half of the world's population, women and children, live in social and economic slavery, controlled by governments and the religious institutions that are revered by so many. This repression has been held in place for tens of thousands of years by entrenched patriarchy.

I do not propose to eliminate patriarchy and replace it with matriarchy which could become as repressive as what it replaces. The fact is we need to recognize and invent a new paradigm, an egalitarian culture, based upon respect and equality, a true balance in all things. We need Wonder Woman as a role model for our children alongside G.I. Joe, so when she uses her "Lasso of Truth" instead of a weapon, they can learn the difference between justice and violence, something that is not clearly defined today.

Along with the comic books I read in secret at school, at home

I was reading the Bhagavad-Gita and the Vedas, discovering the gods and goddesses of the Hindu religion. I was entranced by the myths and grew up wanting to know more. I explored many religions over the years but did not resonate with any of them because women were still treated with less importance than their male counterparts. Depending upon the religion, women continue to be constrained in their life choices, dress and comportment, and until recently women ministers were not easy to find in any church.

In my adult years I discovered the Hindu Goddess, Kali-Ma. She is a triple Goddess that cares for birth, life and rebirth that women look to when they require strength and courage to face the challenges life brings to them. Kali is widely worshipped in India, and every village has their own version of the Goddess and her attributes. Kali has been openly worshipped by men and women for countless thousands of years and survived the centuries when many other gods and goddesses have fallen into obscurity. In fact, the myth of the Age of Kali is that time when women are recognized as equal to men, when the balance of the universe shall be restored, with women returned to the revered status they used to have centuries ago. I believe we are living in the beginning of this age as more of humanity becomes aware of life's injustices and acts to right these wrongs.

Still, there is much work to do. We have hungry, homeless and desperately ill populations of men, women and children all over the world due to careless and incorrect political decisions usually made by men who do not care about the average person. Some people say this is "fate" and cannot be changed. A business deal made on a global basis may make a profit of billions for an elite few while leaving millions of people without shelter or food. Sometimes these decisions close the doors of manufacturing and service industries, leaving hundreds, sometimes thousands, of hard-working men and women out of work, frequently in geographical areas where there is no alternative source of employment at that skill level. Many productive and useful lives are cast aside into the abyss of despair and loss due to greed and the all-consuming desire to attain more wealth. This destructive use of power must end because our world can no longer survive the disruption and destruction that continues every day in the name of profit. We are defiling our earth which is the only home mankind has.

Because of thousands of years of repression, some subtle, some not so subtle, our human race has become seriously out of balance with one half of the population subservient to the other half. Women have been relegated to the back of the bus for many centuries, though we can thank Rosa Parks and others like her for standing up for all women of every culture and color who were so downtrodden we did not even realize we were considered second-class citizens, just because of our gender.

Getting back to Kali, a source of hope to combat the afore-mentioned woes and injustices, she has been found all over the world in many ancient cultures and has been worshipped as a nurturing mother, a benevolent Creatrix and as a Mistress of Time. She is recognized as the cause of all change and development in the universe. In Hindu stories when she is needed to fight evil in any form, she appears and fights alone. If she requires assistance she turns to other females, never to men or gods, for it is the Feminine Aspect of divinity that will always prevail over evil in all forms.

Kali is usually seen with four arms. Her lower right arm bestows boons or gifts, and her upper right arm promises fearlessness and courage. Her upper left hand holds a sword to cut the thread of bondage, and the lower left holds a severed head, indicating the annihilation of ego-bound evil forces such as greed, or lust. Kali-Ma also wears a garland of fifty skulls; this represents the fifty letters of the Sanskrit language that she gave to mankind to facilitate communication, civilization and accumulate knowledge. Some images of Kali show her wearing a girdle of human arms cut off at the elbow; the arms represent the capacity of all work or action because Kali is the source of all energy and power in the Universe.

Kali has called to many women and men over the years to become her devotees and assistants in bringing the universe back into balance, beginning with humanity on this earth. Another often misunderstood aspect of the Goddess Kali shows her manifesting as the "destroyer" to reveal truth and restore balance to our world in the form of the Divine Feminine Spirituality that has been submerged in the chaos that is our world. Her followers understand it is sometimes necessary for something to end or die so that something new and better may take its place. The Goddess movement all over the globe is rapidly growing and promotes love, peace and equal justice for all persons. Some Goddess women and men are strongly encouraging all of us to use eco-friendly products, and to live our lives treading lightly on this earth as we strive to protect endangered land and sea creatures, along with conservation of dwindling resources. Death of the old ways, of greed, waste and destruction, must come to pass so a new way of life might prevail if this world is to survive and have a future.

Like many others hearing the call, it is my intention to continue to work toward the equality that Goddess promises can be found – and I believe it can be found when each of us looks deeply into our hearts and minds and realizes that we are all part of a vast family interconnected by DNA, traditions and a strong belief in the Divine.

We are all a part of each other and until we can begin to realize this our wounds will not completely heal, nor will we become whole. We must find methods and a desire to bring love and compassion to the hearts of everyone on this planet. I pray that we find a way to accomplish this through the endless and compassionate love of the Divine Mother, Goddess of Ten Thousand Names.

About Rev. Sandra Spencer ...

Ms. Spencer has been associated with the National Organization for Women for most of her adult life and been active in her local chapter as an officer, attending regional and national conventions, participating in clinic defense and local political awareness rallies. She was active in Ventura County for many years, assisting with the Clinton, Feinstein and Boxer elections in the early nineties. In earlier years she supported the work of Cesar Chavez in central California.

During a NOW Chapter meeting, one of the other women present invited Ms. Spencer to a Wiccan ritual, celebrating the season of year. During the event Ms. Spencer realized that all of the searching and research she had done regarding various religions had led her to this particular one. She had "come home." She began a course of intensive study with a Los Angeles teacher for five years. In order to become an ordained woman she then began a course of study with an accredited Thealogical Institute.

Ms. Spencer was an ordained Dianic Priestess of the Sacred Veil in 1999, taking the magical name, Sariel. In 2003 she founded the Abbey of Avalon, a Dianic community of Womyn devoted in service to Goddess. Sandra Sariel has served as Abbess to her congregation and the greater Southern California Goddess community for many years. In 2009 a healing ritual was presented for the men and women in the military community as an outreach to show our appreciation for their brave service. In October 2013 she was ordained as High Priestess of the Abbey of Avalon.

Her vision of Goddess Religion being recognized as important for the evolution of a peaceful and loving society has come into being especially in the last twenty years. She has worked as a mentor for many women in the Goddess community and has seen many women recognized for the benefits they have brought to the community and the world.

Each day at the Abbey Motherhouse, prayers are spoken for peace, health, love, healing for the Earth, and a gentle transition for the terminally ill. It is Sandra Sariel's vision that true spirituality will blossom in our hearts if we recognize the Divine Feminine that is within us all. May Goddess continue to bless everyone in Her service.

Chapter 5

Sekhmet: Powerful Woman

by Candace C. Kant, PhD

Sekhmet is a complex and provocative goddess. The one myth most people know about Her is called The Destruction of Humanity and is from the Book of the Heavenly Cow, found on the walls of Egyptian royal tombs from the 19th and 20th dynasties, around 1200–1100 BCE. In this myth humans have rebelled against Ra. Ra sends the Eye, Hathor, against the humans who rebelled against him. The Eye begins slaying the human rebels who had fled to the desert and it was here that Sekhmet came into being. Ra realized that he did want to rule over mankind after all and that Sekhmet will destroy the rest of humanity. He commanded his chief priest to grind red ochre to mix with 7,000 jars of barley beer being brewed by women. On the eve of Sekhmet's planned destruction of humanity, the beer was poured into the fields where she would arrive. She saw Her own reflection in the flooded plains, was delighted, and drank until She was too intoxicated to even recognize humans.[1]

Many people refer to Sekhmet as "going on a drunken rampage," but this is not accurate. She slaughtered humans while perfectly sober and with frightening precision. It was the drunkenness, the intoxication, that saved humankind. Certainly, this is a puzzling lesson. In the twentieth and twenty-first centuries humankind has seen the devastating effects of logic and rationality without humanity, without compassion, in the killing fields of Cambodia, the ovens of the concentration camps, the gulags of the Soviet Union, and the impersonal slaughter by "unmanned" drones. Much of what is evil is committed by people who are convinced they are doing something good.

Perhaps we need that moment of inebriation, of intoxication, to reflect upon our actions and to not take ourselves quite so seriously. I believe that it was the Greeks who said, "The God is in the wine." It is interesting that whenever the gods get into difficulties, they call upon a goddess to bail them out. The story of Durga and Kali is another example of this.

While this is the myth most people know, it certainly does not reflect the nature of Sekhmet completely. A glance at her many names tells us much, much more about her. She has been called "The Lady of Ten Thousand Names," but let me relate just a few of them here. She is "The Great One of Magic," "The Mother of the Gods," "The One Who Was Before the Gods Were," "The Lady of the Place of the Beginning of Time," "The Lady of Enchantments," "The Opener of Ways," "The Great One of Healing," "The Great One of the Place of Appearance of Silence," "The Lady of Jubilation," "Lady of Strong Love," "The Reminder of the Sweetness of Life," "Lady of Radiance," and so many, many more.[2] Her priests in ancient Egypt were physicians, healers. Clearly, this is a multifaceted goddess, and much that the Egyptians loved in her has been hidden from us in the depths of time.

She is reappearing in many unexpected places today and is an active, ongoing presence. She is especially cherished by women although she also has many male devotees. She is an archetype of female strength; her name means "Powerful Woman." She is a mother and, in Egyptian mythology, a wife, but there is nothing submissive or docile about her. When she encounters something out of balance, she fixes it, leaving nothing undone. She sets boundaries, showing how to say no without feeling guilty. She is a healer. She represents empowerment.

Women who are drawn to her receive many gifts from her. I asked several women how working with Sekhmet had empowered them. All of them remarked on the courage, strength, comfort and inspiration they received. According to Dot, "She is

44

with me daily on my new path, giving me velvet paws and purrs when that is needed. When needed she roars and uses her claws to get my attention and spurs me to do what must be done for the higher good. Sekhmet is my Sister, my Mama Cat, and my Fire Goddess." Cathy remarked, "When I first dreamed of her in the early 1980s, she taught me self-confidence, courage and fierce love." Another one reported, "I have dreamed of her, and she is beautiful. She gives me strength and I know that she walks with me always. She is always with me. Her name, Powerful Woman, is inspiring and she encourages me to stand up for what I think is right for all her creatures, two legged, four legged, six legged and eight legged." Jackie added: "I turn to her each and every day to help me deal with the difficult challenges that life sometimes drops on my doorstep. I have found Sekhmet to be a very powerful goddess and I believe how we choose to use those powers shows the true heart of a priestess. Sekhmet has empowered me with the strength and courage to point out injustice when harm has been done. She has given me capabilities to help me see others as they really are, not what they pretend to be, and I have learned not to expect too much."

Working with Sekhmet energy can transform lives. Jessica wrote:

It always comes like a smack upside the head, and Sekhmet was no different. I got smacked, and the way was clear to me. I knew what to say and how to say it. She also gave me the strength to do it, because it was still going to be difficult ... by carrying Sekhmet with me, my empowerment as a woman has become deeper and wider, as with my perceptions. I feel secure in my gender identity, and how I define it, even (or perhaps especially) as it differs from societal norm.

Mia wrote:

I walked into the temple and here was this beautiful black statue of a goddess with a lion's head ... I knelt before Sekhmet, I asked her to kill me. I had nothing but bad decisions and sadness in my life. I didn't want to live anymore. I almost felt like I got slapped in the face that day. I went home, still emotional and a complete mess, took some pills and fell asleep. I awoke feeling different. But the logical me didn't think much of it, that the strength I felt was because maybe I needed the sleep. I look back and I see that Sekhmet really did kill me that day! I left that sorry, weak, woman behind in the temple. I feel Sekhmet's fire burning inside of me; I feel her breath deep in my lungs! I feel her rage inside me whenever I start to feel weak and I feel her with me when all is silent and I'm alone. Sekhmet has ripped me apart and put me back together and has given me gifts I never could imagine!

Perhaps we should re-interpret her myth. In our world, humans have upset the natural order just as the humans in the myth rebelled against Ra. War is an ongoing fact of life. Poverty is endemic to almost all societies to a greater or lesser degree. The climate is warming, the waters are polluted and our land is soaked with deadly chemicals. Commercial agricultural areas have a continual haze in their air, the result of toxic pesticides and fertilizers, and this air is breathed by living beings, while the food that is produced in this way is fed to our children. We are eating genetically modified food with no idea of how that will affect us. Species are being extinguished at an alarming rate. The top soil is disappearing. Human rights are suppressed. Animals are tortured then slaughtered. Women are subjected to rape and what is euphemistically called "domestic violence," a clever way to hide the reality of many women's lives. Women do most of the world's work, yet control only a fraction of the world's wealth. There are so many mass shootings and acts of terrorism that it has become standard fare on our nightly news. The world is out of balance. Our existing leaders seem incapable of even recognizing the problems, much less of solving them. We need a change.

Women must become empowered. First, with Sekhmet energy they must empower themselves, taking charge of their own lives. Then, women must step forward and set things right. But this must be done with care, learning from Sekhmet's story. Sekhmet set out to punish the evildoers, but enjoyed the process so much that she lost sight of her purpose. Like many who have great power, the power went to her head, and she was carried away with it. Roynan Steres captured the tragedy of this in her poem, "Daughter of the Sun," in which she wrote,

> Midnight and you slept, your ropey lion's mane matted with blood and blood-colored beer;
> The smell of death around you ... but your golden heart was already broken.[3]

Balance is necessary. In patriarchal dualistic cultures, qualities highly valued such as logic, aggressiveness, strength, emotional reserve, rationality, independence, and autonomy, have been labeled as masculine. Qualities such as expressiveness, emotionalism, needfulness, humility, compassion, intuition, and nurturing have been labeled as feminine. These are all human qualities, however, neither masculine nor feminine. In righting wrongs, women must not get carried away and destroy what they seek to save. They must keep all things in balance. Logic must be tempered with intuition, aggression with humility, strength with needfulness. The Charge of the Goddess says, "Let there be beauty and strength, power and compassion, honor and humility, mirth and reverence within you." Perhaps a moment of intoxication, of merriment, is needed, for in that moment, when all the walls are down, all the safeguards are gone, and one relaxes, letting all the tension fade away, then the truth appears, the truth that we are not separate and alone, we are all interrelated and what hurts one of us hurts us all. Sekhmet is indeed the archetype for our times.

Sekhmet's Charge

Behold, I am Sekhmet,
The Ancient One,
The One Who Was Before the Gods Were,
The Lady of the Place of the Beginning of Time.
I am older than time itself.

I am the Lady of the Red Garment,
The One who brings Justice
And avenges wrongs.
I am the Keeper of the Light,
Protectress of the Divine Order,
Overcomer of All Enemies,
The One Who Holds Back Darkness.
I am the One Before Whom Evil Trembles.
I am the Great Defender.
I protect my children with the fiery passion of a lioness.
I hear your cries.
None shall harm you.
With my mighty arm I shield and defend you.
I surround you with my love.

When you are hurt,
I heal you.
I am the Great One of Healing,
The Drier of Tears,
And My Love never ends.
I am the Lady of Strong Love.

I am the Lady of Transformations,
The Awakener,
The Guardian of the Gates.
I reveal the Ancient Paths.
I am the Giver of Ecstasies and the Satisfier of Desires.
I Enlighten and I Empower.
I Reduceth to Silence, and I Rouseth the People.
I ask only that you love me,
And when you see injustice,
When you see my daughters and sons oppressed, starved,
    harmed,
When you see my Earth devastated and polluted,
Do not mildly sit back,
But rise with My strength
And return righteousness to the land.

Sa Sekhem Sahu.[4]

About Candace Kant ...

Candace Kant holds Bachelor's and Master's degrees in history from the University of Nevada, Las Vegas, and a PhD in history from Northern Arizona University. She has taught history, women's studies, and religious studies courses at the College of Southern Nevada (CSN) since 1976, including such classes as the History of Witchcraft, Goddess Traditions, Introduction to Modern Paganism, and Modern Pagan Thought, all of which she developed. After thirty-two years of teaching she retired and was awarded the title Emerita. She has developed and taught courses in practical Paganism and Goddess Spirituality at the Temple of Goddess Spirituality dedicated to Sekhmet in Cactus Springs, Nevada, and through the CSN continuing education. A devotee of Sekhmet, she served as a priestess at the Temple of Goddess Spirituality and participated in creating and leading rituals there. With Anne Key she is co-managing editor of Goddess Ink,

Ltd., a new press dedicated to publishing high quality, affordable and accessible scholarly and creative books in the fields of Women's Spirituality and Goddess Studies. She also serves as the Dean of Students for Cherry Hill Seminary, the leading provider of education and practical training in leadership, ministry and personal growth in Pagan and Nature-based spiritualities. She is often asked to speak to local groups on the topic of witchcraft and paganism. Goddess history and spirituality are her specialties.

Chapter 6

Mary Magdalene:
Doorkeeper to Ancestral Intelligence

by Joan Norton

Karen asked me a very good question in our first radio interview on *Voices of the Sacred Feminine*: "What do women get from Mary Magdalene?" It caught me by surprise and I probably didn't answer as well as I could. I'm glad to have another chance to answer it in this book.

Reverence, respect, devotion, veneration, curiosity and love of any goddess are a pathway to the archetypal world of earth and to the expanded realms of consciousness of the cosmos. Loving a goddess leads people to love women and to love the earth. Why walk along the Magdalene path in particular? Everyone knows how corrupt Christianity became almost immediately, with its denial of the bride of Jesus and its denial of the feminine spirit in its story and philosophy.

The first thing women receive by embracing the story of Mary Magdalene is to get our true story back. We get what we were always supposed to have, a goddess who loves a god and who walks the path of love and consciousness without degradation. Through this we know it is possible for a woman to love a man and walk together a path of love and consciousness. Mary the Magdalene together with Jesus the Christ represent the archetypal pattern of conscious partnership that germinates, incubates and gives birth to insight, evolution of awareness, and new life on the physical plane. The pattern of archetypal sacred marriage is constellated in couples of any gender. It's the paradigm of conscious partnership.

Mary Magdalene, as an inner story, represents the feminine

spirit within every human being – male or female. In times of oppression of women and the feminine spirit, it's demonized as "the left-handed path," which is a metaphor for right-brain functioning. Right-brain functioning includes feeling, intuition, symbolic thinking and perception, spatial perception of the physical world, relationship to one's instincts, and an orientation towards "the big picture." And did I mention that it's in our right-brain functioning that we seek and reach for meaning? It's responsible in large part for our individuality, our very own personal style of expressing life. It's very independent; one's imagination doesn't usually copy anyone else's imagination. We're free in our right brain, on our "left-handed path." It's a very important seat of our individuality and our personal freedom. The spiritual truths that come to us via our imagination, our intuition and our feeling are apt to be very idiosyncratic – not the party line of the creeds of franchise religions. It's in our right-brain, left-handed path that a sense of believing comes to us. Religious people often struggle privately to experience a sense of belief in their religion because they are trying to find it via the left brain's logic function. Facts and rules don't create the experience of belief. But talk to someone who's had an inner experience of Mary Magdalene or any other spiritual being and you will be struck by their firmness of belief.

That's what happened to me, of course, and that's why I have trod the path of the Magdalene. I'd already been steeped and experienced in the Jungian traditions of using archetypal goddess-figures to understand the depth and range of the feminine psyche in modern women. I used the Inanna myth to talk with women clients about descent and depression and how to value your time in the underworld and maybe even bring back the treasure of new insight or expanded consciousness. I used the Artemis and Actaeon mythogem to talk about the necessity of guarding one's privacy to do the inner work necessary for growth and transformation. It's a dramatic moment to say that the intruder is turned into a stag and killed by his own dogs. We need to guard our inner space sometimes.

And into this comfortable world of Greek goddesses came Mary Magdalene, saying she wanted to tell me how much she was loved and respected by Jesus. This was a truly challenging paradigm shift for me, but it came from my right-brain perceptions of the inner world so it was undeniable.

My own "left-handed path" was developed through dreamwork with a wise older woman mentor-therapist and from the value she placed on my feeling perceptions. They were null and void when I reached adulthood, as it is for many women and sensitive men. I recovered them slowly, learned to perceive intuitively and began to gain knowledge about the archetypal patterns and buried spirituality that were in my unconscious. A hideous and horrible tragedy was the cause of further development of my intuition and the opening of my third-eye perceptions. My eldest daughter was killed in a car accident and I literally chased her into the other world for years afterwards. In trying to see her, I saw a lot more. I think that's how Mary Magdalene got in. It's not a surprise that it happened this way; it works the same way for some women and men who are abused. I've known a lot of women over the years who were abused in childhood – or their feminine sensibilities denied – who developed remarkable intuitional openings. They were using their intuition to assess the physical danger in their surroundings and they were also finding imaginal pathways out of the bleak experience of being molested or controlled in some way.

Many women healers have told me rather shyly that they perceive a Mary Magdalene figure in their healing rooms as part of their spiritual guidance as they do healing work. These women are never committed to Christianity so it creates a conflict about their spiritual beliefs. Who can blame them, or blame me for feeling confused to have the Christian goddess come knocking at your door? But a commitment to consciousness and a commitment to the right brain's spiritual perception require us to find out more about her if she's become a visitor.

I had my first-hand experience of Mary Magdalene and the respect she wanted to tell me about in 1996 but it was not until 2005 or so that I self-published it as *The Mary Magdalene Within*. Something my younger daughter said at that time led me to believe that young women were now interested in the Magdalene and I thought the time was probably right to make the effort to publish.

Because of my personal inner encounter with her, I began to read Margaret Starbird and some others who are the historians of the story of the lost bride and goddess. Through these works I've developed a firm grasp on why Mary Magdalene belongs to us as our representative of the feminine spirit in the religion of the Western world. I don't like what was done with the Christian story but I think there's more to come when the feminine spirit will be included. I'm an optimist. It's painfully slow going but there are feminist theologians who are trying to put her back in the pulpit. But more importantly, there are more and more and more women outside the churches who put Mary Magdalene firmly upon their altars and say prayers to the "Way of the Heart" that she represents. She is a spiritual pilgrim on the soul's journey through an earthly experience. She loves, she suffers, she grows in spiritual perception, and she shares it with her community.

For women and men of our time Mary Magdalene can be an inner guide, a spiritual figure who opens the doors to ancestral intelligence and cosmic perspective. She represents The Mysteries, the continually opening door to further experience and knowledge of ourselves. In my own visionary experience of her I was shown the stories of the sweep of history from the time she lived physically until now and I was told that she simply wouldn't be a part of that particular 2,000-year span but she would be a part of the one coming. I am personally tired of looking for her in the past. I'm also tired of looking for a mother of god figure. I want partnership. I'm looking for Mary Magdalene in the ways women perceive her now and in the communications they are having with her about our present-day world. We're in the beginning of the Age of Answers and we need every single drop of the heart's wisdom and the expanded consciousness of our minds that we can get to help us design our world anew. And in this new design we will not throw away the bride, the goddess, the heart, and the feminine spirit in whose body we live.

Lately I feel grateful that Mary Magdalene has remained hidden for 2,000 years and that the church corporations have not been able to use her to further their own mind- and heart-numbing plans. We can now claim her as our own inner gateway to a new world.

About Joan Norton ...

Joan Norton, psychotherapist, is the author of *The Mary Magdalene Within* and (with Margaret Starbird) *14 Steps to Awaken the Divine Feminine: Women in the Circle of Mary Magdalene*. Joan has practiced Jungian psychology for 35 years and continues to support individuals in their search for individuality and deep spirituality.

The Mary Magdalene Within is a channeled book "received" in 1996. It established a pathway to the creation of the Los Angeles Magdalene Circles and the collaboration with Margaret Starbird on a template book for other women to start circles of study and integration of Mary Magdalene into their own spiritual stories. Mary Magdalene has become the touchstone for many women to find the lost feminine principle in their own psyches, in their own religious lives and in the major mythologies of the Western world. As an archetypal reality, Mary Magdalene carries the energies and the stories of lover, wife, mother and widow. Through her, we can know ourselves in partnership with the sacred masculine.

Chapter 7

The Virgin Mary and Her Many Faces

Transcript of interview with Charlene Spretnak

Interview:

KT = Karen Tate
CS = Charlene Spretnak

Tonight we have as our guest Charlene Spretnak, and we're going to be discussing the Virgin Mary and the Dark Madonna Guadalupe because her Feast Day is Saturday.

Charlene Spretnak is our Foremother tonight. Just in case you aren't familiar with her work, let me tell you a little bit about all her credentials before we start our chat. Charlene is one of the founding mothers of the women's spirituality movement. Her first book in 1978 was *Lost Goddesses of Early Greece*, which presented the research and reconstructed myths of the pre-Olympian (pre-Zeus) mythology of Greece, which was almost entirely Goddess-centered and had not been told for some 2,500 years. Her anthology, *The Politics of Women's Spirituality* (written 1982), presented a framework for understanding the emerging women's spirituality movement by presenting essays in three areas: Recovering a Lost History, Personal Spiritual Development, and Engaged in Social Change Work.

In the 1980s Charlene wrote two influential books on Green Politics and was a co-founder of the Green Party Movement in the United States. She also wrote *States of Grace* in 1991, which includes a chapter on the implications of contemporary Goddess-oriented spirituality. Her most recent book is *Relational Reality* (2011).

She then continued her work on ecological thought with *The Resurgence of the Real* in 1997. More recently, she turned her attention to the fate of the Virgin Mary in the Catholic Church since the great modernizing conference Vatican II. The result was her book *Missing Mary* which was published in 2004 which we will talk about tonight.

Charlene Spretnak is a professor emerita in the Women's Spirituality program of the Philosophy and Religion Department at the California Institute of Intrical Studies, a graduate institute in San Francisco. She lives in Ojai, California, with her husband.

Interview starts:

KT: Charlene, welcome to the show.

CS: Thank you.

KT: It's certainly my pleasure to have you on the show tonight; thank you so much for taking the time to be with us. Let's talk about Guadalupe first, if you'd like, since her Feast Day is Saturday. Guadalupe is connected to the Tonanzin; did you want to talk about that a little bit?

CS: Her story is syncretic, as are all the Black Madonna stories in Europe. It's a matter of the indigenous Sacred Feminine presence, symbols, and totemic animals in various geographic locations merging with the Virgin Mary when she was brought in with the arrival of the Church. So in the case of Mexico, there is the account of Juan Diego, a Mexican man who had recently converted to Christianity. He was crossing by the foot of Tepeyac Hill, a small mountain-hill, which had been a site associated with Tonanzin.

That is where he has the visitation of the Lady, the Luminous Lady. He hears birdsong first on December 9, 1531. He wouldn't be hearing birds at that time normally. He goes up to the top of the hill and sees this vision, and she reappears to him over four days. Even though, as you say, the Feast Day of Our Lady of Guadalupe is this Saturday, we're really in the story right now.

It's very much a merger of two religious traditions, and it probably takes too long to tell the story, but she says to him that she would like him to go into Mexico City and tell the bishop that she wants a church built there on the hilltop.

Juan Diego does this but is sort of given the "bum's rush" in the bishop's outer office because he is a peasant. He goes back twice more and is always turned away. Thwarted, he avoids the Lady, but eventually he has to go by the hill because his uncle is sick and he is trying to get help for him. She draws him to the top of the hill, where he smells Castilian roses blooming in December. She tells him to pick the roses, bundle them in his *tilma* (cloak), and take them to the bishop. She directed him to show the roses to the bishop.

So, he goes to the bishop's mansion, and this time he is admitted. The viceroy happens to be there along with other high-ranking officials, who were having a meeting with the bishop. Juan Diego unties and unfurls his *tilma* so that the roses fall down onto the tile floor in front of him. Immediately, the bishop and the viceroy and all the officials drop down on their knees with their eyes wide, staring at the *tilma*, part of which is still tied behind his neck. On the *tilma* hanging in front of him is the image of Our Lady of Guadalupe – which is still in Mexico City in a frame in the Basilica of Our Lady of Guadalupe.

That scene of the ruling conquistadores kneeling before the little brown-skinned woman is the foundational image of the Mexican Catholic Church. So it's very much a story of the Old World and the New, and the indigenous tradition and the European. Mary – who in the Christian tradition is not divine, although she's more than human but less than divine, at least in the traditional Catholic understanding – merges in numerous cultures with the indigenous manifestations of the Sacred Feminine.

KT: Charlene, let me ask you a question that has always perplexed me. Whenever we have these apparitions around the world, and we've had a lot of these Mary apparitions, they are always "Our Lady" or they don't have a name. People always assume they are the Virgin Mary. What would you say to that? How would you identify who these apparitions are when they appear to people?

CS: It's a very interesting subject. There have been more than 1,000 reported visitations of the Virgin Mary, and most of the time the Catholic Church just leaves them alone and doesn't approve them or reject them. But of the ones that were recognized as the major modern visitations, such as Lourdes and Fatima, beginning in 1830 thru 1917, it's very interesting that she appears only to girls or to a small group that is half composed of girls. And it is usually country people or uneducated people. In the case of the visitation known as the Immaculate Conception, it was a girl who went to Paris to become a nun but was from a poor family.

I think the way to think about the visitations is that some sort of spiritual experience is occurring in those young people, and then they face the problem that all humans do when they have a spiritual experience: it doesn't really translate into one's language system. Especially our Indo-European-based languages, in which the focus is not on process and states of being, but on things and categories. It's nominalized family of languages. So the young people can't really talk about what happened, just as no one can. In addition, because they are children, they are talking to adults, and the adults start filtering what they're hearing through their own frames of reference. The parents go to the village priest, and the account gets filtered again, and then to the bishop. All these layers are put on whatever the authentic spiritual experience was, which should simply be honored as a mystery that doesn't translate.

KT: If I remember correctly, in Guadalupe's appearance, she was speaking to him in his native language. So you had that filter again. It's hard enough to language a supernatural experience, and then when you have languages that don't have similar meanings, it makes it that much more complicated.

CS: That's right. And she said to Juan Diego that she came "from the Great God." There were certain metaphors in her speech that would be familiar to him. It was definitely a bridged experience between two cultures with all kinds of references that would work in both systems.

KT: And then we know too if you are talking to people who are Christian, and they filter it through a Christian lens, like so many ethnographers have done in past cultures, when they are transcribing ancient text. To get to the original meaning, probably most of the time it's really lost.

CS: Yes. It has to be "held" in that spiritual space. We don't have to try to nail it down.

KT: I have often said, "You feel Goddess, you don't think Goddess." And I think that's what we're saying here: you know it intuitively, you feel it, and those details aren't quite so important.

One last question about Dark Madonnas before we focus on Mary, on whom most of our questions are going to lie. Did you want to mention some of the other Dark Madonnas for our listeners?

CS: Every Catholic country in Europe – and Catholic regions of countries that are partly Catholic and partly Protestant – has a national shrine. There is a Mary statue in each of those shrines, and it's always a Black Madonna – in every country in Europe. It's really interesting. There are different explanations for why the Madonna in the national shrine is black. It seems definitely connected with the earlier times. Some are grey and earth-colored; some are black.

KT: Is the Church still trying to pass the idea that it is candle soot or have they given up on that?

CS: I still see that once in a while. Then they clean the statue, and they find it's not only black but she sometimes has kohl rimming her eyes and gold flecks in her hair. These are incidences of the aesthetic influence of the Near East coming across the Mediterranean.

KT: And what's so silly about the candle soot theory too is that interestingly it only affects the skin and not the clothes. The candle soot selectively landed on the body parts.

CS: It's interesting because in southern Italy, there are country shrines that are on sites that are Neolithic excavation sites. The cultural historian Lucia Birnbaum has written a book, *Black Madonna*, which presents evidence indicating that Marian shrines were being built on sites that were already perceived to be holy in the earlier, Neolithic religion.

KT: We know there was at least one Black Madonna in France that when the paint was removed, it was actually Isis underneath.

CS: That was very common because in the countries that were occupied by the Roman Empire, Isis statues were numerous. So they would just change the iconography a little and re-Christen it as Mary, Mother of Jesus.

KT: Why are the Black Madonnas different from the Madonna? How do you explain that?

CS: It's very localized. That Black Madonna in the national shrine in every European country embodies the deepest roots of the cultural identification of the people. There is a town in Italy, cited in Professor Birnbaum's book, where on Pentecost, they have two processions: one group marches behind the White Madonna taken out of the church, and the other group marches behind the Black Madonna statue taken out of the shrine. They meet on the soccer field and have a big soccer game between the White and the Dark Madonnas' teams! In Italy and Spain, they feel the Black Madonna is more "of the people." Anti-clerical feeling is strong in many places there, and the White Madonna considered to be more inside the Church system.

KT: There are a lot of people who connect the Black Madonna more closely to Goddess. Do you think that's accurate?

CS: Certainly in those cases in which it's obvious that statues – of Isis, for instance – were simply renamed, it's clear.

KT: Would her darkness be associated with nature? Or maybe the chthonic (underworld) deities?

CS: It's not only the color of the statue. Birds or other animals and particular symbols or characteristics are pictured with her in the various national versions of Mary. Most of those associations came from pre-Christian Goddess iconography. It brings the continuity forward into this era.

KT: It's like the Goddess is passing her baton on to the Madonnas.

CS: It's interesting – in the modern West, the Sacred Female is reinvigorated by the re-emergence of Goddess spirituality in the 1970s and beyond, but in India, and elsewhere in Asia and other areas she never died. In the modern era, there was no Goddess presence in Europe, but Mary in her syncretic forms made it possible for the extremely ancient attributes to go forward into our time. In the Christian story, Mary is more than human but less than divine. She's not a Goddess; she starts out as a Jewish village girl and goes on to become Queen of Heaven. It's a story that can be understood on different levels.

Everyone has the possibility of growing into your large, cosmological self. Mary has symbolic, mystical, and cosmological dimensions. Yet she's always in that special ontological category that only has one person in it: the person who is more than human but less than divine. I think she's a fascinating spiritual figure.

I would like to say something about her Biblical story because some people assert, "Well, you've got all that folk Catholicism stuff where the Goddess attributes are put onto the spiritual presence of Mary, but if you just stick to the Bible – stick only to the text and scripture – then you get away from all the Goddess stuff and have the true, pure story." Actually, that doesn't work, folks. There are so many attributes *in her Biblical story* that link her to the older Goddess traditions. For instance, she produces a child parthenogenetically.

KT: Which the Goddesses have all done.

CS: Yes. All the Virgin Goddesses – including Isis, Hathor, Inanna, Ishtar, and Demeter – like Mary, produce a child without the benefit of sexual intercourse. It's often a male child, often is born at the coming of the light, and often becoming a powerful leader. They often die and then are reborn. They are often born in a hidden place, like the stable that was carved into the hillside where Jesus was born. So, the textual Biblical story of Mary – not merely the add-ons of traditional Catholicism – has many elements that link her to this continuity of the Goddess spirituality flowing into what's going to come next, the next era in the West.

KT: Speaking of the Virgin Mary and how she's viewed today, in the three branches of Christianity, the Protestants, the Roman Catholics and Eastern Orthodox ... They all look at her differently, right?

CS: Yes, very much so. Although, two of them have branches that have moved closer. Martin Luther initially honored the Virgin Mary, but about ten years into the Reformation, he delivered his famous Christmas sermon, in 1530, during which he said that every birth requires a mother, but she's no more important than a necessary component. He preached that paying honor to Mary subtracts honor from God.

In the Protestant tradition, Mary isn't talked about much except at Christmas. That split in Christianity was traumatic for European culture, because she was the Great Mother who was also the cultural heart as the identity of the people. Traditionally the Roman Catholics have honored the Biblical story of Mary but also the "Biblical-plus," which includes her symbolic, mystical, cosmological dimensions. This was beautifully expressed in so much of the art, the music, and the prayers through the centuries.

And that's closer to the way the Eastern Orthodox view her. They honor the mystical dimension of her spiritual presence as the Mother of God. But they disagree with the Catholic Church over the need for dogma, preferring to leave spiritual communion with her in a realm that isn't so legalistic.

Now let me go back to the second branch I mentioned: things changed radically within the Catholic Church regarding Mary at the world conference known as Vatican II, between 1962 and 1965. The purpose was to bring the Church more in sync with the modern world, to get more rational so they could get more respect from modernity. Very slightly more than half of the bishops favored the rationalist, text-based, anti-aesthetic version of Christianity, which carried the day. The traditional spiritual sense of Mary was thrown out the window. It was the most radical break you could imagine. It's very politicized inside the Catholic Church, especially the American Catholic Church along the left–right axis.

KT: When you say "left–right" you mean Conservative and Liberal?

CS: Yes – because the right-wing Catholics claim Mary as their patron saint of all their right-wing political and social positions. And the progressive-liberal half of the American Catholic Church basically agree with that appropriation. They went along with it and said, "Oh yes, you're right: whenever one sees Mary being invoked, that means it's a right-wing group." This is not at all the association one finds in the rest of the world. You may remember the independence movement to get rid of the dictator Marcos in the Philippines: the people marched in the streets toward the tanks, holding the statue of the Virgin Mary in front of them.

Throughout Latin America and in so many places where there are social change movements, Mary is their Patron. Mary is of the People. They feel she is helping them. But in the United States, the whole association with her has largely been given over to the right-wing Catholics. The progressive Catholics don't want to mention Mary much at all, and if they do, it's in a very literal, historical way.

All kinds of books have been written by my progressive feminist sisters in the Catholic Church about the historical Mary – how big her house probably was, what the dimension of her kitchen probably was, how close the neighbors' houses were. I can hardly recognize this as a religion. It seems more like archaeology or anthropology or something.

It's a literal historical, rationalist way to engage with her. And the reason that a lot of the feminists in the progressive part of the Catholic Church feel that way is that they feel they had to knock her off her throne because she was detracting from the effort to get the Catholic Church to recognize God as being as much female as male. They felt that in order to get the Catholic Church to recognize God the Mother they had to "off" what I call "Big Mary" (in her full spiritual presence).

I don't agree with that analysis. I don't think it's that kind of competition because Mary is "more than human but less than divine." She's not in competition with God as male/female. It's entirely different, but that's how they see it.

KT: That doesn't make a lot of sense to me, quite frankly. I'm curious about the left just giving in and going along with it. I know the women in San Francisco at the Feminist Lutheran herChurch – those sorts of progressive Christian churches – where do they fit into this? Are they very much in the minority?

CS: That's a very unusual church. It's a wonderful church. Most of the progressive feminist Catholic theologians, though, feel that the best way forward was to take this rational historical version of Mary. They want to be known and respected in post-Vatican II theological circles. If you are going to play in that arena, of course, it's going to be by focusing solely on Biblical text and not talking about mystical or symbolic dimensions.

KT: Very interesting. In talking about the Virgin Mary's lineage as a manifestation of the Sacred Feminine, in Ephesus, Turkey, Artemis basically passed all her attributes on to the Virgin Mary. I assume that was very common. I mean, the Virgin Mary has a lot of Isis' attributes too.

CS: Originally the temple in Ephesus was to the goddess Artemis/Diana. Much later, the site became the church. Ephesus was also the city where the bishops had the famous conference in which they declared Mary to officially be the God-bearer, or Mother of God. When they took the vote and made the announcement, the people in the streets around the conference were cheering because they already viewed Mary as the Mother of God. This was the Council of Ephesus.

One of the things I learned in my research is that every time the Church declared another doctrine or dogma about Mary – which gradually acknowledged more and more of her "Big Mary" characteristics (the mystical, the symbolic, the cosmological) – it was always pushed by the people. Its request always came first from the people, and then the "Brass" would come up with some rationalization to make it a new official doctrine of the Church. For instance, in the mid-nineteenth century, when the Pope declared Mary the Immaculate Conception, there'd been millions of letters petitioning for that to happen from the grassroots.

KT: I grew up a Catholic, and my grandmother had statues of Mary in the yard and in the house, and you always hear about the people at the grassroots, they don't care about the Church dogma. She's God. It's irrelevant what the Church wants to put in their rule book.

CS: Yes, the people at the grassroots don't always pay close attention to theological boundaries. The sense of "Big Mary" was very much true in the time when you and I grew up, but that's not true for young people in the Catholic Church now. They grow up regarding Mary in a way that's not very different from the Protestant view. She isn't talked about. She's a nice lady in the Bible. You get out her little statue in the crèche scene once a year at Christmas, and that's that.

KT: And this is all about having to put the emphasis on God?

CS: It's all about being a more rational, modern religion and not having a giant "goddess figure" in the middle of the religion anymore.

KT: Well, if you can have a giant God figure why not a giant Goddess? That would be my question, how would they answer that? If one can be big, why do they have to diminish the other? Is it the patriarchy stuff again?

CS: I propose in *Missing Mary* that several developments converged to result in the big overthrow of Mary in 1962–1965 and since then. It was the post-war period, a time of a macho burst of modernity and rationalist thought. Every institution and field of knowledge was determined to become more streamlined, efficient, and rational. Also, Freudian thought dominated much of intellectual life then, in the 1950s. So the young priests coming out of the European universities were embarrassed to have this giant Mother Goddess in the middle of their religion. There were about five different reasons that flowed together to dethrone "Big Mary" and limit her to being solely the historical village girl. Still, it was a very close vote.

KT: Wasn't Pope John Paul going to elevate Mary while he was Pope but then he changed his mind?

CS: Pope John Paul II was very much into Mary. He came out of the Polish culture and really carried with him the deep, older kind of communion with Mary, but you probably won't ever see that again at the top. He even had an "M" put in his papal seal, much to the distress of his staff.

KT: Do you think the "Big Mary" might make a comeback?

CS: In certain ways she is. The people who were against her have had to soften their position a bit. Feminist progressive academics now say that it's all right that the statues are coming back into many Catholic churches because this is a grassroots practice. After *Missing Mary* was published, when I was invited to speak at some places, I learned that there is kind of a generational split in some of the seminaries and other places – and also in some of the communities of nuns and orders of the priests. Many people in the older generation who grew up with Mary really felt that something went wrong in this one area of Vatican II when they threw her out the window so radically. The middle generation mostly doesn't want to hear her talked about; many of them think she should be reduced even more. The young people, though, feel maybe they have missed something growing up without her. They read about the old practices and the music and the art. They want to learn about Marian spirituality – to learn the rosary and things.

It's very interesting. Before I learned that, it seemed as if all the younger progressive Catholics were pretty much waiting for us older ones to die off, but many of the younger Catholics are changing that.

KT: You also say this comeback of "Big Mary" has something to do with the correction of the sterility of our modern world. Do you want to elaborate?

CS: If you want to modernize an institution, make sure you don't get sucked into the damaging assumptions of modernity, the assumption, for instance, that nothing has value if it can't be measured. Without a critique of what's wrong with modernity, you're going to throw a lot of precious things out the window. This recovery of the mystical, symbolic, and cosmological dimensions of Mary's spiritual presence is situated within the larger correction of modernity, in which all kinds of developments are challenging the mechanistic view of the world. I see a possible recovery of the more mystical, cosmological sense of Catholicism as one of the corrections that are now bringing us out of that mechanistic worldview into a more relational, complex, and healthy worldview.

KT: Just as a practitioner out there, it seems like Mary, and Mary Magdalene, provide a bridge between progressive Christians and maybe also Pagans. Is that an anomaly or do you see that happening other places too?

CS: Mary *is* a bridge figure. She's a bridge figure among religions. Large numbers of Islamic people go to Marian shrines every year. She's really the common ground among the three Abrahamic religions – and also among the three branches of Christianity, if they would see it that way. Instead, they tend to see Mary as the "deal breaker" in ecumenical efforts to achieve greater unity.

KT: When it's really all of the gods [men?] who are fighting it out for dominance, it's the "Mary" that's the deal breaker?

CS: Exactly! Blame it on the woman.

KT: Of course, of course! Thank you. I'm glad you said that. Well, Charlene, this has been fun, and I want to make sure if there was anything important that you wanted to leave listeners with that we haven't talked about... I give you a chance to share it and also mention your website if they would like more information about what you're up to these days.

CS: I have a website, http://www.charlenespretnak.com/ about my books. The last thing I would like to say will bring us back to where we started, with Our Lady of Guadalupe: Pope John Paul II has declared her the Patron Saint of all North America. Still, I think people need to be sensitive to the fact that some Mexicans and Mexican-Americans don't like to see her appropriated by non-Mexican people, while others are proud and happy that her presence is spreading to all of North America. It's important to listen and see how the Chicano people you are talking to feel about it; both of these positions are valid and understandable.

KT: Well, that's good to know because I doubt that everyone is aware of that, quite frankly.

Charlene, thank you for being a guest on the show and for participating in the Foremother Series. We are building an incredible archive here, and I really appreciate, as I'm sure my listeners do, your lending your voice and having it there indefinitely for people to be able to look back on and learn from you. So, thank you so very much for taking your time tonight.

CS: Thank you for inviting me.

Chapter 8

Gossips, Gorgons, and Crones

Transcript of interview with Joan Marler

Interview:

KT = Karen Tate
JM = Joan Marler

Tonight we have as our guest a Foremother of the women's spirituality movement, Joan Marler. Joan is the founder and executive director of the Institute of Archaeomythology (www.archaeomy thology.org) and is the co-author (with Harald Haarmann) of *Introducing the Mythological Crescent: Ancient Beliefs and Imagery Connecting Eurasia with Anatolia* (2008). She is the editor of *The Civilization of the Goddess* (1991) by Marija Gimbutas, *From the Realm of the Ancestors: An Anthology in Honor of Marija Gimbutas* (1997), the *Journal of Archaeomythology* (2005 – present), *The Danube Script* (2008), and (with Miriam Robbins Dexter) *Signs of Civilization: Neolithic Symbol System of Southeast Europe* (2009), and other publications. Joan is currently completing her doctorate in Philosophy and Religion, with a concentration on Women's Spirituality and Archaeomythology at the California Institute of Integral Studies in San Francisco.

Interview starts:

KT: Welcome, Joan.

JM: Thank you, Karen, it's a pleasure to be here.

KT: Tonight we are talking about the Gorgon Medusa. She is an archetype that women might need to embrace in these times, is she not?

JM: Absolutely, and she is recognized as a powerful female figure in Western civilization who has been decapitated again and again. For example, in the mid-sixteenth century, the bronze sculpture by Cellini of Perseus holding the decapitated head of Medusa was placed in the center of Florence in the Piazza della Signoria as the revered image of the hero slaying this potent female power. We might ask, "Why?"

KT: Is it going too far to say this represents the patriarchy taking over from "mother right" or the matriarchy?

JM: I think it IS a takeover, an aspect of what the mythologist Joseph Campbell called the "Great Reversal." He was referring to the rejection of the concept of Goddess, in all her powers, as the Sacred Source at the center of all life – in favor of an external male God, and all of its ramifications. The exquisite photograph of the earth from outer space is an iconic image of this Sacred Source. There she is, teeming with life that arises from her body, then returns to her in death, in a vast cyclic symphony of coming into being, going out of being, and regenerating.

The metaphor of the sacred source of life as female – who gives birth to new life from herself – is a completely different concept of creator than the male god whose domain is outside the world. The male god functions as a craftsman who molds life forms out of clay (which is her substance, although her presence and sacredness are erased).

KT: Concerning the Great Reversal, don't we see the very same thing when Athena is birthed from Zeus's head? Her mother is practically out of the equation.

JM: Absolutely. In fact the story of the birth of Athena encapsulates the Great Reversal. Zeus, the head of the Greek pantheon of gods, enjoyed the sport of chasing and "marrying" the local goddesses. Interestingly, they are depicted as fleeing from him, shape-shifting, and trying to get away. Why? Because "marrying," in this context, is a euphemism for rape.

One of the goddesses Zeus pursued, caught and raped was Metis, whose name refers to the intelligence of the earth, the great inner wisdom within all of life.

Zeus raped her, then forgot about her. After a while, he received a message that Metis was pregnant with someone more powerful than he. Zeus was gravely concerned about this, so he searched everywhere until he found her. Using his magical powers, he reduced her to the size of a fly, and swallowed her.

Sometime after swallowing Metis, the intelligence/wisdom of the earth disagreed with his system, and Zeus developed a splitting headache. He called for his blacksmith, Hephaestus, to break open his head with a double axe to relieve the pressure. Lo and behold, Athena arose out of Zeus's head, fully armed, with a battle cry. She declared that she has no mother and is in full service to her father and to his heroes.

The metaphor of this story is that the ancient matrilineage was broken, literally swallowed by the patriarchy, who claims sovereignty over women, the earth, and civilization. Athena was originally a pre-Indo-European (non-patriarchal) goddess, who is much more ancient than the arrival of the Greek tribes who usurped her tradition.

KT: In her authentic essence, Athena would never have let herself be co-opted that way. This is purely patriarchy at work spinning the story.

JM: Yes, of course, by taking over all that she represents. Athena brings with her the arts of civilization – weaving, all of the crafts, and incredible cultural richness and knowledge that became dedicated to the patriarchal project. But THEN you have Medusa, Athena's alter ego, who wouldn't go along with the program! It's fascinating to see how she fits into this story.

KT: Well, tell us please. Because I think most of us have grown up with the idea that Medusa is evil. She must be slain; after all, she'll cause people to turn to stone if she gazes upon them. She's got snakes for hair that can bite you and kill you. But what was patriarchy really doing? Let's go beneath the sands and see what their twisted logic has done to the REAL Medusa.

JM: Such demonization is a justification for the domination, rape, and destruction of the full, radiant powers of women and the earth.

Medusa is one of the three Gorgon sisters who are related to triple goddesses found in many places of the world. What is this triplicity? Past, present and future – birth, death, regeneration – the different phases of a woman's life – the phases of the moon.

New life and maturation are universally celebrated, but death and disintegration are just as essential for the cycle of life. The Gorgon sisters have the fangs and claws of predators, and huge wings as birds of prey. These features of their iconography represent the death/disintegration aspect of the life cycle, which has been demonized. But old forms must disintegrate so that their nutrients can be released to be reintegrated into new life.

KT: So in a way are you saying this is our denial of death?

JM: It IS a denial of death. I think that the Old European (pre-patriarchal) sensibility embraced the entire cycle, and many indigenous peoples throughout the world understand that you can't just have birth, birth, birth, and continual growth. There has to be a return to the Source for new beginnings.

But one of the big questions that determines the fundamental nature of any society or individual is: How do we face death? What is our relationship to that inevitability? The Lithuanian/American archaeologist Marija Gimbutas wrote a lot about that because in looking at Old European iconography and symbolism, she saw that the aspect of death-regeneration was incredibly important.

Getting back to the Gorgon, let's look at the triple aspects of past, present and future. The past and the future are eternal, represented by two of the Gorgon sisters. The only aspect that exists in the field of present time is represented by Medusa. Actually, the present moment can never be captured; it has no dimensions. It is the fountain point of all that is continually emerging. But as soon as the present appears, it is already past.

Medusa, who exists in present time, is the only one who could be decapitated, but in reality, she (in her totality) can never be killed. The present moment cannot be captured, which is why her decapitation is repeated as a ritual action, again and again, within the patriarchal system.

KT: Just to clarify, her two sisters are the past and the future, right?

JM: They are eternal as the past and the future – but, of course, all three are aspects of one goddess who exists in all dimensions of time. One is named Euryale, the great primordial sea, the ocean from which all life comes. The other sister is Stheno which is the strength at the center of the life force. Medusa is the wisdom of the eternal Now. Their parents are deities of the sea: their father is Phorcys, god of the great and dangerous depths of the sea; their mother is Keto, the primordial sea goddess.

KT: So, their parents come from the living waters. Was Medusa always the woman with the snakes for hair, or is that just a patriarchal concept?

JM: That's a very good question. In one story she was a beautiful young priestess in Athena's temple who was raped by Poseidon in the form of a horse.

Poseidon may originally have been an Old European god of the sweet waters and a consort of the Earth. As a pre-patriarchal god, he would never commit rape, or appear as a horse! Patriarchy was introduced during the process of Indo-Europeanization when the Greek tribes came down into the Balkan peninsula around 2000 BCE. They also brought the horse, so Poseidon's association with the horse is a sign of the Indo-European influence. He later became a god of the sea, and earthquakes.

Poseidon's rape of Medusa, as a beautiful priestess, takes place in Athena's sacred precinct. Athena comes in and sees this going on, but does not become angry with Poseidon. NO. She becomes furious with Medusa, and curses her by turning her into an ugly creature with fangs, claws and snakes for hair. This story contains a pattern that has endured for 2,500 years – blaming women for being raped!

KT: Talking about these myths as metaphors, I'm curious if you agree with this. I had a scholar on the show at one point who was talking about how the Greeks had all of these stories, but we take them too literally. For instance, when Poseidon, Zeus and Hades were battling their parents, it really wasn't one set of gods battling another set of gods, it was really the change from the way people were living into more organized civilization.

He also said that when we hear Greek myths, for instance, a god raping a goddess, rather than thinking of it in a personified way, which comes from Christian influence, he suggested that the deities were really cosmic forces, so if there was a rape, it wasn't necessarily an assault, it was two cosmic forces that came together and created a third. Do you believe that? Is that part of the deeper meaning of the myths?

JM: First of all, I agree with what Marija Gimbutas said, in terms of the Old European imagery (c. 6500–3500 BCE), that "their ties with nature persist." In terms of the Indo-European tradition, the figure who became Zeus, thousands of years later, most likely began as a thunderous sky god. But by the mid-first millennium BCE, the Greeks had personified their deities to an extreme, imbuing them with human-like personalities and complex histories. So when Zeus and the various heroes went on raping sprees, rape was glorified. These stories can be seen as metaphors for the justification of the conquest of the earth and of women.

The story of the decapitation of Medusa is a cautionary tale with many layers. There are deep Old European roots to what constellated into the Gorgon Medusa. She has the sharp teeth of a predator, a lolling tongue, snakes for hair, and iron claws. And when she is fully depicted, not just as a mask, she's in a flying posture with poisonous and life-giving snakes copulating around her waist. Her huge wings indicate that she is not only a bird of prey, but a winged serpent who moves freely in all realms.

The Gorgon started out being just a face, described by Homer (c. 8th century BCE) as rising up from the underworld, making a fearsome gargling, growling, strangling sound that is the root of the word gorgon. Gorgoneia (disk-shaped masks of her face and snaky hair) were installed in high places on Greek temples where she functioned as a powerful threshold guardian and protector.

Her face was used continually throughout the Greek period as an apotropaic form of protection on the shields of warriors, or wherever protection was needed. She is sometimes shown bearded and is referred to as the "bearded Aphrodite" – representing a woman's genitals used as a curse. Freud correctly interpreted her mouth as a toothed vagina. Exposing a metaphor of female genitals lined with sharp teeth is a very powerful image.

KT: So is this a way of saying that the demonizing of Medusa represents men's fear of women's sexuality, fertility, life-giving force?

JM: Yes. And Greek heroes were expected to subdue those female powers. The rise of the patriarchal hero represented a shift of consciousness from being in harmony with the cycles of the natural world, to being expected to dominate the life force. But that stance is ultimately futile because no matter how powerful we think we are, death cannot be conquered. The patriarchal ego fights the inevitability of dissolution, all the way down.

KT: So you have humankind's resistance to death, to the natural cycles of life. It isn't necessarily a gender-thing; it's more thinking you can overcome the natural cycles.

JM: Naturally, we all must face the reality of being recycled back to the Source, but the iconography is highly gendered. Everyone is born from the body of a woman who produces new life as well as the inevitability of death, which the patriarchal ego seeks to dominate. To die in service to the patriarchal world order is to achieve eternal life, but to live in harmony with the cycles of life is anathema to that struggle.

KT: So they can have everlasting life while denying their mortality!

JM: Strange, isn't it? In the story of the decapitation of Medusa, there is a young hero named Perseus who is sent on a mission to kill her. He doesn't know what she looks like, he doesn't know where she is, or even how to do it, so Athena guides him and gives him everything he needs: winged sandals so he can fly, the helmet of invisibility, her own protective shield, a magical purse to hold Medusa's head, and so on.

The Gorgons live in a cave on an island at the far end of the western ocean – the liminal place between death and rebirth – where Hera planted the tree with the golden apples. Although the island is depicted on the far horizon, as though on the periphery, the tree, as the Axis Mundi, marks its location as the Sacred Center.

The Gorgons are asleep in the cave, and Athena guides Perseus's hand so he can cut off Medusa's head. There are many variations to the story, but in one of them, Athena slices off Medusa's skin and uses it as her breastplate. Athena also wears a miniature image of Medusa's face on her chest, claiming this fierce lineage as her own.

Medusa had been pregnant from the rape by Poseidon. When she was decapitated, her two children were born out of her bloody neck: her son Chrysaor, and the winged horse Pegasus, who are forced into Zeus's service. Their birth following her decapitation points to the symbolism of the head as an "upper womb" of conception.

Every part of Medusa's body was plundered in service of the new world order. The flash of her eyes was given to Zeus to wield as lightning. Her roar became his thunder. Her severed head was taken by Perseus and used to petrify his enemies.

The blood on Medusa's left side is poisonous, while the blood on her right is life-giving. Her blood was drained and given to Asklepios, which made him a great healer, possessing her powers of death and regeneration. Asklepios is depicted with Medusa's copulating serpents, which also represent death and regeneration. (Their bites are poisonous, and they return from winter hibernation to emerge from their old skin as a kind of rebirth.)

Medusa's decapitation functions on a number of levels, but most simply it can be understood as a cautionary tale which says that as long as women are in service to the patriarchal father, like the virginal Athena, we will be protected, but if we refuse to relinquish our powers on his altar, we will be destroyed.

KT: And it's choosing the status quo, the patriarchy, or you will see what you will get.

JM: Right. The inquisition was all about that – destroying women's powers as human beings – which created shock waves down through many generations. At one point I thought to myself, "What does the mother teach the daughter, so that the daughter can survive? What are we taught never to reveal about our capacities? What do we conceal about who we really are?"

KT: What do we have in the myths that teach the woman to stand up against the new world order and be your true self?

JM: Interestingly, during the ancient Greek period, women were allowed to practice certain vestiges of the old religion. There were women-only festivals such as the Thesmophoria in honor of Demeter, and other women's rituals. But otherwise, women were expected to behave.

KT: Give you a little taste of it to pacify you.

JM: Yes. I am convinced that women-only rituals continued because women had been enacting seasonal rituals for the earth and for the health of their communities for millennia and they refused to give them up.

I highly recommend a book by Eva Keuls, *The Reign of the Phallus* (1985), in which she discusses the sexual politics of ancient Athens. The Greeks were obsessed with the Amazons, as women who had the audacity to rebel and to fight men on the battlefield. Some of the most prevalent images in ancient Athens were of Greek heroes stabbing and clubbing Amazons to death. This is another example of the Great Reversal.

KT: What do we think was the cause for the Great Reversal? Was it just about cheating death? Or was civilization becoming more sophisticated? Did they delude themselves, thinking that they didn't have to succumb to the natural cycles? As a side question of that, if you weren't a hero, if you were a woman, or a man who didn't fight, what would happen to you if you didn't have the chance to achieve immortality?

JM: In patriarchal systems, women are less important than men, of course, and a man who refuses to fight is often referred to as a negative euphemism for woman. But the question of how patriarchy began is complex. Cristina Biaggi has produced an exceptional anthology concerning the beginnings of patriarchy, *The Rule of Mars*, which explores this subject from various standpoints. I contributed an article about Marija Gimbutas's Kurgan theory which concerns the transition in Europe from the long-lived, egalitarian societies of Old Europe to the imposition of patriarchy which is the Great Reversal writ large.

KT: Like you said, this is a complicated subject so we could talk about it for a long time, but we are starting to run out of time. If someone wanted to read more about this, and go into more depth, which of Marija's books would you recommend?

JM: I recommend *The Civilization of the Goddess* (1991). The book is out of print, but used copies can be found. Chapter 10, "The End of Old Europe," discusses this extremely important transformation. The conflict between the ancient female powers of the earth (such as the Gorgons and other primordial deities) and the patriarchal sky gods and their heroes, began during this major transition which Gimbutas dates between 4500 and 2500 BCE. I also recommend *The Goddesses and Gods of Old Europe* (1982), *The Language of the Goddess* (1989) and *The Living Goddesses* (1999), which are still available.

KT: Also, let's make sure to mention your website.

JM: Thanks, Karen. The website of the Institute of Archaeomythology is: http://www.archeomythology.org. I invite your listeners to go onto the website and register to have free access to all of the issues of the *Journal of Archaeomythology*.

I believe that Medusa has special importance for women of our time: She represents the fierce protection of the lion mother and the Wisdom at the Center of the great cycles of the natural world.

Medusa has been demonized, but it is within our power to restore her decapitated head onto her wisdom body within ourselves, and to have the courage to step forward and speak what is true within us.

KT: I think, too, it's also about not being duped into denying our own power.

JM: Absolutely. Because we, too, have had our capacities reduced in one way or another, but it's time to shake that off and to become whole.

There are beautiful Gorgoneia used as beam ends on a temple from the sixth-century BCE Greek colony of Magna Gracia in southern Italy. These images are quietly smiling, as though they know their full powers. It occurs to me that when we know our full powers, we don't have to be raging all the time. We can be serene and consciously discerning about the expression of our fierceness. Our full potential is within us to be summoned, whenever necessary.

KT: It hasn't done us any good to be good little sheep, either.

JM: No. We have to discover our inner powers.

KT: I'm from the south and I don't know whether 20-year-old girls still get this message, but I was always told not to make waves, and to be polite, which doesn't do us any good.

JM: Exactly. We have to think for ourselves, and to be present with all of our capacities. There is so much more that can be said about the Gorgon Medusa, but at least it's a beginning.

KT: It's a beginning and, Joan, thank you so much for your time tonight. It's been very interesting. I'm wondering if there is some way that people can access your work on the Gorgon?

JM: I published "An Archaeomythological Investigation of the Gorgon" in the Summer 2002 issue of *ReVision* vol. 5, no. 1. I do plan to republish it in a future issue of the *Journal of Archaeomythology.*

KT: Thank you, Joan, because we have to get it through the thick skulls of women out there not to be handmaidens of the patriarchy. You know, don't worry about being demonized, because we DO have to save the world.

JM: Yes, and having the powers of protection is also who we are, which sometimes requires fierceness. We can always express our powers in a way that's appropriate to the situation.

KT: Absolutely, whether we are talking Kali, Sekhmet, or Medusa or the Morrigan, we have to be able to feel comfortable embracing that sacred roar, whether we are defending the earth, or ourselves, or some species that's disappearing on the planet or whatever the case may be.

JM: Exactly. Medusa is the European Kali. There are many parallels, as well as differences.

KT: Joan, thank you so much for the work that you do and I appreciate your time tonight.

Chapter 9

The Queen Solves Everything

by Ava

The Queen in Every Woman Solves Everything

The modern world is a mess. War, violence, oppression, rape. The list is endless. Many women wring their hands and wonder what to do. Here's what to do – find your Queen! That's right. She's in there somewhere and she fixes everything.

Four Archetypes of Woman

Every woman has four archetypes or aspects living within her: The Maiden, the Mother, the Wisewoman, and – the one that is most missing in modern woman – the Queen. This is the reason the world is in such a mess: because the Queen in most women is hidden in the dungeon of our consciousness, banging on the bars, trying to get out. Most of us don't hear her. We are living in a culture that denies our Queen.

The Queen Is Needed for the Good of All

When she is not denied outright, the Queen is demonized. The Queen is always the "evil" one in every fairy tale, so no wonder we have a fear of stepping into our Queen selves. We have not been taught about her and so we do not understand what it means to be Queen in the spiritual sense. No woman can be whole, empowered and happy without her Queen. The world cannot come into balance without the Queen in woman. The Queen in Woman is needed for the good of all.

The Maiden Aspect

The Maiden: the experiencer of life. It's dawning springtime and new shoots are bursting forth from the ground with incredible life force. It's the time of the Maiden. Like the fresh shoots, the Maiden is always coming forward, wild, free and spontaneous. She is whole unto herself (the original meaning of the word "virgin.") She has no "to-do" list, no calendar. There are no post-it notes all over her mirror, reminding her of responsibilities and promises. Her promises are all to herself. She is "for herself." She is adventurous and confident, utterly without fear, exploring and experiencing life on her own terms. Because she is an essence of woman, she is naturally pleasing to people. Everyone wants to be near her, hoping a bit of that wild shakti, or divine life force, will rub off on them.

In modern society, we use and abuse the Maiden aspect, commercializing her, using her qualities of youthful female power to sell everything from beer to cars. When the Maiden in woman is imbalanced, she becomes what we call in The QUEEN TEACHINGS™ the "people-pleasing Maiden," worried about others' approval, trying too hard to be liked ... and fearful of an uncertain future. As women, we know these feelings of insecurity, worry about what others are thinking, and general fear of the future.

The Mother Aspect

The Mother: the creatrix of life. It's bright summer and fruit hangs heavy on the tree. It's the time of the Mother. The Mother is the worker. She is about creating, laboring, and birthing, and then caring for and providing for her creations. She takes care of individuals, providing unconditional love, support and nurturing. She has no boundaries. She loves and accepts all just as they are. Because she is the lifegiver, the "Mother of Generations," all humanity needs her.

In modern society, we have a love/hate relationship with Mother. We love her for all she does, and yet we hate her for the incredible power she has. When the Mother in woman is imbalanced, she turns into what we call in The QUEEN TEACH-INGS™ the "overgiving Mother." The overgiving Mother runs herself ragged, taking care of others endlessly, providing everything they seem to need ... and more. Her own self-care is last on the list ... or virtually non-existent. The imbalanced Mother becomes exhausted, and resentment – then outright rage – is not far behind. As women, we know these feelings of being resentful over having no time to ourselves, having little support and help, being taken for granted. We know the feelings of being very angry much of the time, and not knowing why.

The Wisewoman Aspect

The Wisewoman (also called The Crone in Goddess culture): the wisdom-holder of life. It's the dark of winter and the seed, filled with the information of life, falls to the ground to bury itself and rest. It's time to go inward, to rest in the nighttime of the year. It's the time of The Wisewoman, the deep, dark and peaceful. The Wisewoman is the "library of wisdom" for humanity. She is the one to whom we go for both good advice and that rare experience, "serenity," with her companionable silences. She knows that often it is not frantic activity that is needed, but simply sitting quietly with "what is." Acceptance. Surrender. She is the one in woman who knows when to stop talking, to cease the constant blathering of the all-important opinion.

The Wisewoman is in touch with magic, mystery and eternity. This aspect appears to be close to death, but magically, paradoxically, She also holds the power of conception, for it is in the deep dark of her belly that the new spark of conception happens in a woman – human life, a piece of wisdom, or an idea for a new project or company. Infinite, she spans time, holding both death and life.

In modern society, we have foolishly thrown away our respect for our actual old women. We belittle the elder woman – "little old lady" – we ignore and dismiss her. A woman entering her senior years without the power of her Queen aspect to keep her strong becomes weak and imbalanced. When the elder woman is imbalanced, she can become depressed, dried up, bitter and stony. "What's the use? They never listen." She feels "over the hill," "past it," no longer relevant to a youth-obsessed culture. She is pessimistic and hopeless ... without purpose ... just waiting to die.

The Queen, Architect of Life

Spring, summer and winter. Maiden, Mother and Wisewoman.

What is missing? The season of The Queen – autumn, the time of the harvest.

The Queen: the architect of life. The Queen is the aspect of woman most missing in modern woman today and it is from this that all our troubles stem. In societies where women do not lead their families as Queens, do not live their lives with the knowledge of the power of the Queen in them, society in general falls into despair and disrepair. The Queen is the one who leads civilization. When civilization is behaving barbarously – as ours clearly is in large part – it is because without their Queen, women cannot serve as the natural spiritual authority to lead humankind to goodness.

The Queen has many powers that humanity desperately needs: She is the visionary, the architect of life. What good is the power to create – the power of The Mother – if there is no intelligent vision and direction behind that power? The thirteen-year-old unwed mother is an example of this. She has the Mother Power of creation, but no Queen to serve as architect to sensibly direct that Mother Power.

Many women just sort of "let life happen" to them. In a woman's life, this is precisely what happens when the architect Queen is missing. "No Queen" leaves women constantly unhappy and dissatisfied, wondering what is wrong.

The Queen Is the Receiver

One of The Queen's many powers is her power to receive. Her season is autumn, the time of the harvest. Most women spend too much of their lives in their giving Mother aspect, but we women should be asking: "When does it come back to us?" The answer is, "Without our Queen ... never." This is the condition of the majority of women across the globe today. They do not experience the life harvest, the reward to work, that should naturally occur.

It is the Mother who gives, and it is the Queen who receives. With a strong Queen, a woman knows how to reap the bounty, how to "bring in the harvest" of all her good "Mother Work." As receiver, the Queen is the "wealthy one." Women all over the world are far poorer than men. How can this be so, when woman is the naturally abundant one? It is because we lack our Queen and are ignorant of her powers for harvest, abundance and wealth.

The Mother is the caregiver, and the Queen is the one who is cared for. Think of the typical mom. She has so much to do. She often feels frazzled and overworked. The Queen is never the frazzled one! She is the one who others serve and care for. Why? Because they know they need a strong and healthy Queen to rule the realm for the good of all. It is in their best interests to take care of their Queen. A woman functioning as a powerful and good queen naturally elicits care from those in her realm – and she knows how to receive it.

The Queen Is the Boundaryholder

The Queen holds boundaries. If the Mother aspect is unconditional, unboundaried love, it is the Queen who knows when to say, "Stop! Enough!" Stuck mostly in our Mother aspect of giving, we women often have no proper boundaries. We continue to give to those who are not appreciative – or even abusive! – because we think we have no choice. We do have a choice. We can bring forth our Queen. The Queen is needed to prevent the Mother in woman from being taken advantage of. How many women continue to provide love and care to men and families who take them for granted, who show no appreciation? This must stop. The Queen knows what to do.

The Queen Is the Leader

The Queen is the leader. Woman is the natural spiritual authority on earth, and we see what happens when woman abdicates this position. Men – without woman and her natural reverence for life, without her natural wisdom for living compassionately and well – make a mess of things. Men's egos run amok and life becomes imbalanced – insane, even. Men all over the world are leading politically, spiritually, and economically without woman.

This should not be so. We need the Spirit of the Queen to lead humanity. We have been falsely taught some myths about the Queen ... the queen bee, the diva, the cold one. Yes, the Queen is impersonal, but she is not cold, and she does not lead in the same way that men do – giving orders, using pressure, force and punishment. Rather, she "leads like water," with no ego. She does not lead in a hierarchical way, with "power over," rather she leads from the center, seeing the big picture, holding center for the good of all. When a woman enters her elder years, if she maintains a strong visionary Queen, she will not be ignored, cast out and belittled. She will be heard.

The Dalai Lama famously said that "It is the Western woman who will save the world." Maybe so, but we've had at least a hundred years to do so. I believe: "It is the Queen in the Western woman who will save the world." When the Queen steps forward with her vision, her ability to receive, her boundaries and her leadership, all the ills of the world begin to fall away. With our Queen, we women need no longer wring our hands and wonder what to do.

Women, Let Us Bring Forth Our Queens

We need to bring forth our Queens. Let her out of the dungeon and into the light of our daily lives, and she will fix everything. People won't like it at first. They think they want you to continue to be the people-pleasing Maiden, always nice, always accommodating. They think they want you to continue to be the over-giving Mother, overworking, uncomplaining, washing their socks, cooking their meals, providing everything they need. They think they want you to continue to be the nice old granny, making cookies but never making waves.

But they really don't. A Queen's realm is anything for which she is 100% responsible. Realms run by women who do not understand their Queen are realms that feel unsafe to all within it. The Queen creates a sense of order, safety and a feeling that the future is secure. It is the Queen in woman who is the architect of the good life for all.

The Queen solves everything. With her, life is "as it was always meant to be."™

About Ava ...

Ava is recognized as a leader in the teaching of the Queen archetype in woman with her "Queen of Your Realm"™ classes, convocations and cruises. Says Ava, "When the Goddess got thrown out of religion, the Queen got thrown out of Woman." Ava is dedicated to the return of the Queen in women everywhere, as she believes this powerful queenly quality of woman's natural spiritual authority is exactly what humanity desperately now needs to return to peace, justice and prosperity. She is the founder and Presiding Priestess of The Goddess Temple of Orange County, "a world sacred site of devotional pilgrimage, historical education and spiritual ceremony." The Temple is the only temple of its kind in the world, celebrating its tenth year, a beautiful 3,200 square foot woman-centered space dedicated to Goddess, with all major cultures and times represented in

numinous altars and educational museum displays.
Website: www.GoddessTempleOC.org

Chapter 10

Motherhood and Power

by Barbara G. Walker

Even after men came to understand fatherhood and sought to personify it in a god, it was hard for them to oppose the matriarchate. The act of begetting still seemed trivial by comparison with the mother's extended care and manifold skills. According to the Book of Maccabees, a mother's sympathy for her children was always deeper than a father's. The *Mahanirvanatantra* says, "Mother is superior to father on account of her bearing and also nourishing the child." Menander wrote, "A mother loves her child more than a father does." The Laws of Manu declare, "A spiritual teacher exceeds a worldly teacher ten times, a father exceeds a spiritual teacher one hundred times, but a mother exceeds one thousand times a father's claim to honor on the part of the child and as its educator." As the old Irish proverb put it, "To every cow belongs her calf."

Even as newly conscious fathers, early men feared to oppose the social power of women because of their conviction that women were allied with cosmic forces. In West Africa, men said that "women were more powerful than men, for to them alone the mysteries of the gods and of secret things were known." Women founded the magical Egbo society, but after men learned to practice the secret rites, women were forbidden to participate anymore. Similarly in Queensland, once men learned to practice magic, they forbade women to use it anymore, saying that women had too much natural aptitude for it, which gave them an unfair advantage.

Men of Malekula frankly admitted that all their religious rituals were stolen from women, who had invented them. Men of

Tierra del Fuego said women used to rule the world by witch-craft, and all religious mysteries belonged to their Goddess, who was identified with the moon. Eventually, men adopted the cult of the sun god and under his leadership murdered all the adult women of the tribe, leaving only immature girls who didn't yet know the religious mysteries. A transparently mendacious Iatmul legend said that women invented all the sacred things and secrets of magic, then "gave" these things to men and "asked" the men to murder them, so that no woman would know the secrets anymore.

Similar battles of the sexes occurred in the ancient world. The Norse Vanir or Elder Deities, led by Mother Earth and the Goddess Freya, were overthrown by new patriarchal deities from Asia, the Aesir, led by Father Odin. In the Aegean, followers of Father Zeus attacked the pre-Hellenic worshippers of Mother Rhea (or Hera) and revised scriptures to force her into an unwanted marriage with their god. In Babylonian scriptures, the god Marduk rebelled against his own mother, Tiamat, who repre-sented the sea-womb and its "waters," the mother-essence. Marduk killed her, divided her in two, and from her halves made heaven and the abyss. Obviously, it was from this Babylonian myth that bible writers derived their God who "divided the waters which were under the firmament from the waters which were above the firmament" (Gen. 1:7).

Even modern scholars, who should know better, often describe Tiamat as nothing more than a "dragon" slain by the heroic Marduk, although the old scriptures clearly say that she was the hero's mother and the Creatress of the World, as well as the mother of all the gods. Her very name meant "Goddess Mother" like the Latin Dia Mater.

It was true in antiquity, and it is still true, that male writers tend to diabolize or trivialize figures of the Goddess once she has been declared subordinate to a god. Mexican Aztecs, for example, said the former ruler of all men and beasts was the Goddess

Malinalxochitl; but she was overthrown by her brother, the legendary leader of the Aztecs, and was afterward described as "a bad witch." Innumerable Goddess figures in European history have been assimilated as "demons" (Lilith, Hecate, Hel, Lamia, etc.) or else humanized as saints, or their ancient shrines have been rededicated to "Our Lady" of this-and-that.

The overthrow of the matriarchate was almost always mythologized as a violent attack of men upon women, representing invasions and usurpations of old systems of mother-right. "This legend of leadership being wrested from the women, either by force or coercion, is too widely spread throughout the world to be lightly ignored." According to Engels, "The overthrow of mother-right was the world-historical downfall of the female sex."

However, in ways not immediately apparent, it may have been the downfall of the male sex also. It brought essential changes in social attitudes which may have been destructive. The late theologian Mary Daly points out that matriarchy was not patriarchy spelled with an "m," not a hierarchy preserved by fear, with women on top: "'On top' thinking, imagining and acting are essentially patriarchal." The violence, intolerance, and ruthless power-seeking characteristics of patriarchal societies seem to have been largely absent from those earlier, matrifocal ones, which would have meant more comfortable lives for all.

Matriarchal or semi-matriarchal societies still in existence in the past few centuries tended to show the spirit of affirmation in the behavior of individuals toward one another. Some Native Americans, for example, worshipped the female principle and were ruled by chiefs elected by councils of matriarchs, known as Female Governesses, Mistresses of the Soil, or Life of the Nation. Sometimes the people surprised Christian missionaries with the nobility of their behavior. One missionary wrote, "What is extremely surprising in men whose external appearance is wholly barbarous, is to see them treat one another with a gentleness and consideration which one does not find among common people in the most civilized countries." Much of this behavior seems to have been determined by feminine influences. As one Native American man explained to a white questioner, "Of course the men follow the wishes of the women; they are our mothers."

Examples are numerous in the annals of anthropology to indicate that ideas of the sacredness of motherhood may be one of the few really effective deterrents of violence. Ancient people believed that those who shared mother-blood shared a soul. Real injury to one might mean magical injury to the other. Therefore, the children of one mother couldn't harm each other without putting themselves at risk, just as voodoo practitioners induce the "soul" of an enemy to inhabit a doll, then "kill" it by magical means. Bonds based on fatherhood seemed to lack the basic cohesiveness of those based on motherhood. Egyptians and other ancient peoples often distinguished between children of the same father and children of the same mother; the latter were assumed to be the only "real" siblings. This alone would make a man think twice about injuring anyone related to him in the female line.

It followed that if all people are related by blood to the same Great Mother, from whom all descended, then they are universal siblings, and should not shed the blood of their own kind, and warfare could be seen as a sin against motherhood. Even aggressive savages, like the Dobu Islanders, viewed motherhood as an antidote to war. They believed that mutual trust can be maintained only among members of the matrilineal kinship group, which was known as "mother's milk."

Some past societies dreaded even a temporary loss of the divine mother image. Of the seasonal period when the Goddess departed from the world, Apuleius wrote: "There has been no pleasure, no joy, no merriment anywhere, but all things lie in rude unkempt neglect; wedlock and true friendship and parents' love for their children have vanished from the earth; there is one vast disorder, one hateful loathing and foul disregard for the bonds of love." When the Goddess was permanently displaced, a widespread sense of alienation became a social norm.

Unlike other social animals, human beings engage in mass slaughters of fellow members of their own species, which are clearly related to male dominance and father-imagery within the society. Phyllis Chesler points out that whatever else it may be, war is an expression of Oedipal aggressions: a legal way for dominant elder males to destroy large numbers of younger, more virile rivals. Since the overthrow of matriarchy, "mothers have no power to stop this senseless male killing of the children, their own and the children of other mothers."

The mother figure affects the psyche in a different way from father imagery. There are indications that the human psyche still longs for the vision of its first acknowledged parent. It may be that a return to the Goddess image could ease the modern sense of alienation, as well as restoring to women the former deep sense of their worth rather than their sinfulness. Anthropologist Robert Briffault (1876–1948) gives us food for thought when he says, "The maternal totemic clan was by far the most successful form that human association has assumed – it may indeed be said that it has been the only successful one."

Society becomes sexist when the original Mother Goddess / Creatress is replaced by a father god, who doesn't give birth but creates the world in some more artificial way, by breath or by the use of a magic word, the Logos. Even that, however, was stolen from Goddess traditions that claimed her use of the first life-giving word. In Sanskrit, her word was *Om*. Greek renders it Omega, "great *Om*," placing it at the end of the alphabet instead of at the beginning; but in pre-Hellenic cyclic religious imagery, the Omega and the Alpha were united in endless recurrences of the Great Round, birth and death alternating, for all creatures as well as for humans and even the universe itself.

When all humanity took it for granted that birthgiving was

synonymous with creating, the concept of a creative father god gained credence only with glacial slowness. But once the idea of a supreme creative male power became acceptable, and biological fatherhood was finally understood, the process of denying divine authority to women and repressing ancestral Goddess worship began its long evolution.

A characteristic of patriarchal society is reckless exploitation of nature, another way of enslaving the divine Earth Mother. Biblical Genesis presents this as man's God-given right to "have dominion over" and "subdue" all the natural world; modern men like to call it the "conquest" of nature. The ancients looked upon the Goddess as immanent in nature. For them, the material world was not sinful but sacred. Native Americans and many other "primitive" groups had the same idea.

The patriarchs, on the other hand, declared that all nature was soulless and had little to do with God, who was transcendent, existing apart from the material world, which some Christians claimed was actually created by the devil. Out of disrespect for the earth and for other life forms arose the ruthless exploitation of nature for the benefit of *mankind* alone. This exploitation is a plague possessing serious implications for the future of the planet.

Another characteristic of patriarchy is the "We–They" syndrome: setting up a hierarchy in which invidious compar- isons are always being made. Men are better than women, our country is better than your country, the rich are better than the poor, white people are better than black people, Aryans are better than Jews, Muslims are better than anybody; and so on through centuries of hate propaganda to justify war, oppression and genocide. Goddess-oriented societies were more democratic. Their model was not a pyramid but a circle, indicating the wholeness of all parts.

Among humans, male aggressiveness has been encouraged by religious sanctions to oppress females and children, while the natural family head, the mother, has been disenfranchised. "The subordination of women is not natural at all, and it is different in kind from anything seen in nature among other primates." It exists today in large part because women have been made ignorant of their religious and social history. Gods created in the image of man have plagued human culture for too long a time. Knowledge of the primal Goddess, the natural leader for all beings born of a mother, is coming to light again and might serve in some sense to create a safer, kinder and more tolerant environment for the children of Mother Earth.

About Barbara G. Walker ...

Barbara G. Walker is a researcher, lecturer, and author of twenty-three books and numerous articles on comparative religion, history, mythology, symbolism, mineral lore, the Tarot, the I Ching, a collection of original *Feminist Fairy Tales*, an autobiography, a novel, and her latest, *Man Made God*. Her *Woman's Encyclopedia of Myths and Secrets* has been continuously in print for more than a quarter of a century and was named Book of the Year by the London *Times*. She has received the Humanist Heroine of the Year award from the American Humanist Association, the Women Making Herstory award from New Jersey NOW, and the Olympia Brown award from the Unitarian Universalist Association. She is also listed in that prestigious publication, "Who's Who in Hell."

As an artist, she created seventy-eight original paintings for the Barbara Walker Tarot Deck, and sixty-four more for her I Ching of the Goddess card deck, both published with companion books. She has also worked as a professional knitwear designer, and her books on knitting patterns are American classics. She personally invented more than a thousand original pattern stitches, more than any other single person known to history, and created a new technique that she named Mosaic Knitting.

A Phi Beta Kappa graduate of the University of Pennsylvania, she has worked as a journalist, dance teacher, painter, designer, workshop leader, and mentor of women's spirituality groups as well as a wife and mother, and has presented many talks for Humanist, Unitarian, and Freethinker organizations.

Chapter 11

The Queen:
Empowering Model for Midlife Women

by Donna Henes

Aging and changing might be inevitable, but it ain't easy. It precipitates in us a great uncertainty. The myriad dramatic disturbances of modern middle life – menopause, health concerns, career shifts, the empty nest, divorce and death – create an overwhelming crisis of identity and purpose for each of us.

Who are we supposed to be at this stage of our life when we are less likely to be bound and identified by our kinship connection to someone else – as a daughter, a wife, a mother, a lover? What exactly is our role as older-than-young and younger-than-old women who are still active, attractive and more effective than ever?

Ever since I first started introducing The Queen as a helpful archetype for midlife women in my workshops and articles, I have received thousands of requests for detailed instructions on how to become a Queen. "Dear Mama Donna," women would write, "I want to be a Queen, too. How do I access my power? How can I feel good about myself? How do I change my life? How do I find magic and spiritual wisdom? How do I know what to do? How do I learn how to rule?"

Indeed. How are women supposed to know how to own our own sovereignty? We certainly haven't been taught. World mythology abounds with inspiring examples of beautiful and adventurous Maidens, compassionate and nurturing Mothers (as well as some devouring ones), and wise and wily Crones. But these archetypes don't include me or other women in our middle years. They do not address our issues and needs. They do not even recognize our existence. The old stereotypes simply do not apply to us. We haven't been Maidens in decades, we are no longer Mother material, and we are definitely not old Crones. Where are the archetypal role models for us?

We midlife women today desperately need a new body of role models, ideals, examples and teachers to encourage us to create new and joyful ways of being in charge of our own destiny. In the absence of a traditional mythic example to spur me on and sustain me through my own midlife changes, I perceived the need to invent one. And so I did, thus providing me and other women of my generation with a recognizable role model for our middle years: The Queen.

Was this hubris? Who am I to conceive an archetype? Well, I am in fact, a proud member of the pioneering Sixties Generation, and consequently, I have a certain modest amount of experience in rebelling against the status quo of old systems and beliefs and striving to replace them with new, more inclusive and relevant ones. Bereft of affirming depictions of our lives, today's women-of-a-certain-age are more than ready, willing, and perfectly capable of creating our own.

The Queen paradigm promotes a new understanding of what it means to be a middle-aged woman today who accepts full responsibility for and to her Self. And it celebrates the physical, mental, emotional and spiritual rewards of doing so.

Becoming a Queen is not automatic. The Queen bursts forth from adversity and previous constraints, actual or imagined, to become a proficient player in the game plan of *her* choice. The Queen does not invite hard times and trouble, but she chooses to use them well. Actualized, organized, efficient, self-sufficient, competent, ethical and fair, the Queen has struggled for and earned *her* authority and respect. Determined and firmly centered on *her* own two feet, she dares to climb, step after step, with nascent surety into the heady realm of *her* own highest sovereignty.

This mythic model that I envision is recognizably like me, like us. Not yet old, yet no longer young, still active and sexy, vital with the enthusiasm and energy of youth, she is tempered with the hard-earned experience and leavening attitudes of age. She has been forced to face and overcome obstacles and hard lessons, including her own shadow, and in so doing, has outgrown the boundaries of Her old self.

Agitated with the unessential and restless for authenticity, she sheds all attachment to the opinions of others and accepts complete responsibility and control for her own care, feeding and fulfillment. She is the Queen of Her Self, the mature monarch, the sole sovereign of her own life and destiny. Here, finally, is an archetype that fits.

About Donna Henes ...

Donna Henes is an internationally renowned urban shaman, contemporary ceremonialist, spiritual teacher, award-winning author, popular speaker and workshop leader whose joyful celebrations of celestial events have introduced ancient traditional rituals and contemporary ceremonies to millions of people in more than 100 cities since 1972. She has published four books, a CD, an acclaimed Ezine and writes for *The Huffington Post*, Beliefnet and UPI Religion and Spirituality Forum. A noted ritual expert, she serves as a ritual consultant for the television and film industry. Mama Donna, as she is affectionately called, maintains a ceremonial center, spirit shop, ritual practice and consultancy in Exotic Brooklyn, NY where she offers intuitive tarot readings and spiritual counseling, and works with individuals, groups, institutions, municipalities and corporations to create meaningful ceremonies for every imaginable occasion.

Websites:

www.DonnaHenes.net

www.TheQueenOfMySelf.com

www.mamadonnasspiritshop.com

www.treeoflifefunerals.com

Part II

Embracing the Sacred Feminine
Ritual and Healing

There was a time when you were not a slave, remember that. You walked alone, full of laughter, you bathed bare-bellied. You say you have lost all recollection of it, remember ... You say there are no words to describe this time, you say it does not exist. But remember. Make an effort to remember. Or, failing that, invent.

– Monique Wittig

Chapter 12

Mysteries of Menstruation

by Judy Grahn

My earliest reclaiming of menstruation as a cultural subject – a short poem written in 1970 – was part of a surge of feminism that occurred in the middle of the very unpopular Vietnam War, an example of male bloodshed that was everywhere in evidence and filled us with horror. Surprising even ourselves, a few of us burgeoning feminist cultural leaders turned toward women's blood, expressing through our arts especially that loving and honoring women's blood was a way of loving and honoring women. Though we didn't know it at the time, revising some elements of women's blood rituals is a possible replacement for continuing the rituals of violence that were and are so clearly not working.

The ineffectiveness of the blood ritual of war as a solution to national, community, or personal problems has been displayed repeatedly since the American war on Vietnam, through the US invasion of tiny Grenada, the interference in South and Central American civil wars, and the devastation thrust on civilians and soldiers alike in both the Iraq and Afghanistan wars. In addition, on US soil ongoing gang-violence, and the acceleration of femicide by out-of-control husbands and boyfriends, continue to be powerful reminders that we need better, effective blood rituals, rituals of peace. Many of these can be found within the matrix of women's worldwide coming-of-age rites – sitting mindfully still for days on end, fasting, resting in a steam-bath, being extremely careful with one's gestures, voice, demeanor, and gaze; cultivating service, gratitude and humility without capitulating to tyranny in any form. Passing tests of exertion, personal risk, and endurance. Celebrating the sacred, and making consistent gifts and offerings to nature, rather than passively sucking up all she has to offer, and more.

Beyond that initial burst of feminist enthusiasm for women and our bodies, a second surprise for me has been the sheer difficulty of conveying the contributions of women to culture through our own female rituals. I found that the challenging task of coming out as a lesbian, first to my parents in the fifties and sixties, and then as a public lesbian organizer, co-founding Gay Women's Liberation on the West Coast in late 1969, though difficult, was easier in some ways than it has been to "come out" as a theorist of menstruation's link to culture-making. The reason for this seems to have to do with both patriarchal religion and science suppressing, shaming, or overlooking the subject of women's blood. And of defining "maleness" as having strictly oppositional qualities to this state of shame.

To me a most astonishing aspect of menstrual rituals is that the onset of the flow was celebrated in so many cultures around the world, while in my own Protestant family, I was cautioned not to speak of it, and my mother was obviously ashamed of her own and her daughter's perfectly natural monthly event. That picture is typical in the US, especially in longtime Christian families, yet very different in other parts of the world where, I would gradually learn, menstruation was a woman's power, not shame.

Origin stories reflect the absence of women as positive culture forces – the two stories that I grew up with were Genesis and Darwinian evolution. Neither credits woman with creation of culture; Genesis in fact blames her for humanity's ills while Darwin declares that she would have been too busy caring for her babies to contribute to culture. As eco-feminists point out, women have been mythologized as "nature" in contrast to men as "culture." In the absence of any inclusion of women as positive forces in culture, mass societies have become entirely too dependent on male blood rituals.

Though I use the word "patriarchy" to describe contemporary problems, this is not a call to cast out the many beneficial contributions of men's bleeding rites, originally constructed as "menstruation," and other times more veiled yet imitating the practices deeply embedded in women's menstrual rites. (See Gregory Gajus' article in *Metaformia: A Journal of Menstruation and Culture*, for an example of a culturally aware Gay man examining practices of men's bath houses.) Modern skills of surgery grew from the practices of barbers in war zones, for example.

My studies of menstrual rituals led me to invent a term – metaform – to mean units of cultural meaning stemming from menstrual and related blood rituals. My metaformic studies show that yes, women are identified closely with nature, with trees and plants, various animals, planets, sun and moon, and the earth itself, in countless mythologies, and in art. A premise of metaformic study then became the question of why, and the answer was another surprise. Evidently peoples around the world experienced the beings of nature as menstrual beings, and as mothers like themselves. Women, as gatherers, knew plants intimately, and identified some of them as being like themselves – as having qualities of menstruation, such as red flowers, fruits or sap.

Ancestral women also understood their own bodies as carrying cosmic energies – both beneficial and malevolent, and they understood the world of nature as inhabited by similar charged energies. Through their empathetic identification with natural beings, they spoke to the plants respectfully as mothers who would feel badly about the loss of their children. Women brought plants home as members of their extended family and cared for them the way they cared for their own daughters. They used "menstrual blood" of all kinds of beings – red plant sap, red ochre – as a signal language for this communication. They sang and decorated themselves as a kind of dialogue with the mother plants, asking permission to gather the plants' young without rousing the spirits in nature to harm their own human children, through illness or accident. Thus, the connections of women to nature are always cultural connections, and led directly to the arts of horticulture, as well as other arts and sciences. The connections also show that ancestral peoples understood and in some cases continue to understand natural beings as conscious beings with their own animal, vegetable, or mineral cultures.

If we, people of mass culture, were to revise and continue these traditions, how much easier would it be for us to engage with deep ecology and demand that corporations and governments alter their – and our – behaviors toward the ecosystems of Mother Earth?

These intimate and respectful relationships lead to yet one more mystery – why is it that humankind practices what we call "religion" – a sense of origin coming from outside of ourselves, and complex dialogues between ourselves and the natural world, whether imagined as spirit, or consciousness, or creator beings, or goddesses and gods.

When I did some comparisons of rituals in South India for my dissertation, the connections became crystal clear to me. Maidens at menarche in some communities, even into modern times, are considered goddesses. Menstruation was formerly endowed with astounding superhuman powers – both good and bad, auspicious and destructive – that were regulated through carefully proscribed behaviors.

As patriarchies have encroached on matrilineal cultures, sometimes quickly, or sometimes, as in India, very slowly, the positive and negative aspects of menstrual powers have split apart. Monthly menstruation has picked up the negative taboos, and become considered "dirty," while menarche remained publically celebrated until very recently. Ultimately, as occurred in Europe and the US, male-centered religions and secular societies alike replace women's blood rites with male blood rites, and menstruation becomes shamed for generations, and then as has happened more recently, medicalized, treated as a biological fact related to human fertility but losing its cultural roots altogether.

Hence the obvious turn my activist friends and I effected in the 1970s as we reclaimed cultural and artful meanings of our own blood flow. The journey of menstrual cultural exploration for me has been extraordinary, as I have found that things Metaformic are real; even parts of the theory that seemed a stretch have been demonstrated to the point that I can call it Metaformic Consciousness, an embodied philosophy.

Contemporary women across the globe are engaged in both a reclamation of, and a separation from, ancestral menstrual rites, depending on where they live. When rituals have become hide-bound we must break away from them to find a renewed freedom, and in many countries women are doing just that. They are leaving behind rites that have gone out of date, become quaint or even repulsive, and embracing a more "Western" stance toward independence. But when freedom becomes wild devouring, heedless addiction and out-of-control consumption, accompanied by cruel wars and other violence, as has happened from many long centuries within cultures dominated by the blood rites of patriarchy, then a reclamation is in order, to reassert the powers of the ancestral feminine, renewed, revised, restored for current times and needs.

That is the project students of Metaformic Consciousness have embarked upon.

About Judy Grahn ...

Judy Grahn is internationally known as a poet, mythologist, and cultural theorist. Her writings helped fuel second-wave feminist, gay, and lesbian activism, beginning in 1965 when she picketed the White House for Gay rights, and wrote her first article, "A Lesbian Speaks Her Mind," published the next year in *Sexology Magazine*. She co-founded Gay Women's Liberation and the

Women's Press Collective in 1969.

Judy began engaging with a burgeoning Women's Spirituality Movement in 1972, with a series of thirty-two poems called *She Who*, which have been called "the goddess as a verb." One of the goddesses she has written about extensively and is revisioning through poetry is Helen of Troy, who links to both Sumerian Inanna and Gnostic Sophia. Judy has published two (of an expected four) book-length poems on her, and is currently writing the third, *The Queen of Cups*.

In 1973 she began a lifelong exploration of the relationship between menstrual rituals and human culture, publishing "Menstruation: From Sacred to the Curse and Beyond," in Charlene Spretnak's 1981 anthology, *The Politics of Women's Spirituality*. Judy's Metaformic Theory is laid out in *Blood, Bread, and Roses: How Menstruation Created the World*, published by Beacon Press in 1993. An Indian filmmaker, Vipin Vijay, made a 55-minute film, *Poomaram*, or the *Flowering Tree*, on this book in 2008.

Additional work addressing LGBT as well as feminist approaches to the sacred include nonfiction books *Another Mother Tongue: Gay Words, Gay Worlds*; and *The Highest Apple: Sappho and the Lesbian Poetic Tradition*; and a novel, *Mundane's World*.

Her latest books are a collection of poetry and prose, *The Judy Grahn Reader*, and her memoir, *A Simple Revolution: The Making of an Activist Poet*.

Judy is a professor in the Women's Spirituality Master's Program at Sofia University in Palo Alto, California. She co-edits an online journal based in her theory of ritual origins: *Metaformia: A Journal of Menstruation and Culture*, www.metaformia.com.

Email: judy.grahn@sofia.edu or judygrahn@gmail.com

Chapter 13

Ancient Egyptian Dream Temples: Doorways to Alternate States of Consciousness

by Normandi Ellis

As I have begun more research and thinking about Egyptian states of consciousness, I have come to realize how strongly Egypt understood itself to be "a thought-form civilization" that was both temporal and eternal. They created a long-lived culture, recognizing as they did so that they as individuals were but a part of a vast organization of conscious Mind. They also understood the eternal realm as just as real as the physical.

As above, so below.

As the pharaoh and his court organized life in Egypt – its warehouses of grains, its roads, its towns and seafaring travels – the pharaoh as high priest along with his priests and priestesses organized the work of the gods, made not just supplications but invocations and worked as co-creators of the spirit-filled life of the temples. These temples not only honored the gods through liturgy and rites on a daily basis, but they also held a great many festivals in honor of their gods and goddesses (the *neteru*). These priests and priestesses provided counseling and aid from beyond through healing, personal ritual and dream interpretation.

Over time, certain temples and their priests or priestesses became well-known for their oracular work with dream interpretations and healings. In ancient Egypt there were many active dream temples, and nearly all of them were connected to the divinity of that temple. Among the more famous oracular temples, for example, was the Temple of Amun at Siwa Oasis, which legend says was founded by one of two African sibyls who were banished to the desert from the Temple of Amun in Luxor. The appearance of the lush Siwa Oasis in the midst of the vast Libyan Desert may be one reason why the temple was founded there. Its simple presence in the midst of emptiness seems miraculous, so one might expect other such vibrant miracles to follow.

Possibly, the arduous trek through drifting sand, the blinding sun, and intense heat caused heat prostration that altered one's consciousness. When that exhausted individual, far removed from everyday life, collapsed inside the temple, all manner of unusual visions, spirit visitations, and dreams might have occurred. Led by two magical crows through the desert to the dream temple at Siwa, Alexander the Great supposedly was confirmed as the future king of Egypt by the oracle of Amun.

Another famous dream oracle was connected to Hatshepsut's mortuary temple at Deir el Bahari. A scribe named Kenhirkhopeshef in the nearby village of Deir el Medina kept a library that contained his own dream book. It offers 108 unusual dream symbols and associations to the modern mind, but when one considers that much of dream life, whether ancient or modern, engages in word puns, we might consider that the meanings of a hieroglyphic dream book may be lost in translation.

Certainly some of these dream images also appeared in many chapters of the Book of the Dead, which the workers of Deir el Medina were employed to emblazon on tomb walls in the Valley of the Kings and Queens. The aforementioned dream book of Kenhirkhopeshef, for example, mentions a man eating his own excrement, while in the Book of the Dead there appears an underworld guardian of the gates whose name is Eater of His Own Excrement. In the dream and in the afterlife as well, knowing the name of the formidable shadow figure was a good thing.

The ancient text does give us prescriptions for how to have a dream, or how to dream an answer to a question, for example, how to dream of your future spouse. This dreaming with intention included how to fill out the dream request. In reality, this technique was working with thought form as intention; and a dream intention is really about having your conscious mind tell another part of your consciousness what question it needs to have answered. When you tell yourself in this way you will have a powerful dream. We moderns sleep with a dream journal and an ink pen next to the bed, in case we have a dream. But really, it is the dream ritual that sets the intention to have the dream. And we more often will remember it if we write it down.

It interests me that three hieroglyphic words all use the same root word (*res*), a hieroglyph of a half-opened eye, to indicate the same dreamlike states of being: to dream (*res-t*), a name for the underworld (Res-tau) and an anagram for the god of the underworld Osiris (Auser), a god who used the dreamtime to teach his son the esoteric means of ruling Egypt. This means that the dream state possibly was considered to be another kind of seeing – perhaps a truer form of sight because the ego stood apart from it. Res-tau in fact may be related to an astral dream world to which both the living and the dead had access.

Because many dreams are only partially understood or recalled, dream incubation and interpretation were important temple functions. Most temples offered dream consultations to those who entered as "a pure one, washed and fasted." Revelatory dreams were common in the temples of Isis, Anubis, Amun, and Re – even in the temples of Imhotep at Saqqara and Seti I at Abydos. Often the particular dream *neter* was chosen because he or she was known to provide help of a specific nature. For example, women hoping to glimpse their future children came to the dream temples of Isis.

Some oracular dreams prophesied future destinies, like the dream of a royal son, Tuthmosis IV, who was hunting one day and fell asleep beneath the chin of the Sphinx. The Sphinx told him that if he removed the sand that clogged its neck and body, he would receive the throne of Egypt. Whether the particular dream oracles of Tuthmosis IV or Alexander the Great were actual or part of a hagiography, it is difficult to tell of course, but they do offer some understanding of the importance of dreaming in ancient times.

Some dreams offered transactions with the Divine, such as the forgiveness of sins committed or similar judgments that meant that the gods understood the dreamer's secret needs. Because the gods could peer into one's soul, by interpreting dream images one could divine the future and make amends before things happened. Departed family and friends often appeared in dreams as messengers from the other side. Myrrh was the dream incubation aroma that Isis was said to use when contacting Osiris in the dream world; and the incense was also used in burial and mourning rituals.

Dream time during the Old Kingdom differed from dream time in the Greco-Roman era when dreaming became a kind of national pastime. Skilled priest-dreamers, who acted as shamans for their king, engaged in dream practices that were more along the lines of remote viewing, astral travel, and vision questing. The high priest who performed the secret rites of the pharaoh's renewal festival may have created a mystery play in which the pharaoh experienced his death. With the aid of plant medicines, the pharaoh entered a trance and connected with the ancestral spirits and the gods.

This long history of vision questing here may have led to the Serapeum (built in Saqqara by the high priest-scribe Khaemwast during the Eighteenth Dynasty) becoming known as a dream temple during the Greco-Roman era. Tales of the many astral travels and adventures of Khaemwast, son of Ramses II, caused Khaemwast to reach the level of epic folk hero after his death. And his father, Ramses the Great, the most long-lived pharaoh of Egypt, boasted about having completed thirteen jubilee festivals at Saqqara, the first after his thirtieth year of reign, and subsequent festivals followed every three years thereafter.

The big dreams came only seldom. More often, dreams were of a more mundane, personal nature, such as dreams of overeating, losing status, losing one's teeth, being naked, being elevated in stature. Many scribes kept copies of dream books, in which they recorded their interpretations. Still, dream interpretation was up to the individual consultant to determine the true nature and meaning of the dream.

Dreamers came to the temple to meet with the priest-scribe in the house of life and receive dream charms, healings, dream interpretations, or counteractions against psychic attacks. The temple library contained many sacred texts, including the texts of all the temple rites and secrets, and so, the library was well protected and kept shrouded in great mystery. The sacredness of its contents automatically elevated the lector priests who attended it and who kept the *medjat,* or the papyrus scrolls. From this word, meaning "holy words," we derive the Greek word *magikos* and the Old Persian word *madju,* or magi.

Many dream charms included words directed to the god Bes, an African pygmy god often found in birthing temples to Hathor at Dendera and to Isis at Philae. Bes was such a popular dream god that many people kept a statue of him in their homes. In addition to working with us in altered states, Bes was also a god of childbirth because, let's face it, the process of birthing a child is an altered state. Thus, he also commanded a lot of energy as a protector of sleeping children, guarding them in the dream time. When my own daughter used to suffer from nightmares, I presented her with a statue of Bes who stood guard at her bedside table. And to this day, I work with Bes when I am astrally traveling in the dream time.

One ancient Egyptian dream spell suggested drawing an image of Bes on the left hand in black ink mixed with myrrh, frankincense, cinnabar, and rainwater (hard to get in the desert!), along with the juice of wormwood and the blood of a black cow and a dove. Then, black cloth dedicated to Isis was wrapped around the hand. (The rest of the cloth was wound about the neck!) After an invocation at sunset, the dreamer in total silence went to sleep. If one spent that much energy in the pursuit of an important dream, certainly the subconscious mind would receive a powerful suggestion. Being receptive to a possible appearance, more than likely the big dream would come.

As I mentioned, dreams were important to the Egyptians because dreaming was Isis's preferred method for contacting Osiris. Likewise, dreams were the method in which Osiris trained his orphaned son Horus to defeat Seth, who kept trying to kill him and take his throne. Anyone who has traveled in Egypt for some time knows that upon return home, the ancient world has been imprinted so strongly in the brain that we often dream about and receive nightly visitations from the land we explored psychically and physically by day.

All ancient Egyptians knew that life existed in other dimensions, and that this alternate life was similar to a world already known. Familiarity with the divine beings who peopled the Elysian Fields and the underworld made it easier for them to see the gods in their dreams, or even walking through the streets. They used affirmations to remind themselves that when we sleep our consciousness travels. The body rests, but the mind is at work, learning and exploring in other dimensions.

Dreams always came in service of healing. It's something we moderns forget. In our culture we think of a dream as merely interesting – sometimes disturbing. We tell a dream as if it were a cartoon snippet, then we discount it. We need to remember that a dream is intended for our personal and spiritual growth. These days I find more and more people seeing that dreams come into the service of health and wholeness. Dreams connect us with all our parts: psychological, mental, spiritual and physical.

Edgar Cayce used to visit the astral realm intentionally. He made himself sleep and when he awoke he came back with cures and messages for people from the other side. He said that when he did this, he was tapping into the akashic records, which hold information for us from both the past, the present and the future selves. Dreams tap into ALL the different layers of our existence. Most often on a conscious level, we don't connect to all those multiple levels at the same time. We haven't even begun to touch what really happens in our sleeping lives.

Dream counselors have called them "unopened letters from God," and in the broadest sense I will say they are messages that come from consciousness itself. We are extensions of a much mightier consciousness that is attempting to make itself known to us and through us. Perhaps that just reconfirms the idea that we are a microcosm of the macrocosm. When we sleep we are more able to tap into that greater level of consciousness because in sleep, we let the rational ego go.

Paying attention to our dreams shows us that there is an interconnected web of being that is creation itself – and we are a part of it. More than that, we come to see that in each part of it, the whole is contained. So, in fact, we are consciousness dreaming itself whether we are asleep or awake. Knowing that helps me to make meaning of some of the dreamlike states of being that occur when I am actually awake, such as synchronicities, or what we would call nothing more than our imagination.

Now, we come to see that creative types of any stripe know that the imagination can be and often is more real than what we mistake as "ordinary" reality. Let's face it: If I am going to have a reality, why would I want to have an ordinary one?

I have begun to see that the imaginal realm is the inheritance of the visual and creative artist. In ancient Egypt art functioned as spiritual landscape. The beautifully constructed and painted temples of the ancients are the dreamscape in real time through which the Egyptians walked and in which they lived. Thus, it became easier to tap into the collective dream because on a daily basis they were living right inside it.

About Normandi Ellis ...

Normandi Ellis is a spiritualist medium and the author of ten books of fiction and nonfiction. Her nonfiction is rooted in her studies and travels in Egypt and includes the spiritual classic *Awakening Osiris,* and most recently *Invoking the Scribes of Ancient Egypt* and *Imagining the World into Existence* (Bear & Co). Her recent fiction, *Going West,* was published by Wind Publications. She facilitates spiritual travel through Egypt.

Website: www.normandiellis.com

Chapter 14

Honoring Goddesses Reawakens Women-Honoring Multiculturalism

by Elizabeth Fisher

Around the globe, those enthusiastic about earth-honoring spirituality openly praise female deities without reservation: in essence they Rise Up and Call Her Name.[1] Even in more conventional religions, the female images, like the Virgin of Guadalupe, have been reclaimed by those who advocate for full equality and freedom for women. The Female Divine has made her impact on the modern human psyche, adding fuel to the worldwide effort on behalf of women's human rights. When these female deities are truly honored, the misogynous aspects of diverse cultures are often challenged. Interpretations of what is valuable in human society are revised to incorporate universal human rights and environmental justice. So, what are the characteristics of this Global Goddess and earth-centered spirituality?

The One and the Many

I am sometimes asked, "Is this belief in a Great Goddess just another monotheistic conceptualization, only now with a female face?" Earth-centered concepts of the divine are both/and constructs. She is both diverse and united. Some understand these diverse images from many cultures as faces of the One Great Goddess. In my experience, while she carries quite varied personas, her overarching presence gives her a monotheistic tone qualitatively different from male-centered monotheism.

Thealogically, she is the cosmos of which we are all a part – multifaceted yet integrated. Because I am describing a belief system that is unique to this planet, the term "earth-based" is used, though the concept of Goddess, for those who honor her, invariably incorporates an appreciation for the vast universe as well.

New Ways of Knowing

Western societies are frequently called modern. Indigenous cultures that maintain practices that are more closely aligned with pre-industrial ways of living are labeled primitive. In these traditions, the Goddess or Spirit is immanent in all creation: animals, plants, rocks. The elements of water, fire, earth, and the air we breathe are the Goddess manifest. To know the Goddess calls us to seek to know all creation. As communication and knowledge about the earth-based worldview continues to cross the artificial constructs between cultures, earth-based beliefs are flowing into the Western post-industrial culture at a rapid rate.

Medicine Stories

Serving as scripture for the feminist spirituality movement, these stories of goddesses are pieces of an improvisational pattern that is inspiring fresh discourse, ritual practice and personal transformation. It is said in indigenous cultures that stories are medicine. For example, one Native American deity honored in the Southwest of the United States, Spider Woman, a Creatrix, sings the world into being. The world she creates is an interconnected web of all existence. Actually, thousands of female and woman-honoring sacred stories from numerous cultures, past and present, exist. From the Outraged Ancestral Mother of African and African-American origin to the Egyptian Isis who migrates across Europe as the Black Madonna, and from Aphrodite of Ancient Greece to the Celtic triple-goddess Brigit, these deities offer powerful role models.

By Calling Her Name in many forms a wider range of qualities are identified as suitable for the female divine. Knowledge of these stories provides inspiration and better equips us when seeking appropriate ways to live in the diverse world society and sensitive ecological system in which we all find ourselves. A richer array of behavior then becomes available for women to emulate, and men to appreciate in women. Men also are freer to overcome their own gender typing.

Ample testimony verifies the healing power stories characterizing the female divine offer. Working on a deep psychological level, these sagas give permission to fully express parts of ourselves we have not been able to access because of patriarchal conditioning that still lingers in most of us. Some who discover these stories say they have developed stronger senses of themselves. Others have been aided in finding their voices. Freedom to move in new directions often follows this increased awareness.

Patriarchal Overlay

Does honoring goddesses ensure honoring women? The answer to this question is mixed. Over centuries patriarchal social structures have assumed control in most societies around the globe, recasting religious teachings in ways that lowered the status of women, and modified the original intent of ancient stories so they reinforced male supremacy. In some practices, the female deity is appropriated in ways that leave women out completely.

One example of a culture where goddesses are prominent but women are not always respected is India. Even though the vision of women's equality is part of the constitutional fabric of modern India, women there are too often the victims of violence. Accounts of bride burning, gang rapes, and other atrocities against women continue in this country where multiple Hindu goddesses are revered.

Other societies around the globe with religious traditions which include honored female deities also report violence against women. Many begin to assume that the often told stories about goddesses are actually conveying misogynous messages to a dominant male culture. This causes those, particularly in the

West, who value women to feel alienated from cultures around the world even when they seem to practice religions where female icons of the divine do exist.

Feminists who are familiar with Hindu culture, however, have revealed that patriarchal religious practices often distort the intended qualities of goddesses, as well as sever the connection between women and goddesses. Scholars are finding that female-honoring interpretations continue, both in India and elsewhere. For example, Laura Amazzone, author of *Goddess Durga and Sacred Female Power*,[2] tells how she has gained power by exploring Indian goddesses including: Durga – Goddess of Justice; Saraswati – Goddess of Sound and Speech; and Lakshmi – Goddess of Beauty, Commerce, Spiritual and Material Abundance, among many others goddesses. As these woman-honoring versions of the stories become more known, the impact on the status of women is often positive. Change is always possible if efforts are made to present alternatives to ingrained prejudices. Values have the power to re-shape religions just as religions can form social norms.

Earth-Centered Values

In my experience, earth-centered spirituality as it is developing in contemporary societies celebrates these qualities:

- A holistic individuality that values both uniqueness and the commonalities existing among people of varied backgrounds
- A relational feeling regarding the earth and other people
- A mystical view which asserts that sacred and secular are one
- A diversity honored through use of a broad array of sacred imagery
- A humanity integrally embedded in the natural world, not separate and above

The Interconnected Web

In their healthiest forms, natural systems are complex, subtle, diverse and inherently beautiful. To respect this beauty and to feel a part of it is to be earth-based. Ancient cultures as well as contemporary ones have been studied with an eye to interpreting the meaning of iconography. Judging from the art they created and the evidence they left behind of their ways of living, when the Goddess was held in esteem, humans in these cultures felt comfortable seeing themselves as part of nature. Animals, plants, minerals, trees are all part of the same sacred spiral. There was a sense of reciprocity both within the human community and among all that formed the living web. Time was cyclical, not linear.

Patriarchal religions, on the other hand, often suffer from a split between matter and spirit. These religions honor a male god – a father – with no female aspect of the godhead. Spirit is often perceived as limited by the body. Nature is a demon to be overpowered, contained, and re-directed. As a result, around the globe we are struggling with violence, wanton destruction of ecosystems, a social climate of disrespect for women's rights, and over-production of goods at the expense of service and creative expression. Much of this results from a profound feeling of human alienation from nature. Death, if we are lucky, is an escape to Heaven after living a pure life untainted by the realities and callings of nature.

By contrast, those of us who honor goddesses respect the processes of nature as valuable teachers. We venerate both conti-nuity and change, in proper balance. We accept the primary process of nature which is birth, life, decay, gestation, and rebirth, remembering new life grows from the spent energy of previous effort. This is not to say that death caused by neglect, waste, and outright arrogance is accepted. Rather, we assert that assaults on the earth, now rampant, have thrown the natural processes out of balance.

Archaeologist Marija Gimbutas – a pioneer in fusing knowledge from linguistics, ethnology, folklore, religion and literature – who devoted the last three decades of her life to an exhaustive study of the earlier Neolithic culture in Europe, says this: "We must refocus our collective memory. The necessity of this has never been greater as we discover that the path of 'progress' is extinguishing the very conditions for life on earth."[3] These interpretations of matriarchal proto-Indo-European societies which Gimbutas gave us are ones this culture sorely needs, and which can indeed provide a vehicle for health against all odds. For Gimbutas, and those convinced by her research, remembering her is at the core of our very survival.

Men Coming to Know Her

This exploration into the effects of goddess veneration is not concerned with women alone. Rather, within this movement there has also begun a keen inquiry into false gender expectations for men as well. According to author Christine Downing, feminist writer and mythologist, the healing of men's relationship with the feminine also has profound implications for the healing of the earth. She says:

> Earth-based spirituality, with its emphasis on living in harmony with the natural world, speaks powerfully to men as well as women. Although men and women relate differently to the Goddess, we all need to embrace the emerging consciousness to avoid ecological catastrophe. In this endeavor, no one sex has exclusive rights to the Goddess's blessings.[4]

Opening to the Future

The world desperately needs a multifaceted and multicultural countenance of the Spirit. We know we cannot escape into a romantic vision of the past and that we must cope with modern realities of technology. We who value Western technological advances and seek to practice earth-honoring spirituality must advocate for the use of technology and science to create human harmony with the natural world. By seeing ourselves as a part of nature we are motivated to protect her.

We also realize we need to be able to nurture ourselves and others. To overcome isolation and move into connection we must be able to truly feel compassion, joy in community, and empathy for others – all traditional female qualities that have, from time to time, been honored in religious life. A female aspect of the Divine can aid in re-engaging these. An increasing appreciation for Kwan Yin, a well-known Asian female deity of compassion, is one example.

Cross-cultural goddess stories and woman-honoring practices then are among the threads from which to make the fabric of our renaissance. They are gifts from the goddess(es) of many times and places. This tapestry of female-honoring images provides prompts to the imagination we all can employ to expand possibility.

By prominently including in our personal religious iconography goddesses from a variety of traditions, we are more able to appreciate multicultural beliefs and practices, connecting with the female-honoring and earth-based aspects they contain. As these links expand, many women find it easier to claim a feeling of belonging often denied them under patriarchy. Then, the nameless essence of the universe becomes available to each of us.

About Elizabeth Fisher ...

Elizabeth Fisher is author of two widely used curricula: *Rise Up and Call Her Name: A Woman-honoring Journey into Global Earth-based Spiritualities* and *Gender Justice: Women's Rights Are Human Rights*. She has been active in the Women and Religion movement over many decades, contributing insights from cross-cultural feminist spirituality combined with international human rights considerations. Her programs are designed as vehicles for educating, healing, and encouraging people to think more deeply about spiritual questions which impact their personal and community life. Currently Liz is creating a trilogy of interactive, multimedia internet novellas. This series models knowledge-exchanges across cultural and class divides, recasts gender stereotypes, explores historical roots, and addresses life-cycle challenges. Liz has worked professionally in the areas of social work, law, and publishing.

Website: www.RiseUpAndCallHerName.com

Chapter 15

Healing, Freedom and Transformation through the Sacred Feminine

by Jann Aldredge-Clanton, PhD

For more than twenty years I have researched, preached, taught, and written books to persuade people that we need to include biblical Divine Feminine images in worship if we are to have social justice, equality, and peace. I am an ordained minister, and my call has been to contribute to the transformation of the Christian church as well as the wider culture.

When I was ordained as a Baptist minister, I thought the barriers to women's equality were finally breaking down. But I soon discovered that breaking free to become all we're created to be in the divine image is a continual challenge. Patriarchal religious and cultural traditions are constantly trying to stifle our gifts and our voices, to put us back into boxes we've broken free from. External and internal forces are formidable.[1]

The more I tried to live my call to pastoral ministry and my call to write in support of women in ministry, the more I realized that the resistance to ordination of women is just part of a larger patriarchal culture that gives greatest value to white, straight, able-bodied, financially privileged males. Other people are considered "other" and marginalized and oppressed. I was realizing that the ordination issue is just the tip of the patriarchal iceberg. At the foundation of our patriarchal culture is an image of a male God, sanctioning patterns of dominance and submission. More and more I was understanding that the strongest support imaginable for the dominance of men is this worship of an exclusively masculine Supreme Being. So my call expanded to writing, preaching, and teaching on the importance of including the Divine Feminine.

My feminist writing began with biblical, theological, and historical support for inclusion of female divine names and images. My intention was to change the church by changing the minds of a wide audience of clergy and laypeople through persuasive discourse. I quoted chapter and verse to support the inclusion of female language and imagery.[2] In my unquenchable idealism, I believed people would be convinced of the truth of my words in these books and turn from their patriarchal ways.

When my writing, teaching, and preaching didn't bring the changes I longed for, I realized the missing piece was ritual. Sacred symbols must take root in our imaginations as well as our intellects if they are to shape our values. For inclusive spirituality to become the foundation for a new egalitarian culture, we need to go beyond biblical and theological explanation to ritual experience. I began with that part of liturgy I love most: hymns. I began writing hymn texts in 1994 in the Advent season when all the masculine images in traditional carols felt like stones pelting my spirit. From experience I knew that words sung in worship carry great power to shape belief and action. My book *Praying with Christ-Sophia: Services for Healing and Renewal*[3] includes my first hymn texts to familiar tunes, along with other worship resources. In the following years I wrote two inclusive hymnbooks[4] and an interfaith book of inclusive blessings and prayers drawn from my experience as a hospital chaplain.[5]

One of my hymns that has been featured on Karen Tate's radio show, *Voices of the Sacred Feminine*, is "We Sound a Call to Freedom," sung to the tune of "Battle Hymn of the Republic":

We sound a call to freedom that will heal our broken land;
as the call rings out more clearly, violent forces will disband.
Prison doors will open; bonds will loosen by the Spirit's hand;
the truth will set us free.

We are tired of idle promises and token words and deeds;
we want equal rights and benefits for every race and creed.
Cries of women, men, and children we want everyone to heed;
the truth will set us free.

Our recovery is coming as our eyes receive new sight;
we are moving out of bondage; we are bound for freedom bright.
As we claim our fullest powers, we walk on into the light;
the truth will set us free.

Now our joy breaks forth in dawning of a free and glorious day,
and our healing springs up quickly as our talents we display.
Come and join our celebration; come rejoice and gladly say:
"The truth has set us free."

REFRAIN:

Free at last, O Hallelujah! Free at last, O Hallelujah!
Now, Sophia, you have freed us! Your truth has set us free.

Words © Jann Aldredge-Clanton

These lyrics draw from the Gospel of John: "You will know the truth and the truth will make you free" (8:32), and from the words in the book of Isaiah on breaking "the bonds of injustice" and letting "the oppressed go free" (58:6).

"We Sound a Call to Freedom" also brings the freeing truth of Divine Wisdom to light. Even though Wisdom is a prominent name for Deity in the Bible, Divine Wisdom is ignored and excluded in most churches. Just as women have been excluded from leadership and still are in numerous churches, Divine Wisdom may be excluded from worship because the Bible presents Divine Wisdom as female and refers to Divine Wisdom as "She." Also, people don't always want to know about Her paths of peace and justice (Proverbs 3:13–18; 8:1–20). Divine Wisdom (*Sophia* in Greek) is one of many biblical female images of Deity. Including these female images along with other biblical divine images to create gender-balanced worship will expand our spiritual experience and contribute to equality and justice in human relationships.

"We Sound a Call to Freedom" celebrates the power of *Sophia* to bring healing, justice, peace, and freedom to all people and all creation. "Now, *Sophia*, you have freed us! Your truth has set us free."

In my research I have discovered biblical and historical links between *Sophia* ("Wisdom") and Christ. The apostle Paul refers to Christ as the "power of God and the Wisdom (*Sophia*) of God" (1 Corinthians 1:24), and states that Christ "became for us Wisdom (*Sophia*) from God" (1 Corinthians 1:30). The book of Proverbs describes Wisdom as the "way," the "life," and the "path" (4:11,22,26). The Gospel of John records Jesus' saying, "I am the way, and the truth, and the life" (John 14:6). The Bible describes both *Sophia* and Christ as having creative, redemptive, and healing power. In the Gospel of Matthew, Jesus identifies with Wisdom (*Sophia*): "the Son of Man came eating and drinking, and they say, 'Look, a glutton and a drunkard, a friend of tax collectors and sinners!' Yet Wisdom (*Sophia*) is vindicated by her deeds" (Matthew 11:19). Many early Christian theologians, including Augustine and Aquinas, equate Christ and feminine Divine Wisdom. Origen, another prominent "church father," declared *Sophia* to be the most ancient and appropriate title for Jesus. Nevertheless, in all Christian churches Christ is worshipped, but *Sophia* is ignored in most. Language and visual imagery in the majority of churches reveal worship of an exclusively male God.

However, my research has recently led to the discovery of some churches and small communities who do include female divine names and images in worship. I have collected their stories in a book entitled *Changing Church* and in a blog with the same title.[6] These stories show the strong connection between inclusion of the Divine Feminine and social justice. These people who include the Divine Feminine are changing church and society as they take prophetic stands on gender, race, ecology, sexual orientation, economic justice, interfaith cooperation, and other social justice issues. Ebenezer/herchurch Lutheran in San Francisco is one of the churches featured in the book. The pastor of this church, Rev. Stacy Boorn, believes that the church must change in order for there to be justice in the world. "I don't see how the world is going to change until the religious institutions change because they are so much a part of who the world is."[7]

As I have interviewed people for my book and blog, I have identified with their passion for including female divine names and images in worship, coming from their call to work for the ideals of justice, peace, and egalitarian human life. I share their belief that our language and visual symbolism for the Divine carry great power. Our sacred symbols reflect and shape our deepest values. At the foundation of our patriarchal culture is an image of a male God, sanctioning patterns of dominance and submission. Exclusively masculine divine language and symbolism devalue the feminine by ignoring it. Women receive the message that maleness, since it is used for references to the Supreme Being, is worthy of greater respect than femaleness. Divine Feminine symbolism and language are vital to the revaluing of females. Since male and female are in the divine image, as Genesis 1:27 states, then divinity includes the female, and should be named and imaged as female.

Naming the Divine as "Mother," "Sister," "Sophia," "Hokmah,"[8] "Ruah,"[9] "Midwife," "She," and other female designations[10] gives sacred value to women and girls who have for centuries been excluded, ignored, discounted, even cursed and abused. I've come to understand how worship of an exclusively male Deity forms a foundation for demeaning, devaluing, and abuse of women. In the U.S. alone, every fifteen seconds a woman is battered.[11] One in three women in the world experiences some kind of abuse in her lifetime.[12] Worldwide, an estimated four million women and girls each year are bought and sold into prostitution, slavery, or marriage.[13] "More girls have been killed in the last fifty years, precisely because they were girls, than men were killed in all the battles of the twentieth century. More girls are killed in this routine 'gendercide' in any one decade than people were slaughtered in all the genocides of the twentieth century."[14] Two-thirds of the world's poor are women.[15] There are many more alarming statistics on worldwide violence and discrimination against women and girls.

Men as well as women suffer from the sin of sexism that has foundational support through the worship of an exclusively masculine Deity. Making the Ultimate Power of the universe male gives divine sanction to the dominance of men, stifling their full emotional and spiritual development. Dehumanization results when dominance leads to violence. From patriarchal worship practices follow patterns of dominance and subordination, resulting in the interlocking oppressions of sexism, racism, heterosexism, classicism, ableism, and rape of the earth.

The Sacred Feminine has power to heal our broken world and free all people to be all we are created to be in the divine image. As I continue writing stories about people who are transforming religion and culture through including the Divine Feminine in sacred rituals, hope stirs within me. As I hear their visions for the future of the Divine Feminine, my vision expands.

My vision is for the Divine Feminine to shine forth in all her glory in multicultural visual imagery and in the language of worship, supporting equal partnership of all people. My vision is of a church where the Divine Feminine and women ministers don't have to be defended or marginalized, but are fully and equally included throughout every worship service and every activity of the church. My vision is for the Sacred Feminine to be worshipped not only in Christian congregations, but in every religion all over the world, and for women to share equally in the leadership of every religion. My vision is for girls to believe they are equal to boys because they hear and see the Supreme Being worshipped as "She" as well as "He." The changes that I envision flowing from the worship of the Sacred Feminine will be profound: abuse and violence against women and girls will end because they will be given sacred value; the virtues of peace-making and cooperation, that have been traditionally labeled feminine, will be valued by all; there will be justice and equal opportunities for all women and girls, for racial minorities, for homosexual people, for disabled people, and for other oppressed people; there will be economic justice so that all people have their needs met and share in the world's resources; the earth, traditionally labeled feminine, will be healed and nurtured; all people will experience self-worth and freedom so that we can become all we are created to be in the divine image.

About Jann Aldredge-Clanton ...

Jann Aldredge-Clanton, PhD, ordained minister, author, teacher, and chaplain, currently serves as adjunct professor at Perkins School of Theology and Richland College, Dallas, Texas. Jann is a widely published author and lyricist. Her published books include *Changing Church: Stories of Liberating Ministers; In Whose Image? God and Gender; Seeking Wisdom: Inclusive Blessings and Prayers for Public Occasions; Breaking Free: The Story of a Feminist Baptist Minister; In Search of the Christ-Sophia: An Inclusive Christology for Liberating Christians; Praying with Christ-Sophia: Services for Healing and Renewal; Counseling People with Cancer;* and *God, A Word for Girls and Boys.* Her published music with composer Larry E. Schultz includes *Imagine God! A Children's Musical Exploring and Expressing Images of God; Inclusive Hymns for Liberating Christians; Inclusive Hymns for Liberation, Peace, and Justice;* and *Sing and Dance and Play with Joy! Inclusive Songs for*

Young Children. Her YouTube videos feature her music with Sacred Feminine images. She also writes a weekly blog: www.jannaldredgeclanton.com/blog

Chapter 16

The Little Goddess: Equality through Love

by James D. Rietveld

One day a father tucked his little girl into bed. She put her head down on her big fluffy pillow, wiggled her toes under the cool sheets, and, suddenly, asked: "Why do they say God is a man?"

Caught off guard, the father looked at his daughter for a moment, and returned, "Because he is – that's what we're taught and those people who say he is are a lot smarter than you and me. They should know!"

She paused for a moment. The father thought he was off the hook. But the little girl, propping herself up on one elbow, spoke again. "Did they see what God looked like?"

At this point, the father realized he might be in trouble, for now she fluffed up her pillow, sat up straighter than before, and suddenly became as bright-eyed and awake as ever. The father measured his words carefully: "Well, they read in special books that God is a man."

Tilting her head to the side, her eyes looked a bit puzzled as her little curls fell onto one of her shoulders. "You mean like the books you read to me – about princes and faeries and magic castles?"

The father shook his head sternly, "Oh no, none like that! These books are written by very serious people who saw God."

Quickly she replied, "And they said God was a boy like you and my baby brother?"

The father did not know how to respond. The little girl smiled. He quickly gathered his thoughts and tried to act as smart as possible, "God is described by being called a 'he' and

HE is said to have a big beard and they use lots of other words that make him a man."

The little girl was now confused. "Does God shave like you, Daddy? Does God go potty like you and my baby brother?"

The father responded, "No, he doesn't do human things, because he's God, so he does God things, but is still a man."

The little girl looked sad. "So God is not like me at all? God is only like YOU?"

Now the father felt bad as her eyes started to well up in tears.

"Now, now, it's not like that at all; you see, God made both man and woman in his image – we both reflect God like a mirror, you see? So you and I are both like God."

Now the little girl was more confused than ever, "But – But – if God is a mirror of you and me then he must be both like a girl and a boy, right?"

Now the father was frustrated. "Sweetie, God is a man – that is what those special books written by those very serious men say and that is how he is drawn in pictures too."

She scratched her head. "So there are no happy girls who say God could be a girl too or who wrote books about that or drew pictures of God with long hair and a pretty bow, but only boys who wrote that God had a big old beard?"

The father became concerned, "Well, some people think God could be a girl, even a goddess, but we don't think so. We know better."

She paused, looked down, fiddled with her hands, looked up again, and then stared directly into her father's eyes. "Did God make the world?"

The father immediately responded, "Of course!"

She continued, "Did God make the animals, the mountains, the rivers, the trees, and kitty cats?"

Not sure where she was leading, he again replied, "Yes."

She smiled, "Wow, all of this came out of God?"

Now scratching his head, he nodded in agreement.

All of a sudden with a huge burst of energy, the little girl stood up, threw open her arms and declared, "God gave birth to the world and the animals and the mountains and the streams and the kangaroos and the puppies and even the kitty cats just like a mommy gave birth to me and my little brother!"

Defeated, the father responds, "I suppose so."

The little girl then gives the father a big hug and says, "So God is like a girl and a boy, like a daddy and a mommy!"

Holding his little girl in his arms, he responds, "Yes, God can be like you too."

The little girl kissed her father on the cheek, and said full of confidence, "I knew it!" At last, she again put her head back down upon her big fluffy pillow, wiggled her toes under the now warm sheets, fell happily asleep, and dreamed of a new day to begin.

About James Rietveld ...

Dr. James D. Rietveld received his PhD from Claremont Graduate University School, in Religious Studies in 2006, combining this discipline with History and Archaeology. His specialties include the History of Christianity in the Early, Medieval, and Byzantine periods, New Testament Studies and Greco-Roman religions. Also at Claremont, Rietveld minored in Islam and Hinduism, focusing upon Hindu goddess traditions in the latter field of concentration. He received both his Bachelor of Arts and his Masters of Arts in History at California State University Fullerton in 1991 and 1998. Rietveld is currently teaching at Cal State Fullerton in both the Comparative Religion and the History department. Every Wednesday night, he can be heard on his radio show entitled *Myth & Legend, History & Religion* on Passionate Voices Radio. Rietveld is also an author of numerous publications related to history, religion, and archaeology, many of his articles published in *Sacred History Magazine*, and his latest book is entitled *London in Flames: The Apocalypse of*

1666. He has a passion for studies revolving around Asia Minor, especially focused on the city of Ephesus, and his forthcoming book will focus on Artemis of the Ephesians.

Chapter 17

Woman's Inhumanity to Woman

by Phyllis Chesler

Once upon a time, a long time ago, I believed that all women were kind, caring, maternal, valiant, and ever-noble under siege – and that all men were their oppressors. As everyone but a handful of idealistic feminists knew, this was not always true. Living my life and writing this book have helped me to understand that, like men, women are really human beings, as close to the apes as to the angels, capable of both cruelty and compassion, envy and generosity, competition and cooperation.

One of the reasons it is difficult for a woman to acknowledge that women – including herself – are aggressive and cruel is because these are not socially acceptable traits for women to have and because a woman's best friends and confidantes are usually other women. Most women befriend each other, create female "families" in times of peace and in times of war. Women expect to be emotionally "groomed" (listened to, sympathized with) by those women who most resemble themselves. This is why "difference" (in appearance or ideas) is so threatening to most women who rely upon shoulder-to-shoulder egalitarianism and "sameness" among their female intimates, rather than male-like hierarchies with a leader and a chain of command. To women, even the smallest "difference" signals potential abandonment; to men, it merely clarifies an accepted social arrangement.

Psychologically, seemingly contradictory things can be true. Women mainly compete against other women and women mainly rely upon other women; women envy and sabotage each other through slander, gossip and shunning, and women also want other women's respect and support. Once we learn how to think "in opposites," certain things become clear – including what a woman can do in order to either bond with, or disconnect from another woman with integrity and objectivity.

Female–female aggression and competition is normal and may, to some extent, be "hardwired." In addition, women, like men, have internalized sexist beliefs. We either idealize women as Fairy Godmothers or we demonize them as Evil Stepmothers. Women often have higher and different expectations for other women than we do for men. We tend not to forgive women when they fail us. We tend to have more compassion for male failure or imperfection.

I know this but, for a number of reasons, I clung to my original view of women as perfect victims. Why? Because women are both oppressed and maligned and I did not want to expose us to any further harm. Because it was – and still is – problematic, even dangerous, to challenge the politically correct feminist view of women as morally superior. In the past, women's "dark side" was routinely exaggerated to justify her subordinate status. In reaction, many feminists have tried to focus only on women's "bright side."

Perhaps I was afraid of offending such well-intentioned feminists. But I concluded that women should not have to prove that we are better than men in order to be entitled to equal and human rights. Nor should feminist ideology remain forever fixed and one-sided. We're stronger than that. Most feminists under-stand the importance of acknowledging their light-skin color prejudice, ageism, classism, homophobia; acknowledging woman's sexism is a long overdue, but absolutely necessary, next step.

Still, it's painful for a feminist to acknowledge that, in the course of human events, a woman may steal her best friend's husband, children, job, and other best female friends, that a female relative or co-worker may slander and sabotage women at home, on the job, and in social organizations. It is painful to acknowledge that many women do not believe or support a woman who files a sex discrimination lawsuit or alleges rape, battery, or sexual harassment. Indeed, prosecutors have increasingly preferred men as jurors in rape trials, since women for a variety of reasons (fear of rape, the need to distance themselves from it) often choose not to believe the woman who alleges rape.

My book, *Woman's Inhumanity to Woman*, took me more than twenty years to research, write, and publish. I read thousands of studies and thousands of books – everything from anthropological and primate studies to fairytales, psychoanalytic case studies, and fiction. I interviewed hundreds of women who, although grown, still remembered being taunted, shamed, shunned, and silenced in childhood – not by boys and men, but by other teenage girls and women. I met interviewees whose relationships with their mothers, daughters and sisters were fraught with mutual recrimination, competition, miscommunication, and lethal envy. Most women longed for more positive and redemptive connections with each other but had yet to find them.

I heard similar stories of frustrated love from women of all ages, classes, and races. I heard about how such mother–daughter and sister–sister dynamics invariably surfaced among women in the workplace. I came to understand why many find it harder to work for women than for men, and what kinds of managerial and leadership styles women prefer and admire.

Many writers have written about the "dark side" of female–female relationships. However, their work was either never viewed in this light or was simply kept from view. I acknowledge these earlier works throughout this book. Six months before I published *Woman's Inhumanity to Women* in hardcover, I began calling some of the women whose work had guided me. "Thank you so much for your book and article," I would say. "Are you interested in doing an educational presentation together?" One author said: "Welcome aboard, sister! But wait and see, women will attack you pretty viciously for telling this truth." A psychotherapist-author told me: "I made a vow not to write or speak about this subject anymore. I never want to experience such hostility from women again." A third author: "I've already written about this as truthfully as I know how but it made no difference. Why do you think women will listen to you when they did not listen to me?"

Their comments surprised me, but, as it turned out, what happened to them in the past did not happen to me. Nor did I draw the same conclusions. Sure, some well-known feminists refused to read or review this work (and convinced others to do likewise): and some women who did review this book did so with hostility and contempt. But many more readers and reviewers, both male and female, thanked me for breaking this silence, for confirming that they were not alone or "crazy," that being shunned by other women was not necessarily "all their fault," that women do disappoint and betray each other every day, and that this is not a "small" matter. A retired professor said: "May God bless you for exposing this dirty little secret, this catastrophe." A psychologist who works with adolescent girls described this book as "a prayer answered." A mother wrote that she had read a negative review of this book "but by a woman, so I thought that you might be telling the truth." This kind woman exclaimed: "You are the next stage – after Friedan, but I think that women will continue to deny that this problem exists and will keep playing the game." I hope she's wrong – but it remains to be seen.

One businesswoman thanked me for "finally making sense of another problem that had no name" – another for having the "courage to take the subject on." A doctoral student described this book as a "life-changing experience" for her. Four readers each wrote fairly long reviews – not for publication but for their own communities (which included a lesbian retirement community; a women's business association; a reading club, and an educational retreat center) in the hope that the ideas contained here would help them finally resolve some serious and long-festering problems.

A number of Fortune 500 businessmen wrote to praise my work, agreeing that women sabotaging each other at work is a serious problem. One man wrote: "I watched so many situations where women ate each other for lunch, that I am fully convinced that the 'glass ceiling' is also a self-inflicted problem." (I don't agree – but he may be partly right.) Another man wrote that he hoped women would start learning from men that you can "settle a dispute quickly, loudly, bluntly, by yelling and challenging each other. Otherwise, the resentment and the pretense to friendship seem to simmer for years, as does the revenge – which is exacted slowly."

The online responses were colorful and original. For example, one woman wrote: "This book made me examine my own less-than-ideal behavior towards other women, my inclination to judge women more harshly than men, and resolve to improve on these fronts." Another woman wrote: "If you have ever been the target of female envy, the girl who was never included, the one they called nasty names or wondered why your best friend just ruined your life – in other words if you ever were a girl – read this book!" A third woman ended her long and friendly letter with two final sobering sentences: "I lost my utopian belief in sisterhood when I was twenty-one. I can't say I've missed it much in the twenty years since; it served me badly." A man wrote: "I admire the finesse with which women can insult each other. Men could never be so seemingly diplomatic and mean at the same time: 'Oh, I like what you're trying to do with your hair … Nice dress; black is so slimming, isn't it?'" Or this letter from a woman: "Right now, I am dealing with one of the things I hate most about working with a group of women … the 'we're gonna be best friends and ignore you' thing. These two are mad at me because I called one of my co-workers out on her utter slackitude; now I am big, bad evil Amazon woman."

The most important "reviews" were not reviews at all, but letters in which readers poured out their hearts to me. One never-married woman wrote about how painful it was for her when her married women friends did not include her in social events – but did include unmarried men. Another woman described how a small group of women had ruined her career and how that ruination led to her suicide attempt. A self-described "former food addict" wrote: "Today, eight years abstinent and sober, it is impossible for me to gossip/slander/backstab/exclude and remain abstinent. When I was compulsively overeating I was perpetrator – but always felt like a victim. Today, I am excluded because I have transformed my life and doubly excluded because I am direct and refuse to participate in the vilification of others." A woman who had been sexually, psychologically, and physically abused by her mother wrote about it; her feminist editors would not publish it because it "would hurt the movement." She thanked me for giving her the courage to continue her work on "the reality of women's capacity for violence."

I have been very pleased by the extensive international interest in this book. Almost immediately, I was interviewed in Russia, Australia, New Zealand, China, Japan, Nepal, Poland, Germany, Italy, England, Brazil, Chile, and all over North America. Such interest confirms that what I am writing about is a global, universal phenomenon; the book is about all women. The Chilean journalist wanted to know how I knew so much about the mother–daughter relationship in Chile – and so did the Nepalese journalist! A query from mainland China concerned why women find it so difficult to work for a woman boss; I received the same query in Germany, Brazil, and the United States.

Of course, the book was also damned in some reviews and on several e-mail list-serve groups. Strikingly, the negative reviews came entirely from women. How dare I write about women being violent when men are so much more violent? Didn't I understand that the "near-powerless in society are always forced to fight over the scraps?" Why didn't I show more compassion for incest victims? Clearly, I'd written this book because I was "ready to sell out," "wanted to become a millionaire," had not "gotten over my negative relationship with my mother." And because I "wanted revenge." Some female reviewers were angry I'd gotten published at all given that "they had always known the truth about women; why bother to publish a no-brainer?"

In a sense, I was lucky to have taken so long to complete this work. Had I published this sooner, what I am saying could not have been so well supported by the extraordinary, global research that has only begun to gather steam in the last ten years. Timing is everything, and it seems that I had anticipated a curve. A few months after *Woman's Inhumanity to Woman* came out, a spate of books touching on this topic in different ways were published. For the first time, society in general – and the media in particular – were paying attention.

Where do we go from here? Every interviewer, without exception, ended our conversation by asking me what steps women might take to deal with women's unacknowledged aggression and sexism, and what might the parents of teenaged girls tell their daughters about how to handle female taunting and ostracism. My advice always made the article's final cut. Thus, what should women do?

Humbly Accept That Change Is a Process

We must first accept that change is a process – one that can't be rushed. We will have the rest of our lives to work on transforming envy and conformity into tolerance and individuality, and on doing good, not evil, in the world.

Acknowledge, Do Not Deny, the Truth

Second, we must acknowledge some painful truths. A woman must admit that women are normally aggressive and competitive and that oppressed women are also very angry; as such, they tend to take their anger out on each other. Such an acknowledgement may help a woman become more realistic about what to expect from other women and clear about her own limitations as well.

Become Strong

Each woman must develop a strong self and a sense of her own utter uniqueness. No one can take your "good" away from you. Honor your own ambition; honor other women's ambition. Support strong women who are "different" from you, not only weak women who agree with you totally and who therefore do not threaten you.

Become Strong Enough to Take Criticism

Women often become offended and emotional very quickly. We may be oversensitive to criticism because we have been excessively and unjustly criticized by both women and men from a very young age; we might also have been treated as if we were invisible. Women have been readied to hear unjust criticism where none exist. Therefore, I would like to see women learn how to hear each other gently, respectfully. At the same time, a woman must become strong enough to hear outside, diverse, and critical voices. Asking another woman what she really thinks is not the same as asking her to support you, right or wrong, or to falsely flatter you. A woman has to be able to endure opposing views without feeling personally betrayed by those who hold such views.

Learn to Express Your Anger: Rules of Engagement

A woman may hold a grudge against another woman for a long time; she might turn others against her entirely unsuspecting victim. A woman might instead learn how to express her anger verbally, directly, to the woman who has offended her – and then let go of that anger. This is not easy to do. Perhaps here is where women can learn some rules of engagement from men about how to fight fairly and then, win or lose, move on, befriend our opponents, or at least quit holding a grudge. Men find this easier since they comfortably occupy a psychological middle distance from each other. Perhaps women might have to modify our intense intimacy needs in order to create and maintain more stable or flexible alliances with other women.

Learn to Ask for What You Want: Learn to Move On If You Don't Get What You Want

A woman must be encouraged to put what she wants into words, to ask for it directly rather than waiting for someone to guess what it is she wants. If a woman cannot get what she wants, she does not have to blame herself, give up, disconnect, or become enraged. She must learn that she can get what she wants another day or at another job or with another person. Women must be encouraged to move on as well as to stay the course.

Do Not Gossip

Do not initiate gossip about another woman: if you hear gossip, do not pass it on. Let it stop with you. It's perfectly all right to talk about a woman when she is not present as long as she is someone you like, love, care about, and if what you are saying will not damage her reputation or ruin her life. It is not all right to punish and sabotage another woman whom you may envy or fear by slandering her or by turning other women against her.

No Woman Is Perfect: Apologize When You've Made a Mistake and Then Move On

If you behave badly (see above), apologize directly and move on. Cut yourself some slack and cut the next woman some slack too. If she has slandered or sabotaged you, talk to her about it directly; deal with it quickly. Do not let it fester.

Treat Women Respectfully

Finally, even if we disagree with another woman, we must do so respectfully, kindly. We must cultivate the concept of an "honorable opponent." We should not automatically demonize our opponents or competitors. Women are not obligated to "love" or "hate" each other. We do not even need to "like" each other. I am suggesting that women treat each other in a civilized manner. Finally, women might learn how to thank other women for each small act of kindness – as opposed to expecting everything from other women and being angry when we don't get it all.

These nine suggestions may not seem radical. Trust me: They are. If every reader begins by acknowledging each point as true, and if she vows to bring this newfound consciousness into her daily interactions with other women, she will be part of a profound psychological evolution. It takes many individual ripples to form a wave. The book we're speaking about on Voices of the Sacred Feminine Radio, or the copy you might hold in your hands, is my attempt to rouse the slumber of the briny deep.

About Phyllis Chesler ...

Phyllis Chesler is an Emerita Professor of Psychology and Women's Studies at City University of New York. She is a best-selling author, a legendary feminist leader, a psychotherapist and an expert courtroom witness. Dr. Chesler has published thousands of articles and, most recently, studies, about honor-related violence, including honor killings. She has published many classic works such as *Women and Madness: Mothers on Trial; The Battle for Children and Custody*, and *Woman's Inhumanity to Woman. An American Bride in Kabul* is her fifteenth book.

Chesler pioneered work about motherhood. She published *With Child: A Diary of Motherhood* in 1979, *Mothers on Trial* in 1986, and in an expanded, updated edition in 2011, and *Sacred Bond: The Legacy of Baby M* in 1987. She organized the first-ever Speak

Out of Mothers and Custody in 1986 and spoke at a similar Speak Out in Toronto. She was challenged by the FBI to appear before a Grand Jury in the matter of one particular mother who had run away to protect her daughters from being sexually abused by their father. She also organized weekly demonstrations outside the courthouse in the Baby M case and spoke at the press conference after the New Jersey Supreme Court rendered its verdict which outlawed surrogacy in New Jersey.

Chesler has been consulted by matrimonial lawyers and, in the past, has testified for mothers. Today, she submits affidavits and dispenses advice when asked.

Since 9/11, Dr. Chesler has focused on the rights of women, dissidents, and gays in the Islamic world; on anti-Semitism; the psychology of terrorism; the nature of propaganda, and honor-related violence. She has testified for Muslim and ex-Muslim women who are seeking asylum or citizenship based on their credible belief that their families will honor kill them.

Dr. Chesler is co-founder of the Association for Women in Psychology (1969), and the National Women's Health Network (1974).

Dr. Chesler has published thousands of articles and speeches that have inspired countless people. Her other books include: *Women, Money and Power* (1976); *About Men* (1978); *Mothers on Trial: The Battle for Children and Custody* (1986); *Sacred Bond: The Legacy of Baby M* (1988); *Patriarchy: Notes of an Expert Witness* (1994); *Feminist Foremothers in Women's Studies, Psychology, and Mental Health* (1995); *Letters to a Young Feminist* (1998); *Woman's Inhumanity to Woman* (2002); *Women of the Wall: Claiming Sacred Ground at Judaism's Holy Site* (2002); *The New Anti-Semitism: The Current Crisis and What We Must Do About It* (2003); *The Death of Feminism: What's Next in the Struggle for Women's Freedom* (2005); and an expanded twenty-fifth anniversary edition of *Mothers on Trial* with eight new chapters (2011).

A revised and updated edition of *Women and Madness* was

published in 2005 and a new edition of *Woman's Inhumanity to Woman* with a new introduction was published in 2009. Between 2009 and 2012, Dr. Chesler published three pioneering academic studies on honor killings and an academic article about the *burqa*. All appeared in *Middle East Quarterly*. In 2013, Dr. Chesler was appointed a Fellow of the Middle East Forum.

Website: www.phyllis-chesler.com

Chapter 18

Why Would a Man Search for the Goddess?

by Tim Ward

Why would a man search for the Goddess? Especially a guy like me?

"Oh, I get it! You're getting in touch with your feminine side!" my friends say.

No, I have to laugh. It's just the opposite. It's the darkest part of my masculinity that yearns for her, like a lost lover, like an orphaned child. It is as if a ghost touched me on the shoulder and as I turned she disappeared. Her shadow lured me deeper into the unknown than the gods of my fathers ever did. Jesus and Buddha, they urged me away from the world, taught me to resist the ways of the flesh and seek a Kingdom of God, heaven, nirvana, a higher consciousness. It's different with her. It's visceral, immediate, a matter of the heart, balls and belly.

I caught my first glimpse of her in India as Kali, the black goddess who is both Mother and Destroyer. Her statues there have four arms. The upper right is raised in blessing; the lower right is extended, palm out, as if offering a gift. But the upper left holds a bloody machete and the lower left a freshly severed human head. I once asked one of her devotees how one could get the blessing and escape the machete.

"No, that's not the point," she replied fiercely. "The blessing is only won when you accept both sides of Kali, including pain, sorrow, loss and death. The real death is trying to hold your tiny ego safe from the pain caused by desire and love. Flee from the dangers of life, and you will miss her blessings too. But embrace Kali as she is, kiss her bloody tongue and feel all four arms around you, and then you have life, you have freedom. This, my young friend, is Kali's boon."

On the slum streets of Calcutta, Kali's holy city, littered with human misery and despair, I felt those four arms embrace me once, just for an instant.

When I returned to North America after six years living in Asia, it struck me as strange that we in the West worship only a masculine God. It was not always so. In ancient times, men and women worshipped a pantheon of both gods and goddesses. The Greeks had Aphrodite, Athena, Hera, Demeter, and a host of others. All around the Mediterranean, goddesses appeared as primordial creators, protectors, and powerful forces of nature and fertility right back to the dawn of writing. Thousands of prehistoric statues of women have been unearthed in excavations across Europe back to the Stone Age. Only in the past 1,600 years has Western civilization embraced the religion of the Father as the one and only God. Today, many women are experiencing a spiritual rejuvenation by rediscovering the goddesses of the ancient world. But why not men? These were once our goddesses, too. I wondered what we men might have lost when we turned our backs on the feminine divine, and how this has affected us both spiritually and in our relationships with flesh-and-blood women.

I believe we men have a deep need to connect with women, which for most of us remains profoundly thwarted. This vague feeling that things are out of sync with the opposite sex rumbles around inside of us, mixes with sexual frustration, resentment, anxiety, anger and despair. I felt this even after my encounters with Kali in India convinced me to embrace life passionately. All four of the long-term relationships I had before the age of 35 – including one marriage – ended not just badly, but wretchedly. As things got worse, I could feel animosity towards my beloved growing at the very same time I was trying to "work" on the relationship.

"Why does it have to be so hard?" I found myself asking again and again.

How often we liken the woman we love to a goddess, and how often when the illusion shatters, we turn on her and call her a bitch ...

It's all too easy for men to blame women, as if they are the cause of our suffering. Our myths pin it on the first woman: Eve who conned Adam into disobeying God and got them both thrown out of Eden; or Pandora who opened the jar and released all strife and woe. For thousands of years women have borne the brunt of this blame, taken out on them in oppression, abuse, rape, genital mutilation, sexual slavery, forced prostitution, incest, violence, and murder.

One of the toughest parts of writing this book has been facing my own repressed anger towards women, which came to the surface as I confronted images of goddesses from ages past. My true feelings had been camouflaged well. To speak and write about them honestly has been difficult. Was this just me, I wondered, or was I beginning to uncover a larger link between men's disconnection from the feminine divine and our animosity towards women? Some male readers of my draft manuscript objected to my describing men's anger towards women in generalized terms. Yet many women readers told me male anger towards women was something too obvious to mention. Psychologist Dorothy Dinnerstein claims that "the hate, fear, loathing, contempt and greed that men express towards women so pervades the human atmosphere that we breathe them as casually as the city child breathes smog."[1] She concludes that most of us are so desensitized, we are scarcely aware of it at all. Before work on my book, *Savage Breast*, began, I suppose I too would have rejected the idea I harbored such negative feelings towards women. But in hindsight I can see this animosity in action whenever I have lashed out at an individual woman. We may expunge the biases against women from our laws, change the way we talk, the way we joke, share the household chores, but if we men fail to address this subterranean anger at its root, I believe our desire for intimate connections with women will be thwarted still.

According to Carl Jung, the problem lies in our unconscious. As he put it: "Every man carries within him the eternal image of woman, not the image of this or that particular woman, but a definite feminine image ... an imprint or 'archetype' of all the ancestral experiences of the female."[2] Throughout history these archetypal images found concrete representations in the many faces of the goddess. But with the rise of Christianity, these images have been shorn from Western civilization. As a result, Jung says, men's anima imprints have become stunted in a way that makes a mature connection with women difficult. I think Jung was certainly on to something, connecting goddesses to the anima. But would the revival of ancient goddess archetypes in modern society really make for richer and deeper connections with women? One can hardly look to ancient Greece or modern India as examples of gender harmony. I suspected there was much more to the contemporary problems between men and women than simply the absence of goddesses.

Misogyny's root runs deep. As I worked on this book, I began to hear its echo everywhere, from the lyrics of contemporary rap music to the world's oldest story, the Mesopotamian Epic of Gilgamesh, which was first composed somewhere around 2600 BCE. It recounts the mythic adventures of a historical figure, King Gilgamesh, who ruled Uruk somewhere between 2700 and 2600 BCE. At the story's beginning, Gilgamesh has taken to deflowering every virgin and young bride in the city. Sometime later, Ishtar, the goddess of love, approaches the king and offers to marry him.

Gilgamesh asks her, "What would I gain by taking you as wife?"

"Love," she replies, "and peace."
He hurls back insults.
Just as you loved the lion
And gave him pits to fall in
And the horse whose back
You wounded with the whip ...
Your love brings only war!
You are an old fat whore,
That's all you are,
Who once was beautiful,
Perhaps,
And could deceive
But who has left in men
A memory of grief.
We outgrow our naiveté
In thinking goddesses
return our love.[3]

Here, at the very dawn of literature, man's anger at the feminine is clear to see. It's painful to read, this womanizer's raw hatred, so familiar to me across six millennia. The dark side of my soul knows it well. The story I tell in *Savage Breast* is not just the story of a man's yearning to enter the goddess's world of sweetness and harmony. I wanted to look at her hard and real, not romanticizing, not flinching, not accepting convenient or soothing explanations. I wanted to get to the root of what transpired between men and the goddess that put us so at odds.

In search of answers I traveled to the cradles of Western civilization, to Greece, Crete, Turkey, Israel, Romania, Bulgaria, Ukraine, Yugoslavia, France, Cyprus and Malta. I wanted to walk the ruins of her temples, gaze at her statues and icons. I wanted to see if they held a resonance for me. Just as a harp string will vibrate if another instrument strikes an identical note, I hoped the images created by my ancestors could bring to life a corresponding echo within me. To begin with I sought out the goddesses we in the West know best, the ones from Greek mythology: Gaia, Ariadne, Demeter, Hera, Athena, Hecate, Artemis, Pandora and Aphrodite. But it soon became apparent that each of these goddesses had her own hidden past, and that the Greek myths were just one page in a much longer story. This led me to an era of European prehistory that began more than 5,000 years before Classical Greece. Here there are no names, no myths, only raw and powerful images of women preserved in pigment and stone, clay and bone.

Over the course of three years and thirteen trips to Europe, I encountered thousands of representations of the feminine divine. Facing the goddess allowed me to unleash emotions so threatening and painful I never could have imagined expressing them directly to a real woman. It opened doors that I had long nailed shut. It's one thing to contemplate the goddess as a metaphysical idea or a psychological archetype, but when the feminine divine took shape inside my psyche, she often terrified me, evoking desperate longing, hostility, fear, shame – and also incredible beauty.

So what, in the end, did I learn?

The Goddess as Archetype and Anima

To begin with, in the course of this journey I became aware of my own anima and how it unconsciously projected archetypes of the feminine. When projected onto real women, these archetypes triggered intense and often negative emotions in me. The myths of the ancient goddesses helped me recognize these archetypal patterns for what they were. When I could be conscious that I was projecting, it was as if a spell was broken, and I could shake myself free. For the first time I could see clearly that my relationship problem wasn't just with women. It was with my anima.

When I turned my gaze upon the goddesses directly, I

projected feminine archetypes onto them just as I had upon women. Since there were no real women present, only the archetypes, I could rage and weep and feel these emotions fully, without getting caught up in the drama of a relationship. Through many encounters, this helped me to finally grasp the contradiction at my core: my overwhelming need for the feminine co-mingled with fear that I would be completely engulfed if I ever got too close to her. Trapped between these two responses, I felt anger and hate towards women, and bitter self-loathing. The most amazing thing is that this gnarled psychological mess has been more or less resolved. I have come to see my anima as a blessing, not a curse. I now believe the anima is what makes possible a deep spiritual connection with women – as long as one can keep conscious of archetypal projections. The process of exploring the Goddess helped me reconcile my conflicting fears and desires and as a result, I've found that connection with Teresa, the woman I love, who has been my spouse for over a decade now.

I have come to see men's archetypes of the feminine as perceptual pigeonholes, ways of sorting women into easily defined categories: as wife, mother, lover, etc. We often see women primarily through the projecting lens of our anima, or else like old Hestia, we don't see them at all. Such perceptual shorthand made sense perhaps in patriarchal society where the roles of women were few, and mostly defined by relationship to males. But the feminine archetypes we have inherited do not reflect the diverse capacities and potential of real women. In an age of individualism, we men find our expectations foiled again and again when we attempt to relate to women through the archetypes. They don't fit, and yet it's hard for a man to see the person in a woman undistorted by our projections. I was completely unaware of my own impaired vision when I began to write this book, and I suspect it remains virtually imperceptible to most men.

The Cosmic Goddess

By the end of this exploration, I came to believe in a Goddess who is both energy and matter, who is aware, intelligent, creative, and beautiful, and whose essence connects us all together. When I conceived of divinity as God the Father, the cultural myths surrounding my beliefs left me feeling separated and sinful; at best, forgiven, at worst, condemned. The myths and symbols of the Goddess have helped me better thread my way back to her cosmic embrace. I used to feel severed and disconnected from the feminine and from life. It's as if a wound in my soul has been healed. I am no longer a member of the cult of scarcity. Instead, I feel the Goddess's abundance. I'm overwhelmed with gratitude for the life I have been given.

Of course, someone might point out that the Goddess as I have described her could just as well be a "he" or an "it." Woman is the metaphor for the Goddess, but certainly the infinite divine is not specifically correlated more to one gender than to the other? Well, monotheists have described the divine as "Father" for over 2,000 years. Even if we neutered the God, to be labeled only "It," we would still have the masculine echo ringing in our ears for another thousand years. So maybe it would make sense to call her the Goddess for a millennium or so, if only to even things out. Then perhaps we could move on to something more gender inclusive.

That said, I do believe there is a distinctly feminine essence of the divine. And also, a distinctly masculine essence – one that has long been obscured by monotheistic religion. Discovering the Goddess has helped me begin to see beyond Jehovah. The divine Bull of his Mother, Dionysos, the Minotaur, and the rare male statues of Old Europe point the way to a different masculine god who dwells within me and all men, and who perhaps resonates in the animus of women. This is a new path for me to explore (the first step undertaken in my most recent book, *Zombies on Kilimanjaro: A Father/Son Journey Above the Clouds*).

The Goddess and Moving Beyond Patriarchy

Traveling through Old Europe and the Near East and studying the work of Harrison, Gimbutas, Lerner, Eisler and others has convinced me that men did not always dominate women as they have done in historical times. I do not believe patriarchy is a natural or universal template for humankind. I think the sexual equality we are heading towards in the 21st century is a rebalancing of gender relations that have been askew for some 5,000 years. Patriarchy was a raw deal both for women and for about 95% of all men, most of whom served as the slaves, soldiers and laborers throughout history. It benefits us all to get rid of the social, economic and political biases against women. There can be no true democracy without it.

How can I move beyond patriarchy in my own life? My experiences in writing this book have helped me see beneath the surface of things, to glimpse the myriad subtle structures that keep patriarchy in place. I keep bumping up against male prerogatives I've never noticed, and hearing the subtle language of domination in everyday speech. I'm often appalled at the casual sexism of my own behavior, and I realized after writing *Savage Breast* that I was only beginning to see it clearly.

It remains challenging to speak of this to men. While I believe a substantial number of males do want to move beyond patriarchy, how many are willing to uncover and address their hidden anger towards women? It's so pervasive, so invisible, so disturbing, who among us wants to see it? The key, perhaps, is that like me, many men yearn for a deep and satisfying relationship with a woman they love, and so often feel thwarted. For me this has become a place to start the conversation. In fact, what I believe most is that men and women need to speak more honestly and openly about what divides us, and what it will take to bring us closer together. It's my hope that *Savage Breast* will serve as a good starting point to talk about how we can come together as equal partners in co-creating humanity's future.

About Tim Ward ...

Tim Ward is an author, teacher, speaker, and publisher of Changemakers Books. Deeply troubled by his relationship problems with women, Tim undertook an in-depth exploration of the Goddess from a male point of view. This resulted in the groundbreaking book *Savage Breast: One Man's Search for the Goddess*. For this book, Ward traveled to the cradles of Western civilization to research the history, mythology and archaeology of the Goddess. As a result of this journey, Tim became a Goddess worshipper. He believes that it is in men's enlightened self-interest to get past patriarchy so that men and women can co-create humanity's future.

Websites:

www.timwardsbooks.com

www.savagebreastbook.com

www.changemakers-books.com

Chapter 19

The Red Tent:
Creating a Woman-Honoring Culture

By Isadora Gabrielle Leidenfrost, PhD and ALisa Starkweather

Women who are standing in their power are essential to shifting present paradigms; these pioneers are a balm to an ailing world. But after years of oppression, how do women rise up out of trauma to remember the beauty that lives at one's core? This reclamation work is what many are a part of because when we find our voices, our inspired action, our needed visions then we stand a better chance at creating a world we can thrive in. And it is with this spirit that the Red Tent movement has flourished as a global phenomenon.

A Red Tent is a place where women gather to rest, renew, and often share deep and powerful stories about their lives. The Red Tent is many things to many people: It is a womb-like red fabric space, it is a place where women gather, it is an icon, and it is a state of mind. Some women create red fabric spaces to specifically honor their menstruation. Others create spaces where they can take care of themselves, promote women's conversations, and hold workshops and other events for women.

The Red Tent, a novel by Anita Diamant published in 1997, gave us a story of women who came together in a menstrual hut, known as the Red Tent. The story showed us how the women raised a young daughter who was taught the secrets held for women by women through initiation, stories, and relationships. For many, the story resonated deeply and caused us to question if there was a place like this in our society. Because Diamant gave us a visceral vision of what was possible, many autonomous Red

Tents came into being. The fictitious story was a tool that helped women re-shape their relationships with each other and gave them a vehicle for coming together.

Through the eons, many women have taught about the wisdom of honoring menstruation. In this century, Susun Weed's years of teaching about the importance of the Women's Moon Lodge, Tamara Slayton's Menstrual Health Foundation carried forward by the Red Web Foundation, Linda Heron Wind, Brooke Medicine Eagle, and others too numerous to name gave teachings that influenced the emergence of the Red Tent movement. Early on, Red Tent consciousness spread to many arenas such as the New York Women and Power conference in 2004 where the ABC Carpet and Home Store constructed a beautiful rendition that over a thousand women entered. Other pioneers who have influenced our global dialogue include Eve Ensler's V-Day work, Eryka Peskin's Red Tent Women's Project, Jasmin Starchild's Red Moon Medicine Movement and DeAnna Lam's vision of Red Tents in Every Neighborhood. The Red Tent also inspired conferences, festivals, religious organizations, and plays and fueled our desire to have this place in our modern-day society.

In 2006, having experienced Red Tents and featuring them at her Women's Belly and Womb Conferences, ALisa Starkweather, founder of multiple women's initiatives, heard the internal instruction, "A red tent needs to be raised in every city, village, and town." Though daunted by this clear missive, she allowed her visionary self to go to work on how this could transpire globally. With decades of empowerment work, an expansive network of women, and an ability to speak to large audiences, she founded the Red Tent Temple Movement. Starkweather considered naming it the Red Tent Movement, but believed that the word 'temple' signified the sacred. She hoped that it would remind women of their own body temples where the cycles of bleeding, fertility and menopause could be respected and where the tribulations of infertility, trauma, societal ostracism or isolation could be addressed collectively. Though she was not sure women would resonate with the word, she was inspired by Leah Jeannesdaughter and Astrid Grove's Red Temple concept.

Along with years of creating containers for women's transformations, Starkweather was influenced by another book, *Circle of Stones* by Judith Duerk in 1989. Duerk asked questions about how might our lives be different if we had a place for women, a place to mentor our young, a place to be heard, to be held, and to be known. Starkweather believed that many women yearned for this experience and that the Red Tent Temple Movement could give women momentum to work together. As the result of her work, many Red Tents were seeded throughout the United States, Canada, France, Israel, Ireland, Australia, the United Kingdom, and they continue to spread.

As a visionary, Starkweather set forth the following premises for the movement:

- Red Tent Temples are a place for women of all ages and stages.
- That we be tolerant of one another's differences and make room for diversity where all women are welcomed regardless of age, class, religion, sexual identity, ethnicity, and political association.
- This would be a collective global grassroots initiative sustained by donations.
- Red Tents would be held on or near the new moon.
- That a talking circle be held.
- That we bring soup and tea to nourish each other.
- That a storytelling chair be there for women to organically share stories, poems, and ask questions.
- That the focus be on the honoring of our womanhood journeys versus our spiritual beliefs.
- That this be a place to mentor our young women.

- That the Red Tent could teach us about having non-directed time to simply be.
- That women would wear red as a symbol of our bleeding.
- That the Red Tent Temple is an archetypal womb space for humanity's healing.

Many Red Tents are forming without Starkweather's influence. As the dialogue and the vision are taking root, many women are creating Red Tents, emulating what they envisioned from Diamant's book. Overall this red fabric space acts as a catalyst to women's empowerment. Many people now use the terms Red Tent and Red Tent Temple interchangeably. The growing consciousness of the Red Tent movement is changing the way that women interact and support each other by providing a place that honors and celebrates women, and by enabling open conversations about the things that women don't want to talk about in other venues.

In most cases, women create the space through a co-creative process. Some Red Tents are more elaborate than others; some women lovingly transform spaces like yurts, spiritual centers, church basements, cabins, and bodywork and yoga studios into Red Tents for an evening or a weekend. There are other cases, where the creation is a more solitary experience where one woman transforms her living room or guest bedroom into a Red Tent. While every Red Tent is autonomous, there is a thread that runs through us all and weaves us together. Inside the Red Tent, women feel comfortable to open up to address common personal, cultural, and social issues. The Red Tent fulfills a constellation of gendered societal needs. Behind the veils you may see women dancing, singing, and telling lively stories with laughter and tears. Here is one woman's story:

She had never been inside a Red Tent and did not know what to expect when she arrived to the round yurt building. On entry, she was welcomed. She could barely believe how beautiful it was to enter a woman's sacred space. Women were quietly resting or writing in their journals. One older woman was massaging another's feet, another telling a story in the chair. It seemed so natural as if this had always been true. Never in her lifetime had she seen this before though she heard tales of women supporting each other in the Red Tents. A well of grief rose from her heart and though she barely knew anyone she began to sob aloud. Immediately women knew what to do and they embraced her.

Being together regularly gives women an opportunity to celebrate being women, to have our voices heard, to discuss issues about body image, self-respect and empowerment or to simply relax and take care of oneself. Women promote positive ideals for the young women who gather with them. The Red Tent also acts as an educational place where women share about sexuality, birth, menopause, and the mysteries of our bodies. Here conversations take place that enable women to openly speak of their traumas and losses that need healing. Because the Red Tent is a safe space, stories about rape, infertility, death and illness can arise. All in all, it is a place where women can truly be themselves and talk about anything if they want to.

In 2005, Starkweather brought the Red Tent to a Women's Spirituality festival called Womongathering, in northeast Pennsylvania. A group of four women created their first Red Tent at this festival, inaugurating what has become a dynamic annual event. The Red Temple became a haven for documentary filmmaker Isadora Gabrielle Leidenfrost, whose love of fabric and women's community caused her to spend hours and hours here. In early 2009, Starkweather invited Leidenfrost to consider documenting the Red Tent Temple Movement in a short film, but Leidenfrost's love and dedication to the space fueled her desire to create a full-length film on the movement for her PhD dissertation at the University of Wisconsin-Madison.

In September 2012, Isadora Gabrielle Leidenfrost, PhD premiered her 72-minute documentary entitled "Things We Don't Talk About: Women's Stories from the Red Tent" that she co-produced with Starkweather. The film presents a cohesive, heretofore-undocumented tradition and explores the Red Tent as a phenomenon and a contemporary movement that is unique to women. It weaves together healing narratives from inside the Red Tent to shine a spotlight on this vital, emergent women's tradition. The film chronicles the voices of the Red Tent movement, one that is sweeping the world and signals the clarion call to all who envision a world built around cooperation rather than competition, where all women are respected, valued, and heard. This is the world we want to leave for our children, their children and stretching far into the future. "Things We Don't Talk About" shows Red Tents gifting women with an opportunity to remember, to listen, to know, and to discover what needs to be brought to our communities to help reawaken their voices.

In less than a year "Things We Don't Talk About" has had more than 250 screenings worldwide, been subtitled in five languages, and there are hundreds and thousands of Red Tents that have been inspired by the film. An Israeli woman who purchased the DVD wrote to the filmmaker and said that when she received the disc she was not able to watch it because she was so frightened from hearing military planes flying above, tanks driving by, and cars full of soldiers. She wrote, "I watched the movie and for an hour I did not think of war. I was with my sisters. I listened and cried and laughed."

Another woman wrote to the filmmaker from Chile. She commented, "Traveling around Chile raising Red Tents has been an amazing and powerful experience. Every woman that has set foot inside each of these Red Tents has left her mark, her energy, her story, and her lineage. Wonderful networks of love, healing, creativity and sisterhood have been created. I felt very moved to see that our Tent wasn't at all different from the Tents portrayed in the film, since our stories, tears, joys, and our hearts were the same."

After watching the film, both of these women now facilitate Red Tents in their communities, have translated the film into Hebrew and Spanish, and hosted numerous screenings and Red Tents throughout their countries because they believe in the potential that the Red Tent offers women.

The Red Tent phenomenon is our love in action and acts as a meme for changing culture. We are on a precipice of human history. Building foundations for a woman-honoring society is the priority of many committed visionaries because as the Chinese proverb states, "As sleeping women wake, mountains move."

About Isadora Gabrielle Leidenfrost ...

Isadora Gabrielle Leidenfrost, PhD is trained as a filmmaker, a textile historian, and a feminist folklorist. She holds a BFA from the Rhode Island School of Design and a Masters and a PhD from the University of Wisconsin-Madison. In addition to her educational experiences, Dr. Leidenfrost has owned and operated Soulful Media, her film production company since 2004 and has produced thirteen films since she began. She creates documentary films to inspire people and to show them rare and exquisite fabric traditions from around the world. She is an award-winning filmmaker, whose films have been shown worldwide to thousands of people. She has lived, traveled in, and created films in eighteen countries, including several productions in India and a production to accompany His Holiness the Dalai Lama's teaching at the Alliant Energy Center stadium in Madison, WI. For more information about her 2012 Red Tent movie production, "Things We Don't Talk About" visit: www.redtentmovie.com

About ALisa Starkweather ...

ALisa Starkweather is a visionary with a formidable three-decade commitment to women's leadership. She is the founder of the Red Tent Temple Movement, Daughters of the Earth Gatherings, the Women's Belly and Womb Conferences, and the acclaimed women's mystery school, Priestess Path, founded in 1998 in Massachusetts. Certified facilitator of Shadow Work, ALisa is the co-founder of the archetypal Women in Power: Initiating Ourselves to the Predator and Prey Within, an international women's initiation based in the knowing that women hold immense untapped power in places they have feared to look. She is co-producer of "Things We Don't Talk About: Women's Stories from the Red Tent" and is published in the award-winning anthology, *Women, Spirituality, and Transformative Leadership: Where Grace Meets Power*. Her online Fierce Feminine Life course teaches women to move forward with conviction and vulnerability hand in hand. ALisa has three CD recordings of her chants and spoken word and her voice is sure to move your hearts from love into action.

Website: http://www.alisastarkweather.com

Chapter 20

Goddesses, Dildos and Jesus

by Dr. David C.A. Hillman

Blooming Goddess

Ancient religion is the vocalization of a teenage girl in the grips of sexual ecstasy. Contrary to the assertions of modern classical scholars, there were no religious "fertility rites" in ancient Greece or Rome; Greek, Roman and Etruscan priestesses were not concerned with celebrating crops, animal fecundity, or even personal fertility. On the contrary, the poetry and art they left behind shows an all-consuming interest in capturing the songs of someone they referred to as the "Kore," a goddess in the bloom of life, the singular face of everything divine, the oracular manifestation of cosmic beauty.

A quick look at the appearances of ancient Mediterranean goddesses reveals an interesting, if not culturally disturbing, fact: Almost all of them were teenage girls. Despite the wet-dreams of modern wiccans, herbalists and goddess worshippers, there was no maiden-mother-crone paradigm in antiquity. On the contrary, Greek and Roman myth preserves an infinite number of gods in the forms of nymphs, *korai*, sibyls, and *parthenoi*, all of whom were post-pubertal girls in the grips of sexual development. In fact, it is fair to say that the prototypical female divinity was not a matron or an elderly woman at all, but a girl at the height of puberty.

Like the Delphic oracles, who were themselves the first poets, doctors and philosophers of Western civilization, goddesses were considered the bloom of the universe; they didn't age, they didn't die, they were perfect elements of Nature. For example, the Muses, the teenage daughters of Memory, were cosmic fonts of inspiration who entranced the world of mortals with their seductive midnight bathing and moonlit dances.[1]

Athena, the fearsome aspect of civic justice and ultimately the protectress of democracy, was a young girl who struck horror in the hearts of mortals with – of all things – her naked gymnastics.[2] Persephone, the centerpiece of what ultimately became the most popular ancient cult, the Eleusinian Mysteries, unlocked the secrets of the cosmos for her initiates by means of her annual resurrection as a beautiful, pubertal girl.

The Graces were teenage girls. The Fates were teenage girls. The Seasons were teenage girls. The Furies were teenage girls. Hecate, Aphrodite, Artemis, Selene and Hestia were all teenage girls. Io, Europa, and Semele were teenage girls. Circe and Medea were teenage girls. Even the Graiai, goddesses traditionally referred to as "old hags" by modern translators and feminist scholars, were actually referred to by the Greeks as "ancient teenagers."[3] In an eloquent and succinct manner, the Homeric *Hymn to Demeter* stated this phenomenon best by describing a group of young girls as being "like goddesses, possessing the bloom of youth."[4]

Brides by Penetration

As a mystery religion competing with other mystery religions, early Christianity tried to set itself apart as it strove to boost its membership and to achieve prominence in the Mediterranean world. One way to establish itself as the most popular mystery cult of the region was to condemn the practices of pagan priestesses and their own initiates. For example, early Church fathers closely scrutinized the Roman worship of Priapus, a god with a permanent and huge erection known as the "guardian of the garden." And these same men consistently and specifically berated the veneration of Priapus' oversized erection.

The Church specifically condemned the use of Priapus' divine phallus during ancient pagan marriage ceremonies. Augustine himself was horrified that pagans used large dildos – as representations of the god – while celebrating the sacred institution of marriage. In his famous *City of God*, Augustine wrote with great disgust and revulsion that "in the pagan marriage ceremony the new bride is instructed to sit on the regal staff of Priapus."[5] The Latin verb used by Augustine, *sedere*, can mean simply to sit upon something, but it also connotes the act of performing one's occupation or fulfilling one's natural purpose while seated on some object.

The early Christian leadership condemned the practice of young brides performing their rightful conjugal duties via stone or leather representations of Priapus. According to Augustine, the phallic ceremony did not involve the loss of "sexual purity,"[6] a strange observation that raises an interesting question: In light of the Priapic ritual preserved in ancient literature, does Augustine's comment mean that Roman brides were penetrated anally on the night of their nuptials ... by a large Priapic dildo?

Anal penetration on the night of a bride's nuptial rites may make a modern audience uncomfortable, but it does indeed make good sense within a pagan context. Latin authors, like Martial and Juvenal, reveal that it was acceptable for young brides to offer anal intercourse in place of vaginal penetration on the night of their weddings, in order to allay their fear of painful defloration. And of course, Ovid indicates that brides were given opium, a strong analgesic and euphoric, on the night of their first sexual union with their new husbands: "Without hesitation, go purchase the poppy, carefully rubbed for its snow white latex, and honey flowing from pressed combs, since Venus herself, when first led to her aroused husband, drank this concoction and from that time onward was a bride." [7]

Phallic Punishment

So anal intercourse was an option for brides, but why use a ritual phallus? Augustine calls the marital phallus on which young brides sat a "scepter."[8] This regal imagery was not random, but followed long-established traditions of the followers of Priapus, a quirky group of priestesses, witches and necromancers who considered the god's huge erection to be his weapon – like Hercules' club or Neptune's trident – as well as the symbol of his divine authority.

Priapus' bulbous, red erection was considered his royal seal – in Roman terms his "fasces" – an official rod that represented the justice he meted out to the wicked. In fact, garden statues of Priapus often had detachable wooden penises that could be used as cudgels to chase off thieves. And according to one anonymous Roman poet, the "scepter" of Priapus was a fitting and painful punishment: "This staff of office which, severed from the tree, can now shoot forth no verdure; scepter, which pathic maidens crave, and some kings love to hold; to which patrician paederasts give kisses; shall go right into the very bowels of the thief, as far as the hair and the bag of balls."[9] Priapus' erection was no joke; it was a divine means of enforcing justice.

So was the Priapic wedding-dildo a form of punishment or a sign of divine authority? It turns out that it was a badge of religious honor, a symbol of one's pious submission to the goddesses of creative unions. In fact, penetration with the ritual phallus was an honor that extended to numerous pagan cults and mystery religions.

Phallic penetration of brides and priestesses was never confined to one specific Roman cult. For example, the followers of the secret mysteries of Bona Dea were also advocates of using the Priapic dildo. According to Juvenal, rituals celebrating this particular goddess involved highly enjoyable sexual penetration with a dildo-like rod:

The mysteries of Bona Dea are famous; a time when devotees stimulate their groins with the stiff flute. Plying horns and wine with a singular purpose, these Priapic maenads roll their stunned heads and groan to the goddess. Such a great desire for sex burns in their minds; their moaning is accompanied by explicit gyrations and produces a flood of undiluted sexual desire that flows down their medicated thighs.[10]

It's hard to tell if the female followers of Bona Dea were dripping with their own vaginal ejaculates or the many oil-based sex drugs that were rubbed on the Priapic dildo before it was applied to the vagina and anus. Vaginal and rectal tissues are good sites for absorbing drugs that need to circumvent the stomach and its destructive acid, a fact that did not escape the classical mind.

And this medicated scepter of Priapus wasn't just for girls. One of the most famous myths of antiquity ends with the self-anal-penetration of the god Dionysus. After visiting the under-world to raise his mother from the dead, Dionysus – like the Roman bride – sat on a phallus in order to appease the ghost of the necromancer who showed him the way to Hades. In other words, the ancient world unhesitatingly associated anal penetration with necromantic gods and necromantic practices; the journey to the underworld was marked by ritual penetration with a sacred dildo, and Dionysus adhered to the practice ... as did early Christians.

Sex, Bishops and Corpses

Pagan gods and brides weren't the only ones who practiced ritual sexual penetration. According to Prudentius (fourth–fifth century), an early Christian author, St. Cyprian was himself an avid sex-magic facilitating practitioner of necromancy. Before he became a bishop, St. Cyprian was one of Rome's premiere aficionados of sexual necromancy. And apparently he had quite a following; Prudentius tells us he had a reputation for being better than any of his peers at overcoming prudery in those with hidden appetites for graveyard sex:

Among the youth of his generation Cyprian was the most well trained in perverted magic arts, craftily penetrating a person's sense of modesty, he judged nothing sacred and often even practiced magical incantations in graveyards, and by using his sexual magic on girls burning with lust he was able to dissolve that which is promised to grooms ... but Christ drove out his Bacchic fury.[11]

Like the sex-maddened Maenads, Bacchants, the juice-dripping followers of Bona Dea, and the pathic girls found in poems dedicated to Priapus, St. Cyprian used dildo-applied drugs to facilitate the sexual necromancy at which he truly excelled. And what were the tricks of the trade for the talented necromancer of antiquity? Snake venoms. In fact, snake venoms were among the most actively used sex drugs in antiquity.

Snake venoms were so commonly used as medicines and sacraments in the ancient world that one physician-priest, named Nicander, wrote extensively about the proper antidotes to use in cases of snake venom overdose. And viper venoms appear to be among the most popular of snake-derived drugs, especially when used in combination with oil-based botanicals. This makes good sense when considering all the literary and iconic associations of vipers with ecstatic mystery religions and orgiastic ceremonies.

And according to his post-conversion confession, St. Cyprian was not above using snake-derived sex drugs in his necromantic practices. Like the followers of Bona Dea, Cyprian's midnight sex romps in the cemetery ended up leaving him splattered with drugs: "I myself became a new man, a new Cyprian, whom you, a good God, cleansed when I was smeared with viper venom."[12]

So Cyprian's cemetery orgies were messy, but the problem with snake venoms is that they are inactive when applied to the skin or swallowed – they are impermeable to the skin and being proteins they are easily digested; in other words, in a world that had not yet developed injection technology, snake venoms were only effective when applied to tissues like the rectum and the vagina. And in order to get them into the rectum or vagina, a device was needed ... in this case a rod.

Greeks and Romans had lots of short rods that were used medically. Their *rhabdos*, a short, thin rod, was originally associated with witches or *pharmakeis*, who were known for their in-depth drug knowledge – especially of venomous reptiles. The same device was called a *virga* by the Romans and was used both in the anus and vagina as a medical applicator. Its cousin was called the *ramus* and was used by oracular priestess on special subjects like Aeneas – for the sake of "underworld travel."

Prudentius, the Christian author who relates the necromantic sex-capades of St. Cyprian, tells us that Priapus' erect penis was referred to as a *ramus*.[13] And this makes good sense when we consider that the Priapic phallus was used by witches and followers of necromantic gods in order to apply drugs. So when Prudentius says St. Cyprian thanked God for cleaning off his viper venom, it wasn't because he applied it to his skin; it was because the venom – like that used by the ejaculating women who followed Bona Dea – was drizzling out of his anus.

Shifting Paradigm

So where do we moderns derive all of our misconceptions about Greek and Roman gods? Why do we think of Athena, Aphrodite and Artemis as adult women? From the perspective of those who lived in antiquity, the Christians were to blame.

According to Julian the "apostate," the world of classical mythology was unavoidably – but actively – distorted by Christianity. For this reason, the Roman emperor himself forbade Christians from teaching the classics. Of course, Julian's decree that the followers of Christ should be prohibited from teaching ancient religion and literature was reversed ... following his untimely demise at the hands of one of his own Christian soldiers,[14] but assuming that Julian was right, and assuming that our Christian cultural lens is to blame for modern misconceptions about pagan religion, how then did Western civilization turn from interpreting paganism as a mechanism for harvesting cosmic beauty to a superstitious recipe for promoting fertility?

The answer to this question may ultimately lie with Jesus and the naked boy he was discovered with in the garden of Gethsemane.[15] And working toward an understanding, the Jewish messiah's night of temptation in a garden based in a cemetery must ultimately return to Augustine and his views of Roman marriage. For, while Christian authors like Clement of Alexandria, Origen and Augustine shared overwhelmingly negative views of pagan religion, their understanding of sexuality and marriage became the foundation for modern Western culture and thus help explain our own classically-distorted perspective.

The pre-Christian, pagan world viewed the highest good as the divine voice of a young girl in the bloom of life. The Greeks created oracles and choruses of young priestesses in order to capture this cosmic inspiration. The Etruscans expressed this idea most succinctly by creating rituals that used young priestess sibyls to bridge the gap between the Earth and the underworld. The Romans ran with these Etruscan rituals and even used them to define their own word for religion … in Latin, *religio* is the binding of the ethereal realms to our own by means of the voice of a young maiden.

The modern world views ancient religion through the lens of Christianity, and the impression is fundamentally out of focus with our surviving texts. Greco-Roman religion was centered on the veneration of the eternal song of the budding Muse, not the theological expressions of godhead or the dogma of faith. Christianity, under the direction of Jesus, the apostles, monks, priests and bishops, refocused Western considerations of sexuality as a means of purification from the stain of the pagan feminine voice. When Mary presented Jesus with a medicated dildo – known in Greek as an *alabastron*[16] – before he was arrested with the naked boy in the Garden of Gethsemane – the Western stage was set for a shift in the way we view sex, drugs, religion and most especially women.

About David C.A. Hillman ...

Dr. D.C.A. Hillman is professor of Classical languages at St. Mary's University of Minnesota. He earned his PhD in Classics and his MS in Bacteriology from the University of Wisconsin, where he specialized in ancient pharmacy and medicine. He is author of *The Chemical Muse: Drug Use and the Roots of Western Civilization* (St. Martin's Press, 2008).

Dr. Hillman's research, which the London *Times* has labeled "the last wild frontier of Classics," is always controversial, due in large part to his willingness to investigate the most taboo subjects of antiquity, including the exploits of sexually explicit mystery cults, the use of hallucinogens in Greco-Roman religion, and classical sexual practices including inflammatory topics such as the use of dildos in antiquity and the practice of "sacred sodomy." Dr. Hillman's dissertation committee famously refused to grant his doctorate if he did not remove the chapter on recreational drug use from his thesis on Roman pharmacy. He removed this chapter, received his degree, and then sent the material to St. Martin's Press, NY, where it was immediately published. He has published books on the ritualistic rape of children in the early Christian Church and on hermaphroditic gods from the ancient world.

Chapter 21

Love and the Sacred Female

by Art Noble

I am a man who has been blessed by knowing some fantastic women in my life; I have also been cursed with an infinite curiosity. Although I've met a few people who have shared these experiences, there aren't too many on the planet right now. And most of them tried to explain their responses in terms of woo-woo. As for me, I only do this partially: I believe human beings are fantastic creatures, with women having the edge.

I began studying sexual biology, learning about our potential for these experiences. Sexual science, in its current state, could not offer me reasonable explanations for these events. I looked into anthropology, archaeology and ancient sexual history, finding an absence of knowledge about sexual biology, particularly with responses beyond orgasm. Eventually, it became clear to me when writing about sex, all these "authorities" had their own agenda based on their limited sexual experience. Although my current range is broader than most, I have learned, as Billy Mays used to say, "But wait! There's more!" Just because you or I have not experienced something doesn't mean this experience doesn't exist for us.

Other than the title of my novel, what exactly is *The Sacred Female*, and what does sex have to do with it? Everything and nothing. First, genital contact is not necessary to elicit any sexual response. Sherri Winston in upstate New York teaches men and women how to have orgasms with guided imagery. Dr. Beverly Whipple notes the brain lights up the same way under an MRI on guided imagery orgasms as it does those with genital contact. Orgasm is just the beginning.

"Orgasm" is a catchall term for every thing that happens in the orgasmic experience. Although our hardwiring (nervous system) is generally the same for all women, and for all men (men and women are different), both our DNA coding and our programming is unique. Therefore to say that at any given time a woman or man is supposed to respond in a certain way is nothing but a continuation of patriarchal/political programming. The good news is we can be de-programmed, perhaps un-educated from the centuries of myth and misogyny and we can restructure our DNA coding.

We currently define love as a feeling created by altered brain chemistry. This is like saying we get a suntan because it is hot outside. Further, sexual desire is also a similarly altered brain chemistry coming from the tiny paraventricular nucleus in the pea-sized hypothalamus. (I never knew that something so small could get me into so much trouble!) They are similar, but not quite the same. Here is where I get a little woo-woo. We can look at love as an etheric energy spectrum. It is etheric because we know as much about it as we knew about the Electro-Magnetic Energy Spectrum 200 years ago. It is energy not only within us but all around us, like the Earth's magnetic field.

How do we open ourselves to it? I visualized a door on my back. I figured, at the time, that God could do a much better job of loving my beloved than I could, so I opened the door and let God love her through me. Years later, I learned from a Shamanic Master that humans do have an etheric portal between their shoulder blades. I've looked with a double mirror and haven't seen it, but whatever I did at the time certainly worked.

As an analogy, I modeled love energy after the Visible Light Spectrum (VLS). This is only a start. Unconditional love as a white light hits the prism of our mind where it is refracted into a beautiful rainbow of love. Each segment on the spectrum is then a different form of love.

Of course, the operative conditioning we've been faced with

for centuries, millennia, is like putting chewing gum on the prism, blocking our love and our responses.

Returning to the difference between love and sexual desire:

Romance smells like flowers, candles and wine.
But love? Love smells like sweat and time.

Metaphorically, using the sun as a primary source of light, we know light energy (photons) is not the only energy put out by the sun: beta and gamma rays, radio waves and a host of other things are emitted by the sun. Therefore, the VLS model is only the beginning of what may be found in the love spectrum.

It is the addition of love that restructures our DNA coding. I could be wrong, but something wondrous happens. This does not apply to just erotic love, but also to mother-love and father-love; it entails restructuring, perhaps even un-structuring our DNA coding, which originates from living in a fear-based society. This latter observation was made by Dr. Bruce Lipton, author of *Biology of Belief*. Of course, we mustn't talk about sex, so Dr. Lipton didn't go there.

For me, the most important attribute of sexual congress is attitude: an attitude of love. This is reflected in his or her behavior. This comes from our belief system, which is generally tainted with myth and misogyny. We have a lot of dirt to scrape off our prisms.

I have found the behaviors of love generally fall into six categories: communicating, nourishing, touching, grooming, gazing and playing. There are many variations within each of these categories, but intimacy is a key point. I think it is okay for co-workers to give one another a pat on the shoulder for a job well done. But a pat on the butt would be a violation of boundaries. A violation of boundaries is not a behavior that originates in love.

After the 2013 NBA Championship, Duane Wade kissed

LeBron James on the cheek as they were hugging. Does this mean they are gay? Absolutely not! Over years of practicing and playing they had developed a strong bond, not unlike that of men in combat. Their intimacy and brotherly love ran deep. Had I tried that with LeBron, I'd have gotten cold-cocked. Pow! So we need to communicate in order to learn about the other's boundaries in all the above categories, as well as seek to discover the essence of the concerned person: who they really are. We usually wear masks at first and it takes time and trust to remove them.

The earliest symbol for woman is found in cuneiform. It is the inverted triangle (also the chalice) with a vertical cleft almost bisecting the triangle. It is a representation of the vulva. This symbol also means "giver of life." Most archaeologists believe this refers to childbirth. My opinion is that with our genetic restructuring, or whatever may be occurring, we are given a new life. The chalice may also represent woman's ability to contain love. Since the symbol is for all women, I presume all women have this capacity and for that alone women should be honored as sacred. Of course, "having" and "using" are two different things.

Men also have this capacity and we can show it. I call it the "gotta wannas." We have to desire to do these things, and at the same time not violate boundaries. Now, don't get me wrong. In my experience it is usually triggered by some woman we respectfully desire. Not all men fully tap into this capacity, nor do all women. "Fully" is undefined. I don't know what that is and it may be different for each of us. But, we can give it a shot and that is what counts.

In early Tantra, it was said that a man who worshipped at the Yoni would have all his wishes granted. Yoni is Sanskrit for the vulva and means the sacred place. One does not approach this altar of love with expectations of having one's wishes granted. One approaches it as one would any altar: with respect and reverence and with permission to enter. It's all about attitude.

Your wishes may have little to do with what you receive. As an imaginative example, you may be wishing for a new car, and wind up knowing how to teleport yourself wherever you want to go. That may seem unrealistic, but you wouldn't have to worry about gas prices. We limit ourselves with our visions of "reality."

When our intimacy with a woman grows to where we are engaging in erotic love, we (guys) must accept their responses as gifts of love. They trust us enough to "let go" of all the conditioning that holds them back. I speak here of female ejaculation. At this point, science knows of only two sources, both through the urethra: the female prostate and the urinary bladder. There are possibly two more, with a path through the vagina: ducts connected to unknown glands located on the wall of the vagina and the uterus. (There may be a science on uterine flow in the spring of 2014.) None of this is urine, though some women do feel the urge to urinate just before emitting this fluid.

What science does know is that the fluid from the urinary bladder is mostly water with electrolytes, unused amino acids, proteins and other good stuff. Better than Gatorade. Obviously, they leave a bigger wet spot than we do. If you can't handle that, grow up!

Another group of responses is known as transcendent sex. Many men and women have this experience and don't realize they are having a transcendent sexual experience. No one told them such a thing existed. There could be sensations of electricity, shooting stars, buzzing vibrations other than the involuntary muscle contractions; or sensations of being one with the Earth or a specific plant or animal, shape-shifting into the animal or being in the presence of God, or merging with a beloved in a way you never dreamed possible. These along with out-of-body experiences and others are transcendent sexual experiences.

One transcendent experience described that I found rather weird is Trespasso. This is when you see a different head, or a succession of various heads, where your lover's head is supposed to be. You may or may not know these heads and some may be animal heads. In Western culture, the animals are usually bird, bear or wolf. Bizarre as it is, Trespasso offers an alternative explanation for animal-headed totems and petrographs as well as Anubis, the Egyptian god of death who wears the head of a jackal. There are other transcendent experiences, all scientifically attributed to altered brain chemistry.

Is love a part of this? I would now say yes, but it doesn't have to be the boy–girl erotic love we normally think of. Indigenous cultures from the American Indian to the Australian Aborigine have their "visions" or transcendent experiences in sweat lodges for example. They receive permission to enter and treat the entire experience with reverence and respect. (Sound familiar?) For most of us in the Western world, a woman revered as sacred can do the same thing – maybe even better.

The last response I will address here is bio-luminescence. This is not the contented glow on the face of our beloved afterward. This is the actual emission of photons from the skin; enough to light up a room like a 10-watt light bulb. It took years for me to track this down, so if you think I was hallucinating, at the time, so did I. Or maybe the rods and cones in my eye expanded so I could see better?

Most animal life uses Adenosine Triphosphate (ATP) as an energy carrier. This is energy from the food we metabolize and other sources. In the process of transmitting love (energy) we may build up an excess amount? Also, I learned of a Shamanic breathing practice called Dragon's Fire/Breath that offers the same result.

Now, let's think about it: We are physically bonded probably with the joy of love in our entwinement. As we approach orgasm our breathing rate increases, perhaps mimicking the Shamanic practice. Our cells are super-oxygenated and the ATP, traveling throughout our bodies, is overloaded with energy. It is given off as photons, just like fireflies and various marine organisms glow.

I have only seen a yellowish-tinged, white glow, but I have heard of red, blue and green. It seems the color is determined by our diet and perhaps our particular state of love.

There is no scientific validation of human bio-luminescence. The only experiment I have read about was conducted in a dark room with a special camera. The subjects were inert, not meditating, or making love or even breathing hard. When this happens, the Mk 1, Mod 0 eyeball is sufficient to see it. This also offers an alternative explanation for halos. (My real goal is to see the world alight with this glow!) Many of us believe we "should" have a goal in sex, ranging from getting off to getting her off, or some practice sex for the various transcendent experiences. My thinking is if we focus on transmitting love (open the door on your back) and let our bodies determine the results, they will be beyond our wildest dreams.

My journey into sexual biology is simply to show the potential women have to offer men, and themselves, and why it is in our best interest to consider them sacred. Napoleon Hill said in his 1937 publication *Think and Grow Rich,* "The combination of love, sex and romance can raise a man from mediocrity to the altitude of genius." Were it just sex and romance, we would all be geniuses. It takes love.

About Art Noble ...

Art Noble is the author of *The Sacred Female: A Sonata of Sexual Love and Spirituality.* Born in Los Angeles, Art grew up in Key West where he lived four years in the Hemingway Home. He is the son of internationally known artist, Van Noble, who opened the Hemingway Home as an art gallery before it became a museum. On moving, he acquired a lamp from the home. He still writes under the lamp.

Noble holds a BS in Ocean Engineering and an MBA. Professionally, he was an adventurer on the cutting edge of technology, an executive engineer and a teacher. Like Robert

Service and scores of other poets and authors, he has acquired and held many jobs, including technical writer and commercial diving in the offshore oil field. This gives him an eclectic view of life. He ended his diving career as an Associate Professor of Underwater Technology at Florida Institute of Technology, Jensen Beach. His poetry is published in South Florida publications, anthologies, international magazines, and read on National Public Radio.

Noble appeared as a bit actor in movies and made commercials. After his participation in the H-Bomb salvage and the first 650-foot saturation dive, he made an appearance on the *Today Show* and his photograph is in *National Geographic*.

Website: www.thesacredfemale.com

Chapter 22

Intelligent Evolution and DNA Repair

by Nicki Scully

Mutate or die. We, as a species, no longer have the luxury of time for evolution. Nothing short of mutation can give us time to adapt to the situation that we've created on this planet and survive long enough to change our destructive ways.

Mutate or die. That was my mantra during my bout with cancer in 1992. My husband and I were shamanistically observing the entire treatment and healing process using Alchemical Healing modalities. The actual experience of the mutation came during a spontaneous meeting between a gene, perhaps the BRCA gene, and me during an Alchemical Healing I received following a chemotherapy session. There was no doubt about what happened during the experience. It is only in the years since that I have encountered scientists who can validate my personal experience and articulate how it worked when viewed through a scientific lens. Science is, as it must be, relegated to measurable information duplicated under strict rules for research in order to become credible. Alchemists and shamans are working with different laws and rules that vary according to their specific traditions.

The discovery of the human genome and DNA was a great milestone in cell biology. Many scientists believed that genes were self-actualizing; they were able to turn themselves on and off, in regulating the development and function of cells. That led to the belief that genes control life and our fate. The new science of epigenetics has since found this belief to be faulty. Empirical evidence shows that the power of belief and perception, whether through traumatic necessities, shamanic journeys, prayer, or placebos, provides the ability to mutate our cells – belief in change and healing causes change and healing.

Epigenetics describes how one's thoughts and perceptions of the surrounding environment influence the mutation and adaptation of our DNA. Just as the fate of each cell in our body as a community reacts to our environment around us, we as "cells" in the larger community of humanity are controlled by our beliefs and perceptions. Correspondingly, shamanism works because it operates from an inherent respect for the power of our thoughts and perceptions. Simply stated, the underlying essence of the words "epigenetics" and "shamanism" means the same thing, although they have very different contextualizing backgrounds to describe their modalities.

From my own experience as a shamanic practitioner using guided visualizations that include self-initiations and empowerments, the subconscious mind that directs our ordinary responses does not distinguish between what is being imagined or visioned and what actually happens. What is visualized will be treated as though it is happening. For example, in Alchemical Healing, if a person experiences the perception of a spirit spider stitching up an inner or outer lesion, or weaving a supportive cast around a broken bone or torn ligament; if they are applying all available senses to perceive and feel every footfall of Spider's eight legs, every squirt of the medicated web and the weaving that is the result of Spider's work, then their subconscious mind informs the body to respond as though it happened in this physical plane.

Through this epigenetic–shamanistic approach and the power of our perceptions, we have a strong possibility for immediate physical change such as decrease or elimination of pain, greater range of motion, or other significant changes.

This convergence of science, shamanism and alchemy invites us to articulate how healing and transformation works. However, it is only through direct experience that we fully understand the incredible potential for self-healing and transformation that lies within the human psyche. Those of us who are awakening and seeking further enlightenment must step up to the task at hand and realize that we have the response-ability to co-direct the future of our personal lives, our species, and our planet. We have no time to lose, and every thought, word and action counts.

In order to provide an opportunity for you to experience directly what we have discovered, I have combined and adapted two journeys from our *Planetary Healing* book. It is useful to have a journal with you when you journey so that you can record your experience as soon as possible when it's complete.

During the first section you will receive a gift from the great Mother Goddess Isis, who helps us find that state of unconditional love through which we can perceive our own healing, and through which we can find new ways to approach healing our world. Within that gift is included the journey that was given to us in response to a direct question we had posed for guidance: "Can you give us a way to alter or repair DNA in order to help us accomplish our goal for speedier, conscious evolution, and to help us adapt and mutate while we are dealing with the changes in our environment?"

In a vision, my husband and co-author Mark Hallert was shown a cell, as if under a microscope. He could see a relaxing of the DNA coil inside the cell. As the coil was relaxing and expanding, the cell itself did not grow. There was a blurring of the DNA information as the unwinding coil stretched beyond the parameters of the cell walls. At this point, Mark could no longer see what was happening: it was as if the coil had moved not only beyond the cell walls but outside of the spectrum of visibility. Perhaps the coil had moved into another dimension to be altered. He understood that when the energy holding the coil together was relaxed and expanded, certain undesirable attributes fell out, and new beneficial codes replaced them. After this, the coil shrank back into the containment of the cell wall, reconsolidating into something slightly changed from its original form. Once the spiral recoiled and tightened again, and everything was back in place, the reconfiguration was complete. No further alterations could take place.

In order to translate these images into the empowerment exercise that follows, Mark was given a metaphor that is revealed at the end of the journey. This allowed us to recreate his experience in a guided journey so that you can change your physical body at the cellular level.

It is important that you be in a state of communion with love when you take this journey, for love ensures that our direction for change is toward healing, surviving, and ultimately thriving.

DNA Repair through Isis's Magic Diamond

Close your eyes, relax, and breathe deeply. Focus your attention on your heart center. Direct love to the eternal flame within your heart and observe how it grows ... Love is the fuel. Feel as the radiance from your heart flame expands to fill your entire being ... Breathe the Heart Breath, simultaneously inhaling the power, vitality, and intelligence of Earth and Sky, up from the heart of the earth and down from the heart of the cosmos, meeting in your heart and mixing with your love before exhaling it out in every direction ... During several heart breaths, as your radiance expands and as your heart flame grows and glows, invoke the great Mother Goddess Isis ... Within the glow of your heart flame you will first feel the love of Isis, and then her exquisite being comes into view, her rainbow wings surrounding you in love's embrace.

However she appears to you, Isis is a wise alchemist and mentor for this work. She is pleased that you have invoked her presence, and hands you a gift. It is a magic diamond, a large, sparkling stone with many facets. As you hold it between your forefinger and thumb, take in its clarity, beauty and brilliance.

Each facet of this diamond is a window that provides a different view. As you slowly turn the diamond, look through it and focus upon your physical body, as though the diamond was a microscope, revealing a different depth of field with each rotation. You begin to perceive your body as a landscape. As seen from above, its surface textures look like geometric forms. As you continue slowly rotating your diamond, still focused on your body, you pass through starburst patterns of fractal energy, discovering yet deeper fields of focus, until you find yourself gazing into the night sky, spangled with stars ...

As above, so below: you recognize yourself and the universe within you. Each star, each cell of your body, is a sun with its revolving planets, peopled with abundant life-forms. You are God or Goddess of your own universe, and it is your responsibility to enlighten all life within you. Begin to radiate unconditional love energy through your magic diamond, into the field beneath you, infusing every cell with all the colors of the rainbow, charging all life within with the radiant light of love ...

This energy, this love that you have sent forth, is reflected back to you, magnified by the magic diamond, and you experience waves of bliss and shivers of joy as that which you have sent out returns to you. Feel as it tingles and awakens every cell of your being [Long Pause] ...

Begin to reverse the rotation of your diamond, observing your body becoming solid once more, window by window, as you return through the different levels of perception ...

Now ask to be shown the facet that you will take into your DNA.

Once you are given the window, look through it and bring the image into focus ... You will see a warehouse full of identical round baskets, stacked to the ceiling and filling every available space. The baskets look like those of a snake charmer. They all have lids on them, and you cannot see inside them.

Change the focus of the diamond so that your vision

penetrates the baskets ... Now, you can see that each one contains a tightly coiled cobra, which almost completely fills the space inside. Your vision shifts again so that you cannot see through the baskets, but you can hear that the snakes have begun to move. There is a growing sound, like that of a breeze blowing through dry autumn leaves, as the snakes relax and uncoil, slither and stretch. Then, for a moment, all becomes still ...

In this quiet stillness, imagine changes that would cause your health to improve and your body to thrive. These changes can happen only at the cellular level ... Hold your intention and attention [Long Pause] ...

Hold your vision as the cobras begin to stir and slowly return to the tight coil. For a moment, you can again see within the baskets just as the cobras complete the tightening of their coils; you can see that there is no room to spare. Notice that something about the pattern on the cobras' hoods looks slightly different from before ...

Once again, all is peaceful and quiet in the warehouse. Step back to take in the whole of the building. You need to step back farther ... You are suddenly blown back, like a leaf in the wind, farther and farther, until your perspective changes. You now can see that it is not a warehouse at all – it is you, lying naked in a field in the sunlight. You understand that your DNA has been altered in a way that empowers it.

Spend a moment admiring yourself and the awesome magic of the complex and yet simple components of your DNA ...

Refocus on Isis's Magic Diamond and you will be in the presence of Isis. Ask if she has any further message or teaching for you at this time, or if there is a particular window she wants you to explore. Perhaps you have need of healing that can be addressed this way.

When you feel complete, offer your gratitude to Isis, Cobra, and any other beings present during this experience. As you ground and center into your physical body, feel the love of Isis that continues to surround and enfold you as you return fully into heart-centered presence.

About Nicki Scully ...

Nicki Scully has been teaching healing, shamanic arts and the Egyptian Mysteries since 1983. Techniques from her Alchemical Healing form are used internationally by thousands of practitioners.

In the late 1980s, Nicki founded Shamanic Journeys, Ltd., which specializes in inner journeys in her retreats, tele-web classes and spiritual pilgrimages to Egypt. Her latest book is *Planetary Healing: Spirit Medicine for Global Transformation*, co-written with her husband Mark Hallert. Other published works include *Alchemical Healing: A Guide to Spiritual, Physical and Transformational Medicine; Becoming an Oracle: Connecting with the Divine Source for Information and Healing*, a seven-CD audio program; and *Power Animal Meditations*; as well as *The Anubis Oracle* and *Shamanic Mysteries of Egypt*, both co-authored with Linda Star Wolf.

Nicki lives in Eugene, Oregon, where she maintains a comprehensive healing and shamanic consulting practice.

Website: www.shamanicjourneys.com

Part III

Sacred Feminine Values – Alternatives to Patriarchy Politics and Social Change

First they ignore you. Then they laugh at you. Then they fight you. Then you win.

– Mahatma Gandhi

Chapter 23

Feminism, Patriarchy and Religion

Transcript of interview with Noam Chomsky

Interview:

KT = Karen Tate

NC = Noam Chomsky

Tonight it is my honor and privilege to have as my very special guest, Professor Noam Chomsky. He has been described as a prominent cultural figure, and was voted the "world's top public intellectual" in a 2005 poll, according to the *Guardian World News*.

Noam Chomsky was born on December 7, 1928 in Philadelphia, Pennsylvania. He received his PhD in linguistics in 1955 from the University of Pennsylvania. During the years 1951 to 1955, Chomsky was a Junior Fellow of the Harvard University Society of Fellows. The major theoretical viewpoints of his doctoral dissertation appeared in the monograph *Syntactic Structure* (1957). This formed part of a more extensive work, *The Logical Structure of Linguistic Theory*, circulated in mimeograph in 1955 and published in 1975.

Chomsky joined the staff of the Massachusetts Institute of Technology in 1955 and in 1961 was appointed full professor. In 1976 he was appointed Institute Professor in the Department of Linguistics and Philosophy.

Chomsky has lectured at many universities here and abroad, and is the recipient of numerous honorary degrees and awards. He has written and lectured widely on linguistics, philosophy, intellectual history, contemporary issues, international affairs and US foreign policy. Among his more recent books are, *New*

Horizons in the Study of Language and Mind; On Nature and Language; The Essential Chomsky; Hopes and Prospects; Gaza in Crisis; How the World Works; 9-11: Was There an Alternative?; Making the Future: Occupations, Interventions, Empire, and Resistance; The Science of Language; Peace with Justice: Noam Chomsky in Australia; Power Systems; and *On Western Terrorism: From Hiroshima to Drone Warfare* (with Andre Vltchek).

Interview starts:

KT: I thought we might start with religion, language and culture before we move to the media and politics. Arianna Huffington's Commencement Address to Brown talked about how success as we know it is no longer sustainable and we should gauge our success not just by male standards of ambition, money and power but also by what we might recognize as feminine values – our well-being, wonder, wisdom, empathy and what we give back. Your thoughts?

NC: Well, I would hope that what you are talking about as female values are male values too. That ought to be everyone's values. The idea that we should only be after money and power is a particular form of pathology that our doctrinal institutions try to institute in us but it's completely inhuman and people have revolted against it for centuries. If you go back, in fact it's quite dramatic, how they have, some of the early examples are the early history of industrialization of America, mid-nineteenth century, mostly in eastern Massachusetts where I am, people were being driven into factories. Tenant farmers bitterly opposed the industrial feudal system. They claimed it was taking away their rights as free citizens, their rights, their culture, and values. One of their slogans, one of the things they most strongly were opposed to, was the slogan that they called "Gain Wealth, Forgetting All But Self." They considered this a hideous idea. It did include women like the so-called factory girls, young women from the farms that were going into the textile factories, but it also included Irish artisans coming from Boston. It was just across the board, and I think that's normal human beings. The idea of being dedicated just to money and power is really a pathology and it's been very hard, that slogan, "Gain Wealth, Forgetting All But Self." There have been efforts to drive it into our minds for 150 years.

KT: I think "Greed is Good" is more recently one of the slogans that parallels that. But that used to be one of the Seven Deadly Sins (laughs).

NC: Yeah, but I think that's the way people feel. Take a look at workers, still keeping to the working class, it's just that its overwhelmingly male labor actions from early on have used another slogan, they want "Bread and Roses." In other words they don't just want enough to eat, they want dignity. Taking control over labor, struggling for independence, fighting to control the shop floor, for example, and not to be subjected to managerial control. Now that's as old as industrialization, so I just kinda think it's propaganda to call it a male value.

KT: Okay. In that vein of thought, there's a documentary that's begun making the rounds produced by actress Sharon Stone and filmmaker Emmanuel Itier of Wonderland Entertainment, called *Femme: Women Healing the World*. And no doubt you've heard the Dalai Lama say it would be Western women who would save the world. I wonder what you think of the Dalai Lama's statement and what you think of feminism. Has it been successful? Should it be a force to help re-shape the world toward justice and equality?

NC: It's certainly been highly successful in changing the status of women. Just take the United States, you go back to the time of the American Revolution, the Colonies, American law at the time was taken over from British Common Law, formalized Blackstone's compilation. And women had a specific function in that law. They were property. A woman was the property of her father and that was transferred over to her husband. In fact, one of the arguments at that time against giving the women the right to vote was it was unfair to unmarried men because a married man would have two votes, since obviously the property votes the way the owner does. And it's taken a long time for that to be cut back. It was literally not until the 1970s, quite recently, that women had the legally guaranteed right to serve on Federal juries, meaning the rights as peers, not just property. Well, that's gone. That's had a big impact. In fact of all the activism of the 1960s and its aftermath, I think that the change in the status of women has been the most dramatic and the one that's affected the whole society.

Going back to your point, not just in the rights of women, but also associated ideas about values that ought to be human values. But through cultural pressures and ideological pressures these were sometimes associated with women's values.

KT: It's unfortunate though that feminism gets such a bad rap. It's demonized in some areas of our culture, wouldn't you say?

NC: Yeah, but that's true of every effort to retain justice and equality. Those who were, holding the whips if you like, don't like it. That was true of minority rights or ending slavery. Look how the white slave holders fought bitterly to maintain slavery. In fact, have maintained it long after the Civil War.

KT: I believe someone said women gaining equality would unravel the fabric of society.

NC: It would unravel the fabric of patriarchal society.

KT: Exactly.

NC: But the same was true of, the same argument was given about giving former slaves rights. It would unravel the structure of civilized society. The same is true of children's rights, or animal rights, almost anything. Those in a privileged position are typically going to resist it.

KT: Absolutely. Well, we hear about the innate differences between men and women, those ideas are out there. Left- and right-brained thinking. Men have more linear vision, women think more peripherally, so maybe they think about the consequences of their decisions on more people. If you believe that, wouldn't you say it's vital we have more than 20% representation of women in Academia, corporate America, leaders in religious institutions, so would you be in favor of policies here in the US like they have in Scandinavian countries calling for a 40% solution, where corporations have to have 40% women in top positions in companies?

NC: I'd be in favor of just equal representation quite apart from any ideas about innate differences in cognitive and emotional capacities. Maybe there are and maybe there aren't, but that's independent of equal rights. I'm here at the University and when I got here sixty years ago there were practically no women on the faculty and student body. Practically zero. Maybe none, in fact. By now the student body is about half women. The faculty is varied. My department is half women and a woman chair. That's true of many departments. There are some where it's been hard. There have been real efforts to attract women faculty and open possibilities for them, but in some departments it's just been very hard to do it, math and physics, particularly. In biology it's quite equal, or close to equal, and in humanities, probably the same. You could ask why, but there have been real efforts. And there are problems in the culture which ... When you talk about having laws, rules, maybe it's necessary, but the right way to do it is to just overcome the cultural conditions and the social, even legal conditions of the general society that just impose burdens on women. So for example, you mention Scandinavian countries, there is a rather different legal structure in the whole society. So for example, after a birth, there's paternal leave as well as maternal leave. Here there's no paternal leave and very little maternal leave by comparative standards. Well, if you have both paternal and maternal leave that overcomes the problem, I think it is a problem, when a couple has a child, the mother has to take, is almost compelled to take, primarily or all of the care and the man has to go back to work. I think eliminating that makes a lot more sense than imposing numbers that have to be satisfied.

KT: Right. Maybe we just need to have some real family values. (Laughing)

NC: Well, I think it improves families and family life.

KT: Right.

NC: Frankly, I think there are always going to be the effects of innate differences. So no matter how egalitarian and equally a couple treats a child, it's going to be drawn to its mother in a very special way.

KT: Maybe that's just the way it should be. There's something primal there.

NC: I don't think we actually have scientific knowledge of this but it seems to me very likely. From experience as well.

KT: Well, myself and my listeners are interested in history, culture, spirituality that's been swept beneath the rug whether intentionally or not. Sometimes here we call that "herstory."

NC: Yes.

KT: Because it seems either the conquerors or the men have written the history with a comparable dearth available on women and their contributions. I wonder if you could speak to how patriarchy or the Abrahamic religions have used language to shape society into one that marginalizes women and a feminine face of god.

NC: They do use language to do that but I think that's essentially just a reflection of the cultural practices. Our hierarchal structures, the demands and so on. The language that's used, the assumptions that are there, will reflect the patriarchal structure. It's true of the Abrahamic religions, all of them. It's not true cross-culturally and there are, we may not call them religions, but different spiritual practices that don't have this distinction.

KT: Right. Well, thinking of spiritual practices, considering the importance of spirituality and religion to so many people, would not the world be a better place with beliefs that actually revere the Earth or are life-affirming, inclusive, practice gender equality? Some of us call it eco-feminist or Goddess Spirituality rather than the patriarchal Abrahamic religions that see the Earth, animals and women as commodities or here to serve men.

NC: Well, I think that any form of hierarchy or authority, whether it's patriarchal or some other, should be assumed to be illegitimate unless it can give a strong argument to justify itself. And that is very rarely possible. I can think of a couple instances where it's possible, but not many. With regard for concern for the Earth, and its rights, that's a very significant topic and in fact, the fate of the species may depend on it. And it's kind of striking if you take a look at the, I mean if there's ever a future historian – and it's not certain there will be one, the way things are going – but if such a historian were to look back at what's happening on the planet right now, he or she would see an astonishing spectacle. Take, say, the threat of environmental catastrophe. It's very real. Anyone who has their eyes open can see it. If you read scientific journals it's perfectly obvious. There is just no doubt there is a very serious threat, not far removed, and there are various reactions to it around the world. There are some who are trying to do something to impede it. There are some countries which have instituted rights of nature as legal parts of the constitutional system. Now there are some, there is one oil producer, who is trying to obtain support to keep the oil in the ground, which is where it ought to be. So that's at one extreme.

At the other extreme, there are societies which are trying to accelerate the race to disaster, get every drop of hydrocarbons out of the ground, and are euphoric about using massive amounts of fossil fuels. Well, who are they? The first ones who are trying to do something to retard catastrophe and insisting on the rights of nature are the societies we call primitive, indigenous societies, tribal societies, like the First Nations in Canada, Aboriginal societies in Australia, tribal societies in India, literally throughout the world. They are the ones trying to save the world. Who's racing toward disaster? The richest, most powerful, most educated societies are the ones who think of themselves at the peak of civilization, like the United States and Canada which are just, with this kind of bi-partisan euphoria about what they call "100 Years of Energy Independence." Energy independence is a totally meaningless concept. What it really means is 100 years of massive exploitation of hydrocarbons. So just take a look at the world. The ones that call themselves the most advanced culture, the technologically developed, are leading the race off the cliff like proverbial lemmings. While the ones they call primitive, backwards, pre-technological are the ones trying to save the world. I don't think this is a male–female issue.

KT: No.

NC: I think this is a much broader cultural issue. That is something we ought to be very much worried about.

KT: I think it goes back to the idea of greed. Some people also talk about the End Times theories. They either think God won't allow anything to happen, or "Gee, if it does, we'll meet God" so they don't see a downside to destroying the planet.

NC: That's particularly true in the rich, technologically advanced, most powerful societies. It's most true here in fact. The End Times is mostly a US idea, but it does exist elsewhere. But this is where it originated and flourished. Actually this goes back much farther. Another part of the general background we ought to be well aware of, I think, has to do with Magna Carta, the foundations of Anglo-American law. It goes back almost 800 years. In two years, in fact, it will be the 800th anniversary. Magna Carta has two parts to it. One part is the Charter of Liberties. That's basically concerned with things like due process, presumption of innocence, rights to a speedy trial by peers, things like that. There is another part that has been forgotten. It's called the Charter of the Forests. That's concerned with preservation of things called the commons. The commons were the common collective property. This was England, of course. That people nourished, cultivated, cared for. It provided food. It provided fuel. It provided welfare. For instance, the traditional image was widows taking out of the forest. Well, yes, that's part of the welfare system. Magna Carta insisted the commons be protected from State authority. And authority meant the King. The Robin Hood myths are based on this. Robin

Hood is essentially the protector of the forest. What happened to that?

Well, what happened to it is, as British capitalism developed, with people driven off the land, becoming their workers instead of independent farmers, the commons became privatized and were destroyed. It happened later here. And this goes right up until today. What I just described is a matter of protecting the commons. It's the indigenous societies that want to protect the global commons, our common property, which we ought to collectively care for. The West, led by us, is calling for the privatization of the commons. Put it in private hands. Let people own it so it's not collective property. In fact, there's even a cultural myth, called Tragedy of the Commons, a famous concept, which we are supposed to believe in. Tragedy of the Commons holds that if things are collectively owned they will be destroyed. So therefore they must be privately owned. So they will be preserved.

KT: How convenient! (Laughing)

NC: Yes, how convenient. But if you take a look at the world, it's the opposite. It's when they're privately owned they're being destroyed. When collectively owned, it's common property.

KT: You can look at our National Forest System as an example of that.

NC: Perfect example. Or Arctic drilling. In fact there's a striking example of this right at this moment. In Turkey, it's all over the front page. Take the uprising in Turkey to protect Taksim Square. That's basically about protection of the commons. Taksim Square is the last open, public space, greenery, a meeting space, and so on, in Istanbul, that the public is trying to protect. The demonstrations in Taksim Square a couple days ago when the government sent in bulldozers to knock down the trees in Taksim Square as part of a plan to commercialize it. To turn it into a shopping mall, you know. Tourist attraction. Gentrify it. Essentially keep it, push it, out of the public domain. That's a struggle that goes back 800 years. And right now the fate of the species depends on it. These are not small questions.

KT: No. Absolutely not. And it's quite a shame these rich and powerful have spent so much money to insure we have so much disinformation out there.

NC: Absolutely. They are the ones that control the means of so-called information. It's something we really have to struggle against and I'd say again, that while there may well be, there probably are, values and emotions and so on that are more typically feminine than masculine, maybe that's true, but these things that we're talking about aren't. So for example in Taksim Square, it's men and women. Take a look. The indigenous people who want to give rights to nature are no more women than men.

KT: We are naturally segueing into media and politics here. Another question on language. Do you think the lack of civility in the media, the hate-mongering of some religious institutions toward certain groups, even politicians, the Rush Limbaughs and Glenn Becks of the world, that they set a tone, perhaps, giving license to throw manners and civility under the bus, and leave us with a society that mimics their bad behavior rather than talking about real issues and facts to move us forward? Or do you think it is all a distraction?

NC: That's very striking. It should be studied more. I haven't seen a good study on it, but if you go back, say forty to fifty years, there was talk radio, though not on the scale there is now, but it was there and it was much more varied. It probably tended toward nationalist and Right Wing and so on, which you're describing, but it was much more varied, but over the years that's changed. And it's been taken over, not just by Right Wing, but by extreme Right Wing, I mean way to the right of the Republican Party, for example, in its current manifestation. Now, how did that happen? I don't think it happened by accident. I think what happened, I haven't seen a good study so I'm speculating, that apparently what seems to have happened is concentrated wealth seems to have taken this over and it's pretty easy to take over a radio station. You just have to offer them advertising. These are commercial institutions, but they run on a very narrow profit margin, and if they can be guaranteed advertising they'll take the program content. And there are packages that come to stations that say we will guarantee you this amount of advertising if you put on the content we want. Well, who is going to be behind content of the kind you see right now, the Rush Limbaugh, Laura [unintelligible], the rest of them. You know it's not going to be ... uh, uh ...

KT: The Sierra Club for instance.

NC: No, it's not going to be people like you and me.

KT: I wonder if there's an innate political grammar in the human mind that influences politics. I'm thinking again, Fox News, Frank Luntz, the GOP wordsmith who advises on talking points to influence Americans to vote against their economic interests. Do you think historians will look back and say that this daily dose of propaganda helped brainwash people, maybe even helped Americans destroy themselves and their future?

NC: That's exactly what's happening, but the whole history of propaganda is pretty interesting. Modern propaganda, which is a huge industry, I mean the public relations industry, the advertising industry, is basically propaganda. And in fact, in the early years, that's what they used to call themselves. Up until the 1930s, Second World War, gave the word "propaganda" a negative connotation because of its association with the Nazis, so people stopped using it, except for the propaganda of enemies. But if you go back to the 1920s, the founding documents of the public relations industry had titles like "propaganda" so they recognized what they were doing was propaganda. Controlling attitudes and opinions, in other words, driving people toward what they called superficial things of life, like fashionable consumption. The idea was very clear. These huge propaganda machines of the public relations industry, they began in the most free societies, at that time, in Britain and the United States. That's where the origins of these systems were. And there's good reasons. In these societies, enough freedom had been won, so that it was getting hard to control people by force, and therefore you had to turn to other means of control. Natural ones are control of opinions and attitudes and behavior, people's intention to act. And out of these developed the modern commercial advertising system, which then became a much broader system of propaganda, and incidently, these became advocated for by progressive intellectuals, people like Walter Lippmann and Harold Lasswell and others.

KT: What was their thinking? That it couldn't hurt or ...?

NC: These are guys who write books about democratic theory. We know their thinking from their books. I'll quote. The public are ignorant and meddlesome outsiders and, for their own good, policies and decisions have to be in the hands of responsible men – always men. Responsible men like us, because we're the smart guys. We're the best and the brightest and we know what's good for people. As one of the founders of modern political science put it, Harold Lasswell, again a liberal, a Roosevelt, Wilson,

Kennedy-type liberal. His view was we should not succumb to democratic dogmatisms about people being the best judges of their own interest. They aren't. We are. We can make decisions that are best for everyone. We hear this right up to the present, incidently. It's part of the argument given for concentrating power to make decisions in the hands of elites.

KT: We see what Republicans are trying to do trying to thwart the African American vote. I heard a Republican on public television say women should not have been allowed the vote. They are disturbed. (Laugh)

NC: They're supposed to be property, after all. It's not that far back. This recent liberation takes a long time to enter into general consciousness. And it will be resisted as you said before.

KT: News is lumped with entertainment now. News agencies don't have to tell listeners the truth. Where do you get your news? Who do you trust?

NC: Trust your own critical intelligence. It's actually the same when you're doing scientific work. You can't say, you may know that certain people have a history and a reputation for being accurate and insightful so you'll tend to believe them. It's not something that particularly concerns you and it's pretty much the same when you read the newspapers or whatever you're looking for. You just ultimately have to rely on your own critical analytic abilities to discern what's probably significant, what's taken out of context. We have many means to check and evaluate.

KT: But don't you think, Noam, that Americans have gotten pretty dumbed-down? That some don't even have critical thinking skills anymore. They don't know when they're being duped?

NC: Yes, and I think there's a tendency for that to correlate, this might sound strange, but I think it correlates with education. Actually there's strong evidence for it. Take the main domestic issue that's under debate in the United States. Let's just look at that one. The main domestic issue is, how do we deal with the current economic crisis. Okay, there are two views on this. One view is that the main problem is the lack of jobs. The other view is the main problem is the deficit. Well, who holds those views? The general public, the unwashed masses' view is the big problem is jobs. If you go to the wealthy, and the banks, for them, the problem is the deficit. Which is being discussed? We have a sequester now. Is it about lack of jobs, or is it about the deficit? It's about the deficit. And who's right in this incidently? My view is the public is right. The big problem is jobs. The deficit is not a big problem. It is a problem, for say, the banks. They don't like the idea that maybe ultimately there will be inflation. But for the benefit of the entire economy and for the people who live here, the problem is a lack of jobs. That's cutting back economic growth, it's harming lives seriously, for young people it's giving them an extremely uncertain future, it's destroying the lives of older working people. That's the main problem with society, even on pure economic grounds. The deficit isn't, but it's the deficit that dominates discussion and debate because that's the concern of the more wealthy, the more privileged, the financial institutions and so on. It is a good example of how education negatively correlates with sensible positions and it's not the only case.

KT: Missing from the conversation, it seems to me at least, we see what austerity is doing in Europe. It's not working over there, so why try to repeat that here?

NC: It's a disaster in Europe, worse than here, in fact. But nevertheless, it is what the German banks, who are dominant there, the European Central Bank, keep pushing for. They are kind of backing off now because the effects were so awful but I think part of the reason is, what I just mentioned, they are concerned with potential inflation. There is no sign of it, but conceivably it might happen. They want to ward that possibility off. But we should not overlook the fact that the wealthy have made direct gains from it. This was in fact described by the President of the European Central Bank, Mario Draghi, who is one of, who is more opposed to austerity, incidentally. But he described to the *Wall Street Journal* the effect of the austerity programs and what he said is, the European social contract is obsolete. We are going to get rid of the welfare state. That is one of Europe's great contributions to modern society and modern civilization but it is being dismantled as you impose austerity. Growth goes down, the deficit goes up, people are thrown out of work, the younger generation has no prospects, but you do reduce the welfare state, which the wealthy and privileged never liked in the first place.

KT: It seems so savage. I use the expression "People will be living under bridges," and wonder how they expect to survive if there are no jobs? Or they just really don't care?

NC: Take a look at the United States. It's not as destitute as the Great Depression. I was alive then and can remember. In absolute terms it was worse, but it is pretty bad now. But for the majority of the population wages and incomes have virtually stagnated for a generation but there has been plenty of wealth generated, but it's going into very few pockets, and for the very wealthy, that's fine.

KT: Well, shifting gears a little bit. I saw your quote, there's basically one party, the business party. It has two factions, Democrats and Republicans, which are somewhat different but carry out variations of the same policies. Well, I wonder, considering this new Republican party, the extremism, the obstructionism, not to mention their blatant homophobia, anti-intellectualism, anti-woman, anti-worker, anti-immigrant, anti-science, lack of empathy. Do you still see both parties as two sides of the same coin or might that be a false equivalency now?

NC: Actually that quote, which goes back to the 1950s, was accurate then. I don't think it's accurate now. I think now we have one party, the business party, with only one faction. The faction is moderate Republicans, who call themselves Democrats. If you look at the positions of the Democrats today, they are approximately what we would have called moderate Republicans not many years ago. The Republican Party, except for a small fringe, has abandoned the moderate Republicans. It is now a very unusual parliamentary party not like the kind we've had in the past or in other countries. It is almost in lock-step obedience to great wealth and private power at the corporate sector. That's its one position. And you can't get votes that way, so in order to have a voting base, it's been compelled to turn to the kind of groups you were describing: the Religious Right, the Nativists who are terrified someone is going to come and take something away from us. All of the kinds of characteristics you were describing that you hear on talk radio. It's been forced to mobilize them. There is no other way to get a vote basically. You can't mobilize people on the basis of saying, look, we're going to try to impoverish you and benefit the wealthy.

KT: So it's a deliberate strategy?

NC: You can call it deliberate or whatever you want, but it's a natural consequence of moving positions toward what I described. Lock-step service to concentrated wealth. And it is lock step. The Republican Party now has a kind of catechism that everyone has to repeat, otherwise, you're not part of the system.

There are real reasons behind these tendencies. Part of them have to do with major changes in the economy since the 1970s. The economy financialized. Financial institutions got vastly more important. Production was substantially off-shored to exploit the working class. There was a spectacular increase in the price of elections which drives both parties into the same pockets. So this general drift to the Right, toward subordination to concentrated power, that's why I think it would be accurate to describe the contemporary Democratic party as moderate Republicans and the Republican party is just driven off the spectrum.

KT: I believe we're coming to the end of our interview, Professor. I thank you for your time. Really appreciate it.

NC: It was good talking to you.

Chapter 24

The Advent of Patriarchy*

by Cristina Biaggi, PhD

There is compelling evidence that early societies in the Paleolithic and Neolithic periods were peaceful and egalitarian throughout most of the world. At one point this changed, and patriarchy – the rule of men over women – emerged as the status quo. We have been living with this state of affairs ever since.

This change occurred more violently in areas such as Europe and emerged more gradually in others, as in China, but it did occur in most areas of the world. With some exceptions, the change from matriarchy to patriarchy occurred during the Neolithic period, and it was probably propelled by a number of factors – environmental, material, psychological and spiritual.

It is my sincere belief that most of the world enjoyed a pre-patriarchal period wherein women were respected – even revered – and when the numinous power that people worshipped was female. Compelling evidence for this statement can be found in the archaeological remains of the beginning of the Upper Paleolithic period (35,000 BCE) in Europe, the Middle East, and Asia. Additional evidence has also been gleaned from anthropological analogy and from the mythology of societies that, until recently, remained in a Paleolithic state of existence.

This evidence clearly substantiates the fact that worldwide, early societies in the Paleolithic and Neolithic eras were egalitarian and peaceful. But at some point, a change occurred in many of these societies that caused patriarchy to emerge as their status quo. Scattered societies still exist in the world today that are matriarchal (my definition of matriarchy follows), but for the most part, patriarchy is the rule.

I define patriarchy as the rule of men over women but I do not define matriarchy as its mirror opposite. Instead, I employ the definition of matriarchy developed by the anthropologist Peggy Reeves Sanday. She defines matriarchy using the Greek root meaning ARCHE, meaning "origin" or "archetype." Thus matriarchy is a social order where women are at the center, and where, as Sanday says, "accommodation and synthesis of difference in a partnership arrangement is the solution for reconciliation of contestation."

I decided to write a book on the advent of patriarchy. This idea came as a result of writing a paper on the aggressive patriarchal Kurgan societies of the early Neolithic that, according to the archaeologist Marija Gimbutas, invaded the Goddess-worshipping centers of Southeastern Europe during the same period. My presentation of this paper at the second Archaeo-mythological Conference (held at the Liguria Study Center in Bogliasco, Italy) generated a lot of lively and compelling discussion from the other presenters and it began to dawn on me how important this topic was, especially in the light of what's happening in the world right now. The patriarchal polarization in the world at this moment seems to be more extreme that it's been in a very long time. I began to realize that a book devoted to the topic of patriarchy would be a valuable contribution to people's understanding of this social system and how its continued unquestioned existence impacts our lives today.

In addition to the discussion at the conference, the chief inspiration for this book is the remarkable work of archaeologist Marija Gimbutas who transformed our thinking about the Neolithic and about patriarchy and matriarchy. Gimbutas was a world-renowned archaeologist and leading international figure who changed perceptions about the ways in which early societies functioned. I believe that her immense contribution, which will become more fully recognized as time passes, has helped and will help change our thinking about prehistoric societies.

Unlike her predecessors, who assumed that patriarchy had always been the status quo, Gimbutas believed that before patriarchy there existed, in the early Neolithic era, societies which comprised a true civilization with women-centered social structures, well-organized cities, highly sophisticated and beautiful art, and no evidence of warfare. The discovery of thousands of female figurines from the Neolithic, fashioned in many forms, indicated to her that the primary deity at that time was a multifaceted Goddess, and that women were respected and perhaps even accorded reverence. Gimbutas theorized that this early matristic civilization was based on a partnership between women and men and only came to an end with the invasions by patriarchal Indo-European tribes riding horses and armed with bronze weapons. These tribes subsequently imposed their gods, economy, and hierarchical social structure on the egalitarian, peaceful people she termed "Old Europeans," dwelling in what she termed "Old Europe."

Gimbutas is widely recognized for the revolutionary "Kurgan Theory." According to this theory, archaeological evidence shows that around 65,000 BCE, the peaceful agricultural communities of Old Europe were invaded by non-indigenous people we now know as Indo-Europeans. Recently, geneticist Luigi Cavalli-Sforza confirmed Gimbutas' theory with his findings that there was indeed a mixing of different biological types in that part of Europe at that time. Recent research and discoveries around the Black Sea by geophysicists Bill Ryan and Walter Pittman also seem to confirm Gimbutas' theories. The importance of Gimbutas' "Kurgan Theory" and the creation of the term "Old Europe" to describe the cultures of early Neolithic Europe cannot be emphasized enough.

Gimbutas also created a new field of study, archaeo-mythology, as an interdisciplinary mode of research combining the field of archaeology, mythology, linguistics, ethnology, folklore, comparative religion, historical artifacts, and early documents. This new field is in direct contrast with traditional archaeology, a discipline that has become increasingly specialized and narrow in focus. Archaeomythology expands the traditional parameters and perimeters of the study of prehistory, and contradicts the traditional concept of human beings as war-like, hierarchical and patriarchal.

Because Gimbutas' work was so original and revolutionary, it elicited much controversy even while she was alive; when she died, the backlash and the attempt to discredit her work began in earnest. This attempt reminds me of the backlash against another strong original woman, Margaret Mead, which also occurred after her death. Serious scholars and accredited archaeologists have joined the bandwagon to try to discredit Gimbutas' work, often not even including her in their research or bibliographies even when they are examining her specialty – the Neolithic Era in Southeastern Europe. As is the case with all great and original thinkers, Marija Gimbutas not only elicited jealousy and envy because of the extent of her fieldwork and the power and origi-nality of her insight, but also inspired a new wave of research and writing under the rubric of the new discipline of archaeomythology.

About Cristina Biaggi ...

Cristina Biaggi, PhD, has achieved international recognition for her varied and significant contributions to the field of Goddess-centered art and scholarly studies. Her works are a reflection and an extension of her lifelong interest in art, archaeology, women studies, literature and classics, acquired at Vassar, Harvard and New York University.

When she isn't preparing new pieces for an exhibition, Dr. Biaggi is writing and lecturing. She continues her studies in Kung Fu (Black Sash) and teaches Tae Kwon Do as a Fifth Degree Black Belt. She has just finished writing her autobiography, *Art and Activism*, and is seeking a publisher. Her artwork has focused on creating bronze portraits of people and their animal companions, and abstract collage. In talking about her creative process, Dr. Biaggi says, "As an artist, I enjoy transitioning from realistic work to abstract work. Creating my bronzes requires my total immersion in contemplating and rendering the physical, psychological and spiritual aspects of my subjects – a process where I must concentrate on capturing the minute details of a face and the soul beyond it."

Chapter 25

The Essence of Good Business: Companies That Care*

by Riane Eisler

The essence of good business is caring. This is not only a spiritual issue or a matter of doing what is right; caring business practices benefit all stakeholders: employees, customers, shareholders, and communities.

Caring business policies and practices are actually highly profitable in purely financial terms. The SAS Institute, the world's largest privately-held software company, illustrates this point. SAS has the largest on-site daycare operation in North Carolina. Its cafeteria has high chairs and booster seats for children so they can eat with their parents. The company pays the entire cost of health benefits for employees and their domestic partners. Workers are only required to work a seven-hour day, and employees get unlimited sick days, which may be used to care for sick family members. And SAS has had nearly twenty consecutive years of double-digit growth.

What SAS does is to create a work environment that supports employees' well-being on all levels. It leaves them time and energy to have a healthy family life, offers them preventative health and wellness care (as opposed to just sick care), provides education and caregiving for everyone in their families, and helps them with housing. It further offers them stability of employment, an ergonomically safe work environment, and respect for the work they do.

Not surprisingly, applications for jobs at SAS come in by the thousands. Also not surprisingly, SAS workers are committed to making the company successful – and to staying with SAS to enjoy this success. Employees also like the company's more participatory or partnership management style, which encourages communication and is yet another factor in SAS's success.

Companies That Care

SAS is one of a growing number of companies that are making more money by giving real value to caring and caregiving. In 2004, the Winning Workplaces' *Fortune Small Business* award went to Carolyn Gable, CEO of New Age Transportation. Gable, a former waitress and single mother of five children, started New Age Transportation out of her home. Thanks to her innovative leadership in creating a tightly knit workplace of intensely loyal workers, it is now a $25-million company. Gable fosters an environment where employees, particularly those with children, can focus on their jobs while still maintaining a healthy employment/family balance. She encourages her staff to take care of themselves outside the office by paying for health club memberships and offering employees $250 per quarter for up to a year to quit smoking. And rather than being a drag on profits, these policies led to an average 37% yearly growth.

Statistics show that caring business policies sharply reduce employee turnover, saving companies millions of dollars. The cost of replacing hourly employees is equivalent to about six months of their earnings. The cost of replacing salaried employees can be as high as eighteen months of their salary. Job turnover can cost as much as 40% of annual profits.

There are also high business costs from absenteeism, which is often the direct result of workers' family responsibilities. For instance, Chemical Bank discovered that 52% of employee absences were caused by family-related issues.

Businesses that have more caring policies radically cut turnover and absentee-related losses. Intermedics, Inc. decreased their turnover rate by 37% with on-site childcare, saving 15,000 work hours and $2 million. Virginia Mason Medical Center in

Seattle reported 0% turnover among employees using its on-site childcare center, compared to about 23% turnover among other workers.

Johnson & Johnson found that absenteeism among employees who used flexible work options and family leave policies was an average of 50% less than for the workforce as a whole.

Difficulties securing childcare are a particularly important factor in the high rates of absenteeism, turnover, and as a consequence, overtime costs, in companies with extended hours operations. A 2003 report by Circadian Technologies, Inc. found that extended hours childcare reduces the absenteeism rate by an average of 20%. Their study, "Cost Benefits of Child Care for Extended Hours Operations," found that turnover rates among extended hour employees also decreased substantially when childcare services were available – from 9.3% to 7.7%. Since on average it costs companies $25,000 to recruit and train each new extended-hour employee, this too was a big saving.

Caring Private and Public Policies

Of course, these savings don't show the enormous benefits of childcare services to the approximately 28% of American women who regularly work nights, evenings, or weekends. Nor do they show the benefits to society at a time when latchkey children are a major US concern. As emphasized by Professor Joan C. Williams, Director of the Center for WorkLife Law at the UC Hastings College of the Law, support for caregivers in the formal workforce is not only a business issue but a public policy issue. Today, 37% of the workforce has children under age 18. Small wonder that in a Radcliffe survey, 83% of women and 82% of men aged 21–29 put having time to spend with their families at the top of their priority list, way ahead of a high salary and a prestigious job.

The number of caregivers in the workforce will rise even more dramatically as Americans age. By 2020 the US over-50 population will increase 74% compared to 1% for those under 50. Polls show that 54% of US workers anticipate caring for an elderly parent or relative in the next ten years.

Reports from the Families and Work Institute and scores of other organizations, as well as books such as Sandra Burud's and Marie Tomolo's *Leveraging the New Human Capital*, show that factoring these realities into workplace policies is not only socially essential; it makes good business sense. A study of clients of the KPMG Emergency back-up childcare program, for example, showed that offering employees childcare yielded a 125% ROI (return on investment) within six months and that by the fourth year, the ROI was a whopping 521%.

A General Services Administration Child Care study found that 55% of workers who were offered a childcare subsidy were better able to concentrate at work. A study of users of the Bristol Myers Squibb childcare centers showed they had a deeper commitment to the company.

A Bright Horizons Child Care survey showed that even employees without children feel work-site childcare has a positive impact on their workplaces. In short, caring policies make for happier, more productive workers, stronger families, and more fulfilling lives. This leads to higher financial profits, thus, a stronger, more productive economy.

Changing Our Values

Yet many businesspeople still believe the only possibility is a dog-eat-dog, uncaring economics. They think of caring as "soft" or "feminine" – whether it's by a woman or a man – and dismiss it as counterproductive, or at best irrelevant, to business success. The same kind of thinking has distorted national funding priorities.

Many politicians have no problem with huge deficits and large budgets for weapons, wars, and prisons. But when it comes to investing in caring for people – healthcare, childcare, paid parental leave, and other investments in a better quality of life – they claim there is no money. Of course, the issue is not one of money; it's one of priorities and values.

The Real Wealth of Nations

Ultimately, the real wealth of a nation lies in the quality of its human and natural capital. I should here add that an investment in human capital is an investment in human beings. It is the enhancement of the quality of life of human beings, of human happiness and fulfillment, not just of the ability to earn income in the market. I should also add that by natural capital I don't just mean a nation's natural resources, but also our planet's ecological health. Without this we risk losing everything, including our lives.

This investment is not only the right and just thing to do. It is essential in purely economic terms as we shift from the industrial to the post-industrial knowledge/information era where "high quality human capital" is the most important capital. Already knowledge and service work represents the vast majority of jobs (85% according to business expert Peter Drucker), and even the remaining jobs (15% in manufacturing and agriculture) are becoming more knowledge-intensive and interactive.

America and the world are in the midst of a sea change as we shift from the industrial to the knowledge/information era. Many of the jobs being lost in manufacturing and other fields will be gone for good as we move toward more automation and robotics. Economists tell us that the most important capital for the post-industrial economy is "high quality human capital."

Children are the real wealth of our nation. Investing in a caring society will both stimulate economic recovery and develop the high-capacity human capital capable of pioneering new frontiers of innovation in every sector of society: culturally, socially, technologically, and environmentally. It will lead to a more just world, and more fulfilling lives for us all.

About Riane Eisler ...

Riane Eisler is a social scientist, attorney, and author best known for her best-seller *The Chalice and the Blade: Our History, Our Future*, now in twenty-three foreign editions, including most European languages and Chinese, Russian, Korean, Hebrew, Japanese, and Arabic. Her newest book, *The Real Wealth of Nations: Creating a Caring Economics* – hailed by Archbishop Desmond Tutu as "a template for the better world we have been so urgently seeking," by Peter Senge as "desperately needed," by Gloria Steinem as "revolutionary," and by Jane Goodall as "a call for action" – offers a new approach to economics that gives visibility and value to the most essential human work: the work of caring for people and the planet.

Her other books include the award-winning *The Power of Partnership and Tomorrow's Children: A Blueprint for Partnership Education in the 21st Century*, as well as *Sacred Pleasure*, a daring re-examination of sexuality and spirituality, and *Women, Men, and the Global Quality of Life*, documenting the key role of women's status in a nation's general quality of life. She is the author of over 300 essays and articles in publications ranging from *Behavioral Science, Futures, Political Psychology, The Christian Science Monitor*, and *The UNESCO Courier* to *Brain and Mind*, the *Human Rights Quarterly, The International Journal of Women's Studies*, and the *World Encyclopedia of Peace*.

Chapter 26

Antidote* to Terrorism

by Jean Shinoda Bolen, MD

antidote: 1: a remedy to counteract the effects of poison. 2: something that relieves, prevents, or counteracts.
– Webster's New Collegiate Dictionary

The premise: A world that is safe for children will not breed terrorists, a world that is safe for women is a world where children are safe. For this to come about, the feminine principle expressed in circles and the masculine principle of hierarchy must come into balance, otherwise the acquisition of power over others prevails and no one can be safe.

Second premise: The war against terrorism bears great similarity to metastatic cancer that has spread beyond the reach of allopathic medicine's solutions of surgery, radiation and chemotherapy. Conventional armies are finding that their superior power doesn't help when insurgency and terrorists are the enemy, and that their efforts to destroy the enemy are destroying the country and causing more malignant terrorist cells to be created.

Third premise: A critical mass of women in circles with a spiritual center is the antidote to the patriarchal model of domination that becomes the breeding ground for terrorists and terrorism. It is possible to bring about the remission and healing of metastatic disease through strengthening the immune system, improving overall health, and having reasons to live. These are analogous to what a demoralized society, living with terrorism, must acquire to resist further proliferation of terrorists. The antidote, and the deficiency, is the missing feminine principle.

When power over others is the model in families and societies, female children are not important, and male children are taught to dominate others or be dominated; they learn that one is either a strong winner or a weak loser, and that practicing dominance through ridicule, physical means, intimidation or acquisitions means you are respected. Boys who are unprotected from being bullied fantasize about getting even. They can grow into men who do to others what was done to them (identifying with the aggressor), or can seek revenge to counteract feelings of helplessness, lack of worth and humiliation. This is how patriarchy socializes its boys and men. The power to destroy others, using weapons or explosives, then becomes the equalizer. Humiliation of one group of men by another competing group of men leads to turf wars in American inner cities, to civil wars in Africa, to religious wars in the Middle East, or genocidal wars in which total obliteration of the enemy is the goal. In patriarchy, women are defined by their relationship to men, and are the means through which men humiliate other men by raping their women.

The antidote to this dominator model as described by Riane Eisler in *The Chalice and the Blade*[1] is the potential of a partnership one. For this to be achieved, differences between masculine and feminine (as genders, as values, as principles) would be complementary, rather than one ranked higher over the other.

In *Urgent Message from Mother: Gather the Women, Save the World* [2] and in *The Millionth Circle: How to Change Ourselves and The World*,[3] I maintain that a critical number of women gathered together in circles with a spiritual center could bring the feminine principle into consciousness and action. Just as consciousness-raising groups in the late 1960s and 70s transformed women's roles and opportunities in the United States, and became the women's movement which rippled out to influence the world, this would be a women's peace movement, a means to end domestic and global violence.

Invisible Power of Women's Circles

The intention to be in a circle with a spiritual center invites the invisible world of spirit or soul to be in the center of the circle and in the center of the psyche of each person in the circle. Through meditative silence or silent prayer, wisdom and peace enters. Circles foster both the ability to voice what matters and say out loud what is in the heart and mind, and an equally important ability, to listen with compassion. Circles evoke a sense of sisterhood, and also a feeling of being in a maternal space. There is a deep sense of being connected to one another, at an archetypal level.

It is this sister archetype and the mother archetype in women that make it possible for most women (but not all, because these are not the active archetypes in some women) to identify with other women across national, racial, and religious boundaries, without even meeting. It is empathy that makes women able to imagine what it would be like to be on either side of the Israeli–Palestinian divide, or be a woman under the Taliban, a refugee or an abused mother in the United States or a vulnerable and abandoned child. It is a point of view that doesn't see war as something to be won, but as a cause of death and suffering for everyone, especially innocent women and children. Mothers are also concerned about their sons who become soldiers. A soldier is taught to kill, which is also what a terrorist is taught. These are not lessons maternal women want their sons to learn. The original Mother's Day Proclamation, written by Julia Ward Howe in 1870, was a call to mothers to gather together to end wars, so that their sons will not be taught to maim or kill the sons of other mothers.

Historical Power of Women's Circles

Women have never been given rights, nor have they used violence to get them. They have made demands to get the vote, worked together for social and economic justice, and broken through resistance to change by peaceful means. Women's movements are grassroots, they are not financed from above, and grow through the invisible and non-hierarchal network of women's friendships and the ability of women to bond with each other through the medium of conversation and then to have an influence on men and institutions.

Women in circles have raised awareness of what needs to be changed in society as well as in personal situations. The ringing theme in the 1970s, the decade of the women's movement, "the personal is political," grew from women telling their personal stories to each other in consciousness-raising groups, and finding that personal problems and economic, social and political inequality were related. Women made changes in their personal lives and made huge egalitarian changes in American society through the rapid proliferation of small groups of women and ideas that became a movement.

Critical Mass and the Millionth Circle

Two mechanisms to do with critical mass explain how cultural change can come about through women's circles. Rupert Sheldrake's Morphic Field Theory[4] provides one explanation. Sheldrake is a biologist, who describes how a new attitude or behavior becomes normal once a critical number of a species adopts it. In Sheldrake's theory, as the millionth circle movement grows through the formation of new circles, it will draw upon the energy or patterns of similar present or past circle movements, which could include Alcoholics Anonymous. Sheldrake's model suggests that each new circle will draw from all the circles in existence before it, and that the more circles there are, the easier it is for still more to form, which increases the momentum as a movement grows, until a critical mass tips the scales and changes how we act.

Malcolm Gladwell's *The Tipping Point*[5] contributes a second model of how an idea can spread and take hold based on epidemics. The name given to that one dramatic moment in an epidemic when everything appears to change all at once is the "tipping point" or the moment of the critical mass. His thesis is that social epidemics behave similarly with the appearance of sudden change, and that like its disease equivalent, it takes a small percentage of the population to bring it about. Epidemics depend upon the people who transmit infectious agents, the infectious agent itself, and the environment. Social epidemics work in the same way, with it mattering who spreads the idea, that it takes hold, and the receptivity of the environment or context. Using Gladwell's criteria, for there to be a millionth circle tipping point, the idea has to be spread by three types of people, some who are enthusiastic and energetic, are widely known and held in high regard by their peers, by others whose knowledge is valued and who pass on information about the millionth circle with the sole purpose of wanting to help others, and by still others who sell the idea and overcome resistance. All types need to believe that change and transformation is possible through circles, and want to make a difference through what they are doing to further the goal of reaching a critical mass.

When a virus spreads through a population it doubles and doubles again. Geometric progression is responsible for the suddenness in which something can manifest. When an idea spreads by geometric progression through the population, it becomes irresistible. As Victor Hugo observed, there is nothing so powerful as an idea whose time has come.

An idea whose time has come depends upon a critical number of people embracing a new way of thinking, feeling, or perceiving. Once that critical number is reached, what had been resisted becomes accepted. What was once unthinkable, and is then adopted by more and more people, reaches a critical mass, and then becomes a commonly held standard of belief or behavior.

It has been predominantly women who have grasped the idea

of the millionth circle. While the feminine principle is potentially present in the psyches of both women and men, women have a gender and cultural advantage. Women use conversation to bond. Their friendships are based on conversations that build up trust and similarities. Men, in contrast, use conversation to determine hierarchy.[6] Women react to stress (fear, anxiety, pressure) differently than men do. Men respond with a physiological "fight or flight" response with an increase in adrenaline that is enhanced by testosterone. This makes it likely that they will either become more aggressive or withdrawn. In contrast, women react to stress with a "tend and befriend" response which is supported by an increase in oxytocin, the maternal bonding hormone that is enhanced by estrogen. Oxytocin increases and stress is reduced when women talk to each other and take care of children, pets, home, garden or workplace.[7]

In *Urgent Message from Mother: Gather the Women, Save the World*[2] and in *The Millionth Circle: How to Change Ourselves and The World*,[3] I maintain that a critical number of women gathered together in circles with a spiritual center could bring the feminine principle into consciousness and action. Just as consciousness-raising groups in the late 1960s and 70s transformed women's roles and opportunities in the United States, and became the women's movement which rippled out to influence the world, this would be a women's peace movement, a means to end domestic and global violence.

Once this critical mass is reached, the physical and psychological health of children would have the highest priority. Just as healthy bodies and minds have healthy immune systems that are resistant to disease, so it is that children – who are loved, cared for and protected, have good nutrition, clean water, medical care, and education that fosters emotional as well as intellectual development – will develop a resistance to becoming terrorists. This is the antidote.

About Jean Shinoda Bolen ...

Jean Shinoda Bolen, MD, is a psychiatrist, Jungian analyst and an internationally known author and speaker. She is the author of *The Tao of Psychology, Goddesses in Everywoman, Gods in Everyman, Ring of Power, Crossing to Avalon, Close to the Bone, The Millionth Circle, Goddesses in Older Women, Crones Don't Whine, Urgent Message from Mother, Like a Tree* and *Moving Toward the Millionth Circle*. She is a Distinguished Life Fellow of the American Psychiatric Association, a former clinical professor of psychiatry at the University of California at San Francisco, and a past board member of the Ms. Foundation for Women and the International Transpersonal Association.

She is in two acclaimed documentaries: the Academy-Award winning anti-nuclear proliferation film *Women – For America, For the World* and the Canadian Film Board's *Goddess Remembered*. The Millionth Circle Initiative (www.millionthcircle.org) was inspired by her book and led to Jean's involvement at the UN as the leading advocate for a UN 5th World Conference on Women (www.5wcw.org) which was supported by the Secretary General and the President of the General Assembly on March 8, 2012.

Website: www.jeanbolen.com.

Chapter 27

Making the Case: Pagans, Women and Those Valuing Religious Freedom Should Vote Democratic

by Gus diZerega

We Pagans are a diverse lot, and I have more in common with some than others. But I think there are two qualities central to the beliefs of almost all of us that prevent any honest and informed Pagan from voting for virtually any Republican at the present time. First, almost universally we honor the sacred dimensions of the feminine and how those values manifest in and on the Earth. Second, we honor the Earth itself as a direct expression of the Sacred.

What follows is not a brief on Obama as a wonderful president or the Democrats as an inspiring party. Neither is true in my opinion. Both are corporatist, putting the interests of the largest corporations and banks ahead of the interests of Americans. But in that respect they are no different from Republicans, and perhaps more humane. Just as a cat burglar is not as dangerous as a serial killer, so I believe the Democrats are a far better choice for being in office than are Republicans. And that is the choice we have. Not voting, when there are only two choices, is effectively voting for the candidates you dislike most.

While there are many reasons, I will focus here on only one that by itself demonstrates all decent and informed Pagans will not vote Republican for *any* office until the party repudiates those who have dominated it in recent years. Again, my argument has nothing to do with the virtues of the Democrats, although there are a few I could happily vote for. My argument is entirely defensive.

The War on Women and the Feminine

Pagan spirituality in almost all its forms praises feminine values, usually through a Goddess or Goddesses. The Republican Party has demonstrated over and over again that even during times of high unemployment, attacking anything that empowers women takes precedence over *all* other issues. Most of my readers will know of Todd Akin's comments that women when raped cannot get pregnant, along with Richard Mourdock's "insight" that when they do get pregnant from rape, it's God's gift.[1] (Theological coherence is not a right-wing trait.) Recently Republican darling Ted Cruz considers contraception, in violation of all logic and truth, to be "abortifacients."[2]

The Republican and right-wing attack on a woman's right to choose whether to be a mother when she finds herself pregnant is of long standing. But this past year it has broadened enormously and ominously to assault anything that empowers women except as obedient servants to right-wing values.

- The Republican-controlled House passed a bill with overwhelming Republican support that would allow hospitals to let pregnant women die rather than give them an abortion if they thought it a matter of "conscience." [3]
- The Republican Party and its theocratic allies, Catholic and Protestant alike, are now attacking contraception. Contraception causes no abortions and gives women control over their lives more than any other single development in human history. Honest conservatives (there are a few) admit as much.[4]
- This attack on contraception is relentless and implacable even though abortion rates drop when birth control is easy to get.[5] Better pregnant women should die if their doctor or hospital dislikes abortion, but women should not have free access to contraceptives. *Nothing* proves more clearly than this that these people are in *no* sense "pro-life."

- Republicans argue that women who have abortions should face criminal charges.[6] Some might dodge the issue, but this conclusion grows out of their arguments and some have made the implications explicit.

- Republican legislators have intervened into women's relations with their doctors, forcing by law physicians to perform unnecessary vaginal probes of women seeking legal abortions.[7] Far from wanting small government, they want theocratic domination over every woman in the country. As a start:

- The Republicans and their religious right allies lie and lie and lie regarding giving people medical information about abortion and other issues specific to women.[8]

- The religious right and their Republican allies fought the HPV vaccine that reduces the chances of a woman getting cervical cancer because they argued more young women would have sex if they felt it was safer.[9] Some might say their motives were based on uncertainty over the vaccine. They will be lying. The Republican theocratic right admitted alleged health uncertainty was a smokescreen and their opposition to HPV vaccination was due to opposing measures that would make sex safer. Tony Perkins of the Family Research Council said, "Our concern is that this vaccine will be marketed to a segment of the population that should be getting a message about abstinence. It sends the wrong message." He was not alone.[10] Again, for them, better women dead than powerful.

- Republican-dominated states with strong anti-abortion laws provide less funding per child for foster care, *smaller* stipends for parents who adopt children with special needs, and *smaller* payments for poor women with dependent children than do states with strong abortion rights laws. In 1999 Louisiana had America's strongest anti-abortion laws and spent $603 annually for each poor child. Liberal and Democratic Hawaii spent $4,648, almost eight times more. [11]

- Nearly half the states with the strongest anti-abortion laws did not make it a crime for a third party to kill a fetus of *any* gestational age so long as a deliberate abortion was not the reason. But six of the strongest anti-abortion states that do not criminalize fetal battering prosecute women for prenatal drug use.[12] Violence does not concern them nearly so much as independence for women.

There is a pattern here that only someone in deep denial could miss: an attack on women as independent and self-governing beings. In their place they praise "manliness," which involves talking tough, never serving the country, and debasing being a strong man to, in Neoconservative Harvey Mansfield's words: "the claim to protect is the claim to rule. How can I protect you properly if I can't tell you what to do?"[13] Michael Ledeen, another leading Neoconservative, says Americans "must *not* be left to our own devices. We must be forced or, under ideal circumstances, convinced or inspired to do good."[14] On the religious right, theologian Bruce Ware tells us: "If it's true that in the Trinity itself – in the eternal relationships of Father, Son and Spirit, there is authority and submission, and the Son eternally submits to the will of the Father – if that's true, then this follows: It is as Godlike to submit to rightful authority with joy and gladness as it is Godlike to exert wise and beneficial rightful authority."[15]

Religion and Politics

The theocratic right's stranglehold on the Republican Party is a threat to Pagans and to all Americans who value anything but the most vicious and depraved forms of religion dominating this country. That people like Todd Akin and Richard Mourdock have a chance at national office is powerful testimony to the debasement of the Republican Party and the peril we all face as a result. The Republicans are powerfully influenced by an organization, "The Family."[16] It includes a high number of Republican Senators and Representatives, and explicitly seeks to establish theocracy in the United States.[17] John Cornyn, a member, has defended Mourdock's argument that women must be forced to carry to term babies conceived during rape.[18] "Family" leaders have *praised* the ruthlessness of despots such as Mao as necessary for them to realize their goals and are central players in the modern Republican Party.[19]

Nor is this just a matter of Fundamentalist viciousness. Many Catholic bishops have been urging their parishioners to vote Republican as well. These bishops have been in the forefront of Catholic attacks on the gains women have made in this country since the 1960s.[20]

Be they secular or religious, the Republican right is a clear and present danger to all Pagans, and for most, to the values we espouse as central to almost all our traditions. As individuals, Pagans have a wide variety of views about public policy issues. This is to be expected. But *as Pagans* we share in common a desire for practicing our religion in peace, and in almost all cases the importance of the feminine as an expression of the sacred is central to our beliefs. Until the Republican Party changes, it seems to me no Pagan can intelligently vote for one of their candidates. It would be as if a Jew voted for the National Socialists under the old Weimar Republic.

About Gus diZerega ...

Gus diZerega combines a formal academic training in Political Science with decades of work in Wicca and shamanic healing. He has long been a Third Degree Elder in Gardnerian Wicca. He studied closely with Timothy White, who founded *Shaman's Drum* magazine. He also studied and practiced Brazilian Umbanda intensively for six years under Antonio Costa e Silva. He has given workshops and talks on Pagan spirituality and healing in the United States and Canada.

diZerega also holds a PhD in Political Theory with extensive teaching and publishing experience in mainstream academia. In this capacity he has organized international scholarly conferences and taught in Canada and Europe as well as the United States.

His newest book, *Faultlines: The Culture War and the Return of the Divine Feminine* (Quest, 2013), is an in-depth study of the crisis in American society and government from a Pagan perspective. His first book was on democratic political theory and practice. His second, *Pagans and Christians: The Personal Spiritual Experience*, won the Best Nonfiction of 2001 award from The Coalition of Visionary Resources. His third, *Beyond the Burning Times: A Pagan and a Christian in Dialogue*, was co-authored with Christian, Philip Johnson.

His articles have frequently appeared in *Shaman's Drum*, and the ecological journals *Wild Earth* and *The Trumpeter*.

Chapter 28

Media and Politics:
Left, Right, We're All at the Tea Party!

Transcript of interview with Laura Flanders

Interview:

KT = Karen Tate
LF = Laura Flanders

Tonight I have with us a woman I suspect many of you already admire. She's Laura Flanders, and in case that name does not ring any bells with you yet, I'm sure you'll be following her work after tonight. She is a former Air America radio show host and right now she is the host and founder of GRITtv, a nationally syndicated daily talk show for people who want more than talk. She writes for *The Huffington Post* and *The Nation.com* and she's a regular contributor on MSNBC. She's appeared on shows from *Real Time with Bill Maher* and the *Tavis Smiley Show* to *Larry King Live* and the *Bill O'Reilly Factor*. You can follow her on Twitter by following @GRITLaura and you can watch GRITtv daily online at GRITtv.org. She's also an author and that's what we will be focusing on tonight. She's the author of the *New York Times* best-seller *Bushwomen: Tales of a Cynical Species* and *Blue Grit: How True Democrats Take Back Politics from the Politicians* but it is her new collection we are talking about tonight, titled *At the Tea Party: The Wing Nuts, Whack Jobs and Whitey Whiteness of the New Republican Right and Why We Should Take It Seriously.*

Interview starts:

KT: Laura, welcome to *Voices of the Sacred Feminine*.

LF: Oh, it's great to be with you.

KT: I just saw you on *The Ed Schultz Show* and I was cheering you on. You stood up to that Republican woman with her distractions and I want to thank you for being one of the ones who doesn't let them get away it and instead hold their feet to the fire.

LF: I really appreciate that. It's really amazing how they can come up with two women, finally, in conversation but of course we have to be at each other's throats. And they find a woman of color, they find a conservative; Amy Holmes has played that role for years. It's been an interesting few decades watching how cable has opened their doors to women, but which women? That's the question.

KT: Yes, definitely, and that said, I'm really interested in your other book, *Bushwomen: Tales of a Cynical Species*, because I don't really understand that brand of woman very much and it seems like maybe you've done a study.

LF: It sounds like we're talking about women in Africa, but no, we're talking about women in the Bush Administration. The cabinet members and inner circle members, Condoleezza Rice, Gail Norton, Karen Hughes, that crowd. It was a great opportunity to study some strange characters quite closely. And the book still holds up. I think it prefaces a lot of what we've seen since with the treatment of Michele Bachmann and Sarah Palin.

KT: Okay. And thank you for clarifying that point, too. Your book titled *Bushwomen* is not about women in Africa. Or Australia for that matter.

LF: There are some people who may have thought I'm now an expert on pygmies of the Kalahari.

KT: Maybe some would think you went on an extended vacation or something. (Laughing)

LF: If only. (Laughing)

KT: Tonight we're talking about the new book though, titled *At the Tea Party: The Wing Nuts, Whack Jobs and Whitey Whiteness of the New Republican Right and Why We Should Take It Seriously*. It's a collection of articles from folks from *The Nation, Mother Jones, Truth Out, The Progressive*, and many other sources. These experts come together to shed light on the Tea Party so we can dissect who they are. You can't get it in stores though. You can download it.

LF: You can't get it in stores, which means it's special. It's available to you when you go to the website Orbooks.com. Think of it as "sandwiches or books": Orbooks.com. You can download an electronic version or you can get a paperback sent directly to your home. It's an effort to do an end-run around companies like Amazon that are driving prices down for books and contributing a portion of their profits to conservative causes. And to save the environment so we're not sending lots of books all across the country to bookstores only to have the excess sent back. It's an on-demand book. You get the book when you want it. It's a real book. I guarantee it will be indistinguishable from the other books on your book shelf.

KT: I have a copy here in front of me and another thing I love about it is, besides all the different "voices from the Left," each essay stands on its own. You can put it down, then come back to it a week later or an hour later and you haven't lost the thread.

Each author is talking about the Tea Party, but their essays cover a different topic within that subject.

LF: I appreciate that and I will say that while there are in indeed lots of your most popular Left voices, with people like Melissa Harris Perry and Chris Hedges and Jim Hightower and Glen Greenwald, some of the pieces I'm most happy about are transcripts from conversations we've had on the GRITtv show, some of which include people who are members of the Tea Party or sympathize with the Tea Party. Those have been some of the most interesting conversations that we've had. And in fact, the whole book was inspired by someone who was in my very close circle, part of my extended family, who I found one day was a Tea Party sympathizer. Yes, there is a Left critique here but progressives are also put on notice that this is not a phenomena of faraway crazy people. It's actually quite close and very important for us to grapple with.

KT: Well, I suspect they're in my family.

LF: Well, there you go!

KT: Let me read something from the back of the book, then we'll get on to my questions for you. The back of the book says:

Something is brewing and it doesn't smell good. It's tempting to see the Tea Party as a bunch of crazies as the widely-celebrated author and broadcaster Laura Flanders argues in this compelling anthology, but it would be a mistake to dismiss the dangers of the meeting of money, moment and media that has produced the Tea Party phenomena. With contributions by a wide range of leading experts *At the Tea Party* looks at who's behind the movement, its rich sources of funding, its extensive use of new technology, its appeal to women, the pervasive racism that under-pins much of its approach and the lessons for the Left of a political program that, though often incoherent, nonetheless taps into genuine anxiety.

So Laura, here on *Voices of the Sacred Feminine* I wanted to talk to you about this movement of these people because they seem to be the opposite of everything myself and my listeners believe in. We care about social justice. We believe in the interconnection among peoples and the planet. We would like to think we could eventually have more sustainability over growth that goes unchecked. We want partnership, not domination or a survival-of-the-fittest culture. Tell me if I'm wrong, but the Tea Party seems to be the complete opposite. They come across as crass, chaotic and a callous bunch. Are my perceptions wrong?

LF: I don't think you're wrong. There are two things here. One, I think the reason I got interested in this subject was not just because of the prospect of yet another Right Wing movement, but because of the way that much of what is the Tea Party perspective is actually the party we're all attending. It is very much the convention wisdom, not just on the fringes of our political scene, but right at the center and we can talk more about that. In the past election, 40% of voters said in exit polls said that they support or sympathize or feel drawn to Tea Party candidates. You can say that's scary or they're misguided or crazy but the reality is we are all grappling with this phenomenon. We are all, if you will, at the Tea Party. As I argue in the introduction of the book, this is not the beginning of something, it's the "Becchanal". It's Glenn Beck, Sarah Palin, celebrating the culmination of a process that I think has been decades in the making of pushing back against exactly that worldview that you described, that would be easy to associate with the civil rights movement, the women's movement, the gay and lesbian equality movement, the anti-war movement, the ecological movement of the 1960s and 70s. It's a backlash against all of that in an effort to replace those values or head them off at the pass, if you will, with instead a very atomized, individual, private realm. We're talking about this in the days after Barack Obama delivered his State of the Union Address where I'm afraid you have to say that worldview kind of rules, the private company will save us, private enterprise will save us. We have to save our entrepreneurs from the onerous burden of increased taxes. In fact, we want to lower taxes on the least taxed sector of our society, namely corporations, and continue on a path that has brought us to a place of complete division in this society where a tiny few are doing very well and the rest of us really struggling to keep our heads above water.

KT: That's the part I don't understand. But first, you sort of dispelled one of my beliefs. I thought maybe if we had a white president this would not have come to be because so many racist elements seem to be in the Tea Party. I thought maybe Obama was the last straw on the camel's back, so to speak. I thought that's why the Tea Party was born, but apparently not.

LF: Well, we can talk about that. I mean let's talk about race and the Tea Party because I believe that's an important part of the story. I don't think it's the explanation for what's happened but racism operates in our society as a kind of lighter fluid. We keep it handy for when we really want to start the bonfire. And progressives, the Left, the Middle, the Right, in our post-apartheid America have never decided actually to put aside the weapons of white supremacy. We have not actually decided to disarm those tools and we bring them out when we need to vilify people on welfare, or to suggest that maybe that other primary candidate couldn't possibly win the Democratic nomination. Those hot buttons of racist attitudes are easy to push and when you spray a little of that fluid on any situation, you can ignite an enormous fire. So, I think it has been an accelerator, of course, the race of the President, and at the same time it has been a wake-up call for us about just how potent those racial resentments and attitudes still are. So that's how I would look at it. Not irrelevant, very relevant indeed, but not sufficient. Adequate, but not sufficient, if you want to talk science, to bring about this Tea Party phenomena.

KT: I'm from the South. I remember what that racism was like. I haven't lived there for twenty-five years. I guess I forget. But when we see the ugly, racist signs at the town halls and at the rallies, I just couldn't imagine that happening if Hillary had won the White House.

LF: Can't you imagine what the signs would have been?

KT: What do you think? Wash my shirts?

LF: Absolutely! I mean sexism is different from racism, but if we were in a moment like we were in in the spring of 2009 or the fall of 2008, with an economy in crisis, and the powers that be in this society realizing that the potential for true unrest in this nation, an unrest that would look at what had caused the economic recession of that season; namely, the deregulation of the profit sector in this society and the deregulation of corporate business, and we'd all conceded to corporate companies that they could privatize the profits with globalization and share the spoils with none of the rest of society. It was a moment of true unrest and I think that if Hillary Clinton had been the president we would have seen the same sorts of tools used against her. Not race, but gender-based for the very same reason.

KT: Okay, I'll go there with you. But the other part of this is, you've already touched on it. It's that they seem to want to perpetuate the very policies and ideas that have gotten us here. Are they that uninformed? How can they want to keep doing the same thing and expect a different result? That's the definition of insanity.

LF: Well, think about it. We have two groups of people here. One, is the Tea Party followers like my friend and your friend, the people all of us know. They're not the leaders. They're not the funders. They're not the ideologues. They're the people who have been looking for some kind of explanation for what's been happening in their lives and maybe they have their own personal reasons to feel uncomfortable with a black President. Maybe they have their own sense of anxiety about change in a multi-racial society. It's all pieced together for them, very conveniently, a worldview, by someone like Glenn Beck. But Glenn Beck or the Koch brothers, or Dick Armey, who are in the leadership of this mobilization, I think they have a very different responsibility and have a very different agenda from most of the Tea Party followers that you or I would bump into, and I think that is very important for us to realize because it affects us as progressives when we think about what our tactics are. Is our neighbor who is the Tea Party subscriber the enemy? If he's the enemy and he's just a racist pig what are our options when it comes to making change?

I prefer to believe, and I think it's true, that our responsibility remains to talk to folks and try to talk some of this through and not just laugh at the ignorance or the arrogance or the failure to understand but try to erode some of that while we talk about the interests of those who are pushing this agenda, because as you say, for you, me and our friends and relations, continuing to do the same has only produced disastrous results while those at the top of society have continued to see wealth accrue to them unlike anything we've seen in the history of the nation. Sixty percent of all profits in this country are going to the top 1% and if you're those people, this has worked for you. We may say, this is very short-sighted because they still live here with the rest of us, as the planet is heating and the people are starving, so what do you think is going to happen ... But in terms of their bank balance, and what they've come to believe about what they deserve, this has all been working very well for them.

KT: I saw four of the so-called leaders of the Tea Party on *The Last Word with Lawrence O'Donnell*. They weren't the Koch brothers or Dick Armey or anyone like that. They were just the public faces of the Tea Party and it was obvious they were not the brains behind the organization. They didn't have a good understanding of economics or politics. They just seemed angry and misinformed. I have to tell you, I almost felt a little sorry for them. But I wonder if they know they're being used by the corporations, the very people they should be directing their anger toward? Do they think they're a grassroots movement?

LF: I think that they do. It's been very important that an economic move for re-inscribing the economy we have here, which is the economy of the aristocrats, the economy of the super-rich at the expense of everybody else, it's very important that they have a populist, a "Joe the Plumber" public face, in the same way a Republican party that was emerging from a history of supporting segregation had a face of women and people of color, as I described in the *Bushwomen* book. It was very important that Ronald Reagan, as he tried to roll back civil rights, had Clarence Thomas at the head of the Civil Rights Division of the Justice Department, working in the Equal Employment Opportunity Administration. Thomas had to be the face in the same way that Linda Chavez is the face of English-Only education and against affirmative action. Ward Connelly, same thing. So we are very familiar with this straw man public face of a very private agenda. But if you said to Clarence Thomas, for example, don't you know you're being used, I think he would tell you the same thing that the Tea Party leaders say, which is absolutely not. I'm part of a movement that values me, that treasures me and in fact, I'm treated very well here and I believe in the cause.

KT: Clarence Thomas and his wife, they're way up the food chain. I'm thinking more about the people down at the bottom, that corporations are hurting, and they're voting against their economic interests.

LF: He's the public face of anti-civil rights. He's working against his own interests and against his own history of how he got to be where he is. In the same way those town hall, Tea Party people are working against their own interests as they scream for fewer taxes and fewer social services, even when we know from some polling, at least, that these are people who send their kids to public school, who are on social security and they don't actually think the taxes they personally pay are too high.

KT: Alright then, we've covered what *is* the Tea Party. Where does the Tea Party really get its power?

LF: I think we have a lot of people troubled in this society and we have a troubled democracy.

And the trouble comes from a big vacuum at the center of our Democratic discussion where there should be some honesty about what needs to go on. So they get their power from a vacuum where the Left would be. But the Left isn't allowed in the public debates so instead you get these shriveled discussions. Think about it: Barack Obama gets elected in the fall of 2008, the long-shot candidate, the guy with the ears and the strange name with Hussein in the middle of it. Nobody thought he would win. He wins with a vast majority. He sees a Democratic shift and comes into power with majorities in both houses, an economic crisis. How does this become a conservative moment? How did this get turned around?

KT: They're masters of the spin. Right after the November election all you heard was, "The people have spoken." Well, did they forget after the presidential election, "The people spoke then too"? Remember all the people crying after President Obama's election, thinking things would finally be different now. They could really have hope that things would change. The Republicans totally took over the spin machine.

LF: You asked where did their power come from. That's what happened. But how did it happen? I think largely, after this great victory, environmentalists were empowered, civil rights leaders were empowered, and all the rest of it. What do we get into? We get into a second bail-out for the banks. We get into a discussion about an inadequate stimulus, but it's preferred to no stimulus at all. We see an immediate rollback of any focus on the potential crimes, and I would say real crimes committed by some of our most powerful institutions – mortgage institutions, banks, bankers, and derivative sellers, people who literally stole people's homes, and savaged our economy. You have a Democratic majority who fails to tell a story that makes any sense to people about what happened and what we need to do next.

KT: They had a perfect opportunity that seemed squandered. Were they taking Barack Obama's lead that they didn't want to come across as divisive?

LF: I think you're seeing the end of three decades of work by the Right. Think about the State of the Union last night. We have tools at our disposal as a society to even the playing field. And these are not socialist, communist tools. These are the standard tools of governance. Look at any part of the world. You have taxation, you have regulation and you have government planning. All of those things have been turned toxic in our society, by I would say, a very concerted campaign of media spin, think-tankery, and control of the discourse, in part by the buying and selling of politicians through our "pay to play" election system. So those three tools that could address the fact that we have 15 million unemployed, more like 22 million unemployed if you count people who have given up or people who don't have the jobs that they need. We have an escalating economic and environmental crisis, and what are we going to do? We're going to embrace private and corporate measures for improving the economy from the very people who are doing fine in the economy as it is. So you have Barack Obama talking, not about a second stimulus, which is what we desperately need, but about trade, and reducing corporate taxation. We've had so-called "free trade" for thirty years, unleashed by NAFTA [the North American Free Trade Agreement] and before. What has happened from all that trade? Suppressed wages in this country. Massive profits, lower production costs and wages overseas and the profits simply hoarded by business. At this point you have something like $3 trillion simply being sat on by private companies in this country or distributed to their shareholders. Not brought back into the economy as new jobs, new investment. None of that, but yet, what is Barack Obama promising last night? More of the same.

KT: So what is the problem? Do we not know who we elected? Or is he trying to get re-elected?

LF: I think we have to look at two things. One, it's not about him. It's about us. My book *Blue Grit* was about the progressive scene in 2006–2007. It started in 2004 when people were discouraged after the re-election of George W. Bush. I was working for Air America Radio and I heard my listeners so horrified by what had happened and giving up, and I thought it's not as bad as all that. I think actually there are some progressive forces organizing around the country; we just don't get to see them on our TV. So I traveled around the country and sure enough, I found progressive things happening in interesting places, like Salt Lake City with an environmental mayor; Montana, where Native Americans securing their right to vote changed the political scene in that state enough to elect Montana's first Democratic governor in sixteen years. I saw immigrant rights groups growing up in Florida, and in Nevada, union organizations making all the difference in some of those battleground states. There was a kind of mobilization that was happening in that moment. One of the reasons I was happy about Barack Obama was I believed he was going to empower that community because his strategy for winning the primary campaign was very bottom-up. It had to be. Hillary Clinton ruled the roost. What I think happened since then, sadly, progressives sat back and tried to let Obama fix it for them. And then judge Obama. What's he doing? How's he doing? Thumbs up. Thumbs down. Really, what we need in this country is a progressive movement that says we have to change our electoral system, fundamentally, because no one can get elected who isn't bought and paid for by the most powerful interests in the land. And when our most critical decisions have a bearing on the profits of the people who are paying for our politicians' election campaigns, we are never going to get any change that benefits the people who need it, because we don't have the power that comes from the massive, mighty purse of a corporation like the Koch brothers or the health insurers or pharmaceutical companies, or law firms. It's the old Gore Vidal line: we don't have two parties; we have one, the party of property. There are some differences between what Vidal would call the "two right wings" of the Property Party, but

I think this last election, and in the period we're living through now, the decision by the Supreme Court in Citizens United, has thrown the fact up in our face: unless we come to terms with money in politics, we can't expect our politicians to be the same once they're in office as they were on the campaign trail. And it's not going to be the powers that be that change this picture. It's going to have to be us. It goes back to that old story. We've all heard it, how many times? FDR telling activists he agreed with their point of view, but they had to make him do it. That's where we are. It's uncomfortable. It puts a lot of the burden on us, but I don't think there are many alternatives.

KT: One of the things I believe is we need our own progressive Tea Party. Call them Green Party, Eco-Feminist Party. Can you imagine Glenn Beck hearing that! (Laughing) The thought of that even happening seems daunting when you have Fox News on the other side 24/7, constantly spewing hate, divisiveness, saying any of these things we want to do would be socialism. They've demonized the word "socialism." They've demonized the Left. It's as if more than half the country is brainwashed. It seems like an incredible task unless we could get a media outlet backed by our own billionaires.

LF: Well, that's the dream, isn't it? I think there are two sides of that story. One is yes, it's all as bleak as we've just portrayed. On the other hand, as Molly Ivins says, you'll look back and say these were the good ole' days. In fact as a media person, as an independent progressive in media, I would say our position today is much better than it was 20 years ago. You and I are talking through a medium that simply didn't exist, even just a decade back. I have a TV show that is able to be broadcast on cable and public television, and online in a way that was inconceivable even as recently as 2000. We have an obligation to keep alternative conversations happening but we have an uphill battle.

We have a culture which has vilified all the things that you mention. In fact, we've vilified everything public. Public workers, public spaces, public art and instead we celebrate this consumerist private culture of each one for him or herself, amass everything that you can, and your value, your size in society is related to how much stuff you have.

I think one of the interesting things about watching the Tea Party is, and again the leadership is different, but many of these people are people no one ever reached out to before. They felt alienated from politics and maybe they felt alienated for racist reasons, or sexist reasons or homophobic reasons I don't want to glorify, but they felt left out. Then Glenn Beck says, I'm going to talk to you for an hour and explain the world. I'm going to give you credit for understanding the complicated map I'm going to draw on my blackboard. And sure, it's propaganda, it's manipulation, but it's a kind of attention to folks, to people in pain and in trouble, that I think there is something there for progressives to learn.

KT: Talking points from your assistant on the Tea Party says they seem to despise the poor and the weak – as if we all have equal access to education and opportunity. They seem unaware of the predator aspects of capitalism, such as the corporate take-over of America. They complain that Obama saved the auto industry but in the next breath they complain we've lost our manufacturing base. They hate Michael Moore, but his documentaries are in large part about corporations abandoning American workers. They seem to be conflicted. Am I confused or is it just not a cohesive group?

LF: They are not always a cohesive group and some of what they believe is not coherent, but again, how different is everything you've just mentioned from the basic assumptions that have become entirely accepted not just on the fringes of our politics, but every day? The idea that if you just pull up on your bootstraps in this society, you can get ahead. That's a fundamental belief not just of the Glenn Becks but of the Ronald Reagans, the Bill Clintons and frankly, the Barack Obamas, too. The idea that the private person has to be freed from the burden of society, meaning the burden of government and taxation and responsibility from your neighbors. Again, that is a view that is protested among progressives, but it is increasingly a view that is mainstream. When was the last time you heard a politician get up and defend taxation?

KT: I wonder if it's become mainstream because it's been repeated over and over and over again.

LF: Absolutely, and not contested. There is a climate of viciousness in our media and politics. There is no echo chamber for the person that gets up and says, actually, taxes are the membership fees we pay to live in a humane society. And I'm happy to pay those fees and we want to be sure everyone pays them so everyone feels they're an equal part of this society, because in helping one another, we help ourselves. When was the last time you heard someone say that? Maybe it's because we have a media playing field, but it is nowhere near balanced.

KT: Yet they're always crying about the Liberal Media.

LF: Yes, well, that is easy to disprove.

KT: I would suspect most of these people are supposed to be Christian, but the Jesus values seem to go out the window when it comes to politics, or so it seems.

LF: Again, I would say, this is what we've been hearing for years. To be a Christian, it's still okay to wage war on your neighbor. It's still okay to resort to armed conflict as a solution for economic divisions, for humanitarian crises: we can be "good" interventionists in Iraq and Yugoslavia. We've heard it on both sides of the political aisle. There's no question, people should pick up *At the Tea Party*, which is not an apology for Tea Partiers by any means, and neither will it lay out all the contradictions. I just thought more and more as I've watched our society go through even these last six months about how much of what we vilify as "over there" is really right here. It's deep in our political culture, and rarely examined so as to be dug up by the roots. It goes back to the fundamental notion of society, and what society is about and what American society was founded about. When you hear some of these Tea Partiers claim the mantle of the Founders, the mantle is, "Save us from big government." Well, actually, it wasn't the individual who created the American society. It was the individual in consort with his or her neighbors creating a government about protecting the everyman from massive power, monarchy, private interests, and private wealth. If you go back and read the Founders, it was about government to protect you, everyman, member of the Democratic society, from the superpowerful. It wasn't about protecting the individual from government.

KT: There again, Laura, just like with the Birthers. I wonder if they are just uninformed or disingenuous? Or it's working for them so they don't really care about their neighbor. And wouldn't McCain or Hillary have dug this up on Obama if there was a real issue of the birth certificate?

LF: Eric Cantor was on *Meet the Press* and David Gregory finally challenged someone, asking Cantor if he wanted to challenge the Birthers' crazy talk. All Eric Cantor, the new House Majority Leader, would say is, well I believe Barack Obama is a citizen but I don't want to call anyone crazy. He called the healthcare plan crazy. It's a distraction. I said it last night. Barack Obama is born and made in America. The real problem we have is very few things are born and made in America. We have an employment crisis. A manufacturing crisis. That's what we need to be talking about, but as long as we keep talking about this and permit this conversation to keep going, it keeps the lighter fluid on the conversation and is a distraction from what we should be talking about.

So what about the birth certificate. It's been found a million times. The Hawaiian state government has been bending over backwards to produce the documentation. It's been produced, but none of this changes the conversation or the reality of people's lives. And Eric Cantor's evasion, that's trying to stay a good Birther Boy and keep the Tea Party crew fighting for you and not against you.

KT: So what do we do? What methods should the Left employ? George Lakoff had an article out on untellable truths, saying we should be changing the message. Our phrasing is important. I believe he's into neural linguistics and he said we should be calling what's happening a greed crisis instead of an economic crisis. We should say blessed immigrants instead of illegal immigrants. Government for profit, not privatization. Public theft instead of tax breaks. Failing citizens instead of failing schools. Corporate cruelty instead of profit maximization. Someone else said, maybe Jeff Chang of the *American Prospect*, said we can beat conservatism with progressive culture and our creativity. These seem like pieces of the puzzle, but I think we need more than that.

LF: We need language but I think we need to bring these corporate criminals from Wall Street into court and out of the dark. We should be talking about deregulation and bringing people up on charges, like the head of Massey Energy, who is responsible for unsafe practices that stole the lives of twenty-nine miners early last year. We need not just congressional hearings, but also legal hearings. We need to take some strong action to repudiate some of the practices of the Bush Administration. But then as we've talked about before, Karen, we need to build an independent media movement that provides a place for some of these conversations like Jeff is talking about to be heard. We get so nervous in our electoral cycle. We can't be critical of "our" guy or "our" woman on the ballot. I think we need to get very critical of our electoral system, and we need to start working with neighbors to change that. We need to be working locally. The answer is the same as it's always been. Think globally. Work locally. In this last mid-term, some of the only victories, some of the key victories for Democrats, were in places like Arizona where you had good progressives challenged at the last minute, and only because they had an existing ground team and long-term relationships with their voters on the ground were they able to beat back Tea Party attacks. The same politics we have to go back to that worked for progressives and always have. Work locally. Talk to your neighbors. Come out with your political views, with your cultural views. Talk to people. And my one fear about the Tea Party phenomenon and our response to it is we will again become terrified of the people we live among and stop talking to each other, which I think is a disaster.

KT: Do you think with the deck stacked as much as it is, with the Supreme Court, with Citizens United, Fox News, all the money that comes into the Republican party from corporations, what are the chances we actually can get campaign finance reform? It seems the way things are is so deeply entrenched.

LF: Ask the people in Tunisia or Egypt if they ever thought they'd be free of the dictators who ruled their governments. There is a sense that we need change and we need it right now! And if we didn't get it yesterday, then it must not work, and we're going to go home. We see at the local level efforts around campaign finance reform, public finance reform. Portland, New Hampshire and Vermont. Vermont passed a law that will demand an exercise in single payer healthcare. There are interesting initiatives happening at the local level that we can learn from. Is it possible today to figure out how to unravel the Citizens United decision? Well, even there, there are initiatives around a constitutional amendment to at least concentrate the mind on where the problem is. We need government for the people, by the people. We needs tools to stop corporations from not just breaking our laws and re-writing our electoral laws, but also from stealing our homes and our democracy. There's work that needs to be done. There's absolutely no question. You and I, people like us, we need to maintain the media outlets that give that kind of conversation an airing. And of course everyone needs to pick up *At the Tea Party* from orbooks.com.

KT: Let's talk a little about the media. What happened awhile back, under the Bush Administration, that even allowed a foreigner to come to own so much of America's media? Wasn't that a kind of fishy arrangement in itself? Or was that above board?

LF: Are you talking about Roger Ailes and Rupert Murdoch?

KT: Yes.

LF: Well, I hate to tell you that much of the damage to our media structure was done under the Clinton Administration in 1996 with the telecommunications law that year for which communications companies paid an enormous amount in campaign contributions to the head of committees of Commerce and other committees responsible for coming up with that law. But it was during that period we saw the most dramatic weakening of regulations of how large a corporation could be, how many television and radio stations a corporation could own, or the cross-ownership. Could you own a radio station and a television station and a newspaper in the same town.

Now we're in a situation where we've leapt forward once again, and again it's under a Democratic President, to a point where you can have a company that produces content own the pipes that distribute that content as long as they promise not to promote their own content over others. Well, I won't believe that for very long.

The question of how Rupert Murdoch got the laws changed was less about his citizenship than about the ownership rules, which were in many cases, throughout that period, until today, written explicitly for his benefit, not to step on his toes. To not roll back the purchases that he'd already made, many of which were illegal when he made them.

KT: I'd like to talk about the media's role in elevating the Tea Party. Last night, after the State of the Union, CNN runs Michele Bachmann's response, as if the Tea Party is the equivalent of the other two major parties. Is that going down okay in your mind?

LF: I think you're absolutely right. I think there are people who are beginning to wake up to this. Sarah Palin is a quitter Governor from Alaska, with no chance in most people's eyes of getting elected President, she's a failed candidate for Vice President, yet she gets more media attention than the actual Vice President. And it's not just the leadership. We saw Wolf Blitzer on CNN rush down to Delaware to cover one of the election debates with Christine O'Donnell. Christine O'Donnell didn't stand a chance of winning, yet here was the media attention. And that goes back to my point: it's not exactly about the person, it's about the politics. And in the attention to these people, we're seeing a re-inscribing of a political point of view that goes way beyond the candidacy of that individual. And it's not just the candidates. As I said in the book, you've got the same media that pay no attention to marches for choice on Capitol Hill, or marches for gay and lesbian equality or immigrant rights, all of which attracted in the last few years, half a million, three-quarters of a million, a million people at a time, yet showering attention on Glenn Beck's rallies which were at best estimates around 100,000 or fewer on the Mall. You're absolutely right, there's a media imbalance, and you've got to wonder at not just the amount of coverage, but the quality of coverage. That goes back to race again. If it were young people of color carrying some of the banners, calling the President a Nazi, calling the President a fascist, or a socialist, if they could just make up their mind, carrying guns, I don't think you'd see the same quality of coverage, but you might see the quantity. But it wouldn't happen twice.

KT: Let's talk a little about Keith Olbermann. Those of us on the Left are lamenting his departure. But worse than his departure, some are worried this is the beginning of the end of liberals actually having a voice, considering conservative Comcast has merged with NBC. Do you think this is paranoia or is this a real worry?

LF: I think there is a real reason to worry and there is reason to believe there was a role played by corporate executives and if they don't want us to believe that, well, hard luck on them. Because whether it's true or not, it's on their back to prove it isn't. This is exactly the reason we're skeptical of commercial media and corporate control of our news outlets. This is the reason we have to maintain independent, non-commercial, community-supported, advertising-free radio and television because there is always going to be the question if it's about something somebody said that's alienating the owners or the advertisers. In this case, I don't think we really know. I think Keith Olbermann was eight years at MSNBC. It's a pretty good long run for him. Was he an irritant of corporate interests? For sure. Were his own interpersonal skills problematic? I've heard that, too. The point is, if we've been thinking corporate media would bring us the liberal voice that will be an alternative to the other guys, it was never true. It wasn't even true when Keith Olbermann was on the air, and it's not going to be true in the future. We have to build our own that's insulated from that kind of pressure and then you don't have to wonder if, when Laura is taken off the air, is it because of some corporate owner, no, it's probably because viewer contributions didn't come in. We have to build an independent media where progressives have a voice which is not at the behest of General Electric.

KT: And it would be nice if the other half of the country might wake up to: we are looking out for them too! So Laura, in closing, is there one final idea you'd like to leave with listeners?

LF: Well, you've asked lots of great questions. But I think we cannot just assert that there is a sensible Middle in society or a benevolent Left. We can't just have marches on the Mall as the folks from the *Daily Show* did to restore sanity. We have to do the local work, like in Arizona, or for the healthcare initiatives in Vermont, and we have to have a counter-media strategy. We can't simply focus on the evils of the other guy. We have to make our own. Finally, we have to convene our own conversations and our own narrative for what's happening. It's easy to critique the other guys. We need to get very clear about what's happened in this country and what possible proposals exist out there to resolve it. Technology alone won't save us. We have to save us and I think that's what this is all about!

KT: Quickly, a listener just shot me an email. Why does the Tea Party appeal to women? Assuming I guess we aren't talking Sarah Palin or Michele Bachmann.

LF: There is a great chapter in there by Betsy Reed, where she says that's simply not true. It's asserted women have flocked to the Tea Party but the numbers don't reflect it at all. It's majority male. It's majority older according to every poll. But if you want to think about why women who do go there, go there, there are a lot of women who feel they've been badly treated in their lives and they've never been involved in anything political and this might be the first group that reached out to them, or it's the first time in this fairly unorganized new formulation women have been able to take leadership roles before the guys take over, or people who are actually frustrated and fed up with how women get treated in the Democratic party. That's another story, but fundamentally, that is not true. It's a male-led and dominated movement with some female figureheads.

KT: One last time, let's tell listeners how to find your book.

LF: It's at OR Books. That's Orbooks.com.

KT: They can find you at GRITtv every day.

LF: Absolutely.

KT: Laura, it has been my real pleasure. Thank you so much for your valuable time. I look forward to watching you tomorrow.

LF: Yes, (laughing) thank you and good night.

Chapter 29

Money and the Divine Masculine

by Charles Eisenstein

I recently attended a ceremony at the Tamera village in Portugal in which the officiant invoked "the healing of money." Immediately a vivid image popped into my head of a man, vast and muscular, bound to the earth with stakes and tethers, straining with every atom of his strength to free himself and rise up. Finally, in a desperate, colossal effort, he bursts free and, standing tall, lets out a triumphant roar before striding purposefully off.

I knew immediately that the man represented the divine masculine and his bonds were made of money.

What is the purpose of men? In some primitive societies they were not of much use at all. In many places women were the center of life, collecting most of the food, looking after young children, and doing the small amount of work necessary to subsist. Subsistence was so easy in many places that, as the anthropologist Marshal Sahlins put it, "half the time the people seem not to know what to do with themselves." Describing the Hadza, he notes one ethnographer's estimate that adults spend two hours a day on subsistence, the women collecting plant foods "at a leisurely pace and without prolonged labour," and the men devoting most of their time to gambling. True, the men made an important contribution to the food supply by hunting, but only a small minority of the Hadza did any hunting at all. The rest, it would seem, were completely superfluous as far as the material needs of the tribe are concerned.

In other societies, instead of gambling, the men would devote most of their time to secret societies, ritual activities, interactions with the spirit world, and so on. Theirs was the realm of the abstract; for the most part, the women and children could get along fine without them. Of course, that might change in times of warfare, but that too we might see as another men's game that bears little benefit to the material welfare of the tribes involved.

Thus it was that the great anthropologist Margaret Mead would sometimes, half-jokingly, order the men attending her lectures to leave the auditorium. "Get out – you are all useless," she would say.

So with some small exaggeration, we might say that human life was divided between the women's world, which was central to material well-being and survival, and the men's world, which was largely inconsequential. What has happened in the millennia since hunter-gatherer days?

Today, as in the past, men are still attracted to the realm of abstraction, of non-materiality, of magic and ritual, of gambling. For example, boys spend a lot more time playing video games than girls do, and men tend more than women to fields like mathematics, accounting and computer science.* Whether this difference is genetic or cultural (and whether the genetic/cultural distinction is even fundamental), it is one of the noticeable differences between the sexes in our society.

One arena where all four of these male pursuits (abstraction, non-materiality, magic/ritual, and gambling) come together is money. This is most apparent at the nerve center of the money system, the hedge funds and Wall Street banks, where the "quants" – almost exclusively men – use computers to manipulate data, highly abstract representations of representations of representations, to make or lose vast fortunes. Their numbers – stock market indices, LIBOR, the CDS spread – seem disconnected from anything material, and their manipulations are conducted according to highly arcane rules inaccessible to any but the initiated.

But unlike the Hadza's games of chance or the secret societies of the native Americans, the games of the financial elites have profound consequences for the rest of society. For these numbers are not actually disconnected from material and social life; rather, they rule it. The men's world has invaded the women's world and usurped its domain. Increasingly for the past several centuries, no function of life can be carried out without money. This abstract game of tallies and chits has taken over everything else.

Outside the extreme case of Wall Street, the same money chase prevails, subjecting men and women alike to the pursuit of numbers. The integration of women into the workforce was considered a great victory of the feminist movement, but today some who call themselves feminists, or post-feminists, would say that it was the last and greatest insult to the feminine. What kind of victory for women is it, to be permitted to join the mad chase for money at the cost of nature, culture, community, family, leisure, beauty, and health? What victory is it to have won the right to be equal partners in the pillage of the planet, which itself is the consequence of a kind of distorted hypermasculinity run amok?

If not enslaved to the pursuit of numbers that is destroying the very basis of civilization, what is the true, sacred expression of the masculine principle? What, we might ask again, is the purpose of men? What does the divine man of my vision do after he has broken the chains of money that bind him? Remember, in my vision I saw him stride off with a purpose.

Whether you are a man or a woman, I'm sure you can feel that sense of purpose or mission inside of you, whether it is in full passionate expression or deep latency. It is the divine masculine. No longer is it content with frivolities, as it may have been in the long hunter-gatherer childhood of our species. No longer, in this hour of extremity, can it be bound to a machine that turns its energies toward domination and brutality. What kind of relationship does it want to the divine feminine – nature, materiality, family, hearth, land, community, water, and flesh?

Here is a hint: In Portugal I received a tour of Tamera's perma-culture farm centered around a "water retention landscape" – a veritable oasis in that drought-stricken land. My guide described how the engineer chose where to site the ponds: "He waited until he could see where they wanted to be." Rather than imposing an abstract design onto the landscape, he put the gift of design and the machines to carry it out in the service of that which wanted to be born. Here, an expression of the masculine – digging big holes in the ground – was an act of co-creative service with the feminine, and something beautiful was born.

The divine masculine wants to make love to the world. It wants to carry and protect what is beautiful. It wants to explore new territories and play beyond the edge of old boundaries. It wants to put its gifts in service with, not domination of, the divine feminine.

Nature and science, substance and form, matter and spirit, the heart and the mind ... each of these relationships mirrors, in our civilization, the relationship that has subsisted between the feminine and the masculine. Science dominated nature; spirit was elevated above matter; the mind trumped the heart; substance was the mere substrate of form. Now these relationships are changing: science in service to nature; form arising from substance; spirit immanent in matter; the mind uniting with the heart.

As with any species, none of our human gifts is superfluous, not even those heretofore used to dominate and despoil. We will still play our number games, we will still play with principles, logic, and abstractions; we will still count and measure things; we will still use money. No longer, though, will we be lost in the map, disconnected from the material world the symbols are supposed to represent. No longer will we seek to force reality to conform to our maps. And no longer will money rule the world. "Only the measurable is real," taught Galileo, setting the stage for a world in which numbers became realer than the things they counted. What was true in science was even more so in economics: what mattered was the numbers in the form of cold, hard cash. Thus it is that we celebrate the rise of a number – GDP – even when it comes at the cost of real well-being and even survival.

I saw the divine masculine freeing himself from bondage to money and all the rest of what Riane Eisler called the dominator paradigm. You may have tasted this freedom yourself, any time you decided to follow your passion despite the money, or to put your money in service to your passion, rather than the other way around. Money and the rest of the symbolic world is meant to be a creative instrument, a means and not an end. As a means it opens up new territory and expands the horizon of the possible. As an end, it enslaves.

The liberation from the bonds of money isn't just a psychological shift; it must also have a social manifestation. Our usurious debt-based system of necessity turns more and more of our creative energies toward servicing debt, because in an interest-based system, the debts must grow and grow, carrying all of life, human and biological, with them into the realm of money. That system is crumbling. We strain and pull against it. What would you do, if not compelled by money? Where will you devote your precious creative energy? What will you do when, with a collective roar, we all break free?

Of course each man has an inner feminine and each woman an inner masculine, and both inner masculine and inner feminine are multidimensional in their expression. I am not saying that a female mathematician is less feminine than a homemaker; her feminine qualities might manifest in a different way.

About Charles Eisenstein ...

Charles Eisenstein is a speaker and writer focusing on themes of civilization, consciousness, money, and human cultural evolution.

His viral short films and essays online have established him as a genre-defying social philosopher and countercultural intellectual. Eisenstein graduated from Yale University in 1989 with a degree in Mathematics and Philosophy and spent the next ten years as a Chinese-English translator. The author of *The More Beautiful World Our Hearts Know Is Possible*, *Sacred Economics* and *Ascent of Humanity*, he currently lives in Camp Hill, Pennsylvania.

Website: www.charleseisenstein.net

Chapter 30

Gifting and Peace

by Genevieve Vaughan

This is a country where trillions of dollars are being spent on wars while most people on Earth do not have enough to eat. Where choices are confounded and democracy is undermined by mainstream media misinformation. Where corporations decide what people want to hear and tell it to them, while covering up the death-dealing but money-making technologies of GMOs, fracking, nuclear power, and the murder-by-pollution of the land and the seas with radioactive waste and plastic detritus.

Fortunately there are alternative media sources like Free Speech and Link TV, Democracy Now, truth tellers like Amy Goodman and Bill Moyers who try to inform the public about what is happening. We are also blessed by smaller alternative news and interview programs like *WINGS*, *Women's Voices*, and *Voices of the Sacred Feminine*. These consistently attempt to give the gift of the truth but it is difficult to pierce the heavy cloud of lies that covers our public mindscape.

Recently we have found out about one more deception, one more double standard – the surveillance scandal – where each one's private truths are vulnerable to government's and corporations' penetrating gazes, while the truths of the government and big money are hidden from view.

How could the ship of state go so far off course? How can the people of a democracy be so gullible and so morally helpless? These sound like rhetorical questions, but I believe some serious answers to them exist.

The increasing depravity of the public and of the government, of business and academia, is due to the co-existence of two ways of thinking: the exchange paradigm and the gift paradigm. The logic of exchange cancels, discounts and conceals the logic of the gift while at the same time creating ways of taking the gifts of the many and channeling them to the few. The logic of the gift, which I believe, is the basic human interactive pattern, allows the givers to unwittingly provide for their oppressors and reward them.

We are familiar with the cold war between Capitalism and Communism, but there is a much longer struggle that has been going on between the exchange economy and the gift economy. The exchange economy can never win this struggle because the gift economy is the source of life and even of profit, the very profit that motivates exchange. The gift economy cannot win it because it is discredited and concealed by the exchange economy and is not even recognized by those who are practicing it.

In fact the apologists for the exchange economy discount gift giving and the other-orientation it requires, decreeing that we are all ego-oriented *Homo economicus*. Recent male philosophers even say there is no such thing as unilateral giving, while many women, with whom I have spoken, especially mothers, believe that they do a lot of unilateral giving themselves on a daily basis but it is worth nothing.

We can understand this disconnect if we see the direct giving of goods and services to satisfy needs not as an ethical issue (as in the ethics of care) but as an economic issue (economic in the basic sense of how the means of life are supplied). We will thus frame the gift economy as an economy embodied in maternal care. Exchange, giving-in-order-to-receive an equivalent, quid pro quo, which is practiced in the market economy, is gift giving doubled back upon itself and made conditional upon a return. The two economies diverge in a very elementary way in everyday life and they have different logics as well as different psychological and relational consequences and connections. While we might read these consequences as ethical, I propose that it is more infor-mative to consider them not in terms of individual propensities for virtue or vice, but as deriving from fundamental patterns of the ways needs are satisfied in a society.

Many Native economies at the time of the conquest had little or no market exchange. Women, mothers and grandmothers were respected and goods were directly distributed to needs. The gift culture produced people with a view of life that simply did not comprehend the reasoning of Europeans avid for plunder.[1]

While it may seem improper to single out one factor from the many cultural factors that influence the way we are, the patterns of the two economies do influence us very strongly. They are the patterns of the economic "structures" from which Marx said that "superstructures" of ideas derive. They are also patterns that we in the West have tended to identify with gender (as for example, independence vs interdependence or competition vs nurturing). However even in the life of the tiny child, before gender becomes an issue, needs must be satisfied, and so the gift economy begins as the first economy, neither male nor female but maternal.

The market has been seen as economic, while gift giving has appeared "aneconomic" or "external". Non-market gift economy practices (such as generalized reciprocity, symbolic gift "exchange", gifting festivals and giveaways) can be understood as elaborations of the maternal economy. Market economies too are based on giving but distort and exploit it, imposing the contradictory logic. Even in market economies there are many free gifts, beginning with the gift of the air we breathe and the language we speak. These are usually unrecognized as gifts, though, and are turned to profit whenever possible (as has happened with the privatization of water and seeds).

The gift paradigm has been interpreted as morality and generosity but it is better understood as the way of thinking appropriate to the gift economy, its "ideological super-structure". The logic of direct giving contrasts in many ways with the logic of exchange. It is transitive, bridges the gap between self and other, and values the other, creating positive relationships. Exchange, by requiring an equivalent, cancels the gift; it is ego-oriented, self-validating, and places people in competition with each other. The gift economy requires a creative receiver who uses the gift or service and/or passes it on, while the exchange economy diverts attention away from the receiver onto the object, and treats the other as means for acquiring it. Giving/receiving is mostly qualitative and directs attention to needs, exchange is mostly quantitative and focuses on equations, measurement and having more. Giving/receiving produces inter-dependence and trust, exchange produces adversarial behavior, mistrust and the illusion of independence.

Because infants cannnot survive without a great deal of maternal care, everyone has the early experience of being the receiver of unilateral giving/provisioning. This is the case whoever actually does the mothering – whether women or men, birth mothers or aunts or grandmothers, whole villages, or even paid caregivers (the child does not know the care is paid). Granted the quality of the care may change according to who does it, but if the child survives, the care must have been adequate. Society usually assigns the job of mothering to the birth mother, and the female gender is usually socially constructed to ensure this assignment.The binary gender construction in the West requires that from very early on, in order to be "male," boys renounce identification with the mother and therefore also with the "female" gift economy, upon which their lives depend. They are trained away from their maternal identities when they are most vulnerable, and are encouraged to construct their gender categorization around an adult model of independence, power over, and ego orientation, which is often also violent. In a kind of distorted image of giving, physical violence reaches out and touches the other person to harm and to establish relations, not of mutuality, but of domination. The renunciation of the maternal identity and economy is a false and problematic necessity, imposed on males, for which females are expected to compensate by giving even more.

Patriarchy and the economy of not-giving combine to appropriate the gifts of women's care. Housework, as Marilyn Waring (1989) taught us, would add some 40% to the GNP in the US, if it were counted in monetary terms, more in some other countries.[2] Add to these the gifts of surplus value, the part of the labor that is not paid for in the salary and the gifts of nature and the future, gifts that are destroyed by pollution, the costs of which the polluters do not have to pay. And all this takes place on the background of the past seizure of the lives and the labor of African slaves, the seizure of the lands of the Indigenous Peoples, the enclosure of the commons, the recent commodification of previously free goods like water, seeds, fertilizer, the patenting of genes and of species and of knowledge, the plundering of the Global South by the North.

All of these are ways in which the market economy takes the gifts of the many and redistributes them to the few. It is this redistribution that creates the scarcity for the many that allows the few to maintain control. If too much abundance accrues, there is a kind of bloodletting and the "excess" is wasted on wars. The wealth of the many is cycled through the war industrial complex; it is redistributed to the arms industries or destroyed on the field. We saw this in the Bush administration when the wealth that had accumulated under Clinton was spent (wasted) on the wars on Iraq and Afghanistan.

Money is the great arbiter, the decision maker as to what is a free gift (so valueless) and what is a commodity (so valuable). Since instead the gift economy as a whole would be much better for everyone, the exchange economy competes with it ... and usually wins. Competition is a behavior that is functional for the market and for patriarchy, while cooperation is functional for gift giving, and for matriarchy (matriarchy seen not as a mirror image of patriarchy but as a possible egalitarian society based on maternal values). In the market, competition wins over coope-ration even if some businesses use cooperation as a tool for greater competitiveness. Similarly in war, in business and in sport, cooperation within the teams of competitors results in greater strength. Hybrids of the two logics maintain the control of the one over the other. The successful participation of women in the market system demonstrates that the opposition at the root of our problems is not binary gender but the existence of the two economies, one of which is parasitic on the other while at the same time sustaining it monetarily at a level of vulnerability for most of its participants.

In spite of its success, the system based on exchange is deeply threatened by the possibility of a gift economy and tries to prevent it. In fact in abundance, gift giving would be easy and delightful and people would not need to submit to working within hierarchies of others' power, but they could simply provision each other according to an adult elaboration of the model of the mothering economy. This is indeed what happened in many indigenous societies and is one of the reasons EuroAmerican Capitalism has tried so brutally to eliminate or appropriate them.

Even within Capitalism though, families are pockets of the gift economy within the exchange economy, usually centered around the free caregiving of the mother. The right wing romanticizes the maternal role while maintaining the patriarchal dominance and submission model, which requires that women give to and serve men while men protect and guide "their" women. What I am suggesting is that we realize that both genders are fundamentally gift giving, and that the patriarchal interpretation is pernicious and mistaken.

By revaluing giving and receiving instead of exchange and domination, we can make the economy of mothering the model for the economy as a whole. Liberating mothering from the paradigm and the practice of exchange, frees everyone to direct the flow of goods to needs instead of to profit.

Understanding this lets us see the long-term burden of misogyny and matriphobia as an economic phenomenon rather than simply a psychological or characterological one, perhaps due to men's bad attitudes or women's masochism. The primary challenge for feminism is not to assimilate into the upper power levels of Patriarchal Capitalism but to substitute a new/old economy based on mothering for the anti-nurturing ego-oriented economy of plunder we are now practicing.

Since the various levels or aspects of society are not separate, we can see this as the creation of an economy that centers on the prototype of abundant Mother Nurturer Goddess(es), whose places have been usurped by the monotheistic gods of patriarchy. Goddess worship weighs the psyche towards nurturing for both men and women while patriarchal religions tend to create women-only nurturers, while men are presumably warriors and heroes. Then the integration of giving and exchange seems to take place in a righteous male god who is said to be also gift giving or at least merciful.

There are a number of cognates of exchange like crime and punishment, where we pay for our sins or crimes. Telling the truth is a gift because it nurtures the listener with information that will help her act in appropriate ways. Lies are based on exchange because they use the communicative nurturing of the other for the purposes of the liar, who gives false information in order to receive what s/he wants.

When our government decides to "punish" another country to "bring it to justice," it is functioning according to the exchange paradigm. When it lies in order to justify the attack (and promulgates its lies through the media), it is again functioning according to exchange. The prototype of the mother is missing here, unless it is the powerless Mater Dolorosa weeping for the deaths of her children in war or even the deaths of the children of the "enemy." But add to this that maybe our "punitive" attack on Syria is only a cover-up for the surveillance scandal. Is it surprising that we grow more and more paranoid? At the macro level money rules and the gift economy is invisible or sacrificial. At the micro level in the market it's dog-eat-dog consumerism.

So the questions that we began with are answered. It is the lack of the Mother that unbalances the ship of state and paralyzes the population, opening the way for money and the men at the top to work their warring will.

About Genevieve Vaughan ...

Genevieve Vaughan (b. Texas 1939) has been working for many years on the idea of a gift economy based on mothering as the basis of an alternative worldview and way of life. She created the international all-women activist Foundation for a Compassionate Society based in Austin, Texas (1987–2005), one of the continuing projects of which is the Temple of the Goddess Sekhmet in Cactus Springs, Nevada, founded in 1992. She also initiated a network: International Feminists for a Gift Economy (2001 – present). Her books are *For-Giving, a Feminist Criticism of Exchange* (1997), *Homo Donans*, a web book (2006), and two anthologies: *Il Dono, the Gift: A Feminist Perspective* (2004) and *Women and the Gift Economy: A Radically Different Worldview Is Possible* (2008). These, a film on her life, her songs, children's books and many articles can be downloaded free from her website:

www.gift-economy.com

Chapter 31

Ways Women Can Think about Power

Transcript of interview with Gloria Feldt

Interview:

KT = Karen Tate
GF = Gloria Feldt

Tonight I am very pleased and privileged to have with us for your listening pleasure, Gloria Feldt. Gloria is a nationally renowned inspirational keynote speaker, activist, and author on women, power, and leadership. Her latest book, *No Excuses: 9 Ways Women Can Change How We Think About Power*, reveals why women are stuck at 18% of top leadership roles and, through both inspirational stories and practical tools, shows how women can redefine power, lead themselves with intention, and reach parity from the boardroom to the bedroom for good – their own and society's. And now, she has co-founded Take the Lead to prepare and propel women to their fair and equal share of top leadership positions by 2025!

Feldt's previous books include the *New York Times* bestseller *Send Yourself Roses*, co-authored with actress Kathleen Turner, *Behind Every Choice Is a Story*, and *The War on Choice*.

People Magazine calls Feldt "the voice of experience." A teen mother from rural Texas, Feldt served as president and CEO of Planned Parenthood Federation of America, the nation's largest reproductive health and advocacy organization, from 1996 to 2005. Her passion for bettering women's lives remains her driving force as an independent commentator on women's issues, politics, media, and leadership. Feldt teaches "Women,

Power, and Leadership" at Arizona State University and serves on the board of the Women's Media Center.

Interview starts:

KT: Gloria, what you're doing in the world is so important. It seems especially right now. I don't know if you heard the opening to the show. We were talking about women's issues and women's rights, and how we equate the ideals of the Sacred Feminine with values that are really under assault today. Equality, nurturing, caring, sharing, partnership. Did you ever think in this day and age we would be fighting these battles we've been fighting these past two years – contraception, abortion, redefining rape and all the rest?

GF: I think, Karen, if we look at what we're seeing right now in politics through the long lens of history we will see they are issues that in some form or another come back over and over and over again. They are about power. They are about fairness and justice and who gets to decide things like what happens with our bodies and who we will have children with and when. Those are the most profound human issues anywhere. I think there are some, I don't want to say that this is a blanket indictment of men in any way, but I think there are some who are so frightened of the changing gender power balance going on right now, that their response is to dig further and further into a very ancient and not fair, not right, not just way of living, in which they held all the power and they didn't have to share it.

KT: We are going to primarily talk about your book, *No Excuses: 9 Ways Women Can Change How We Think About Power*, but let me ask you first, do you think religion is at the root of women who tend to acquiesce to male authority and men being all too willing to grab hold of it and not want to let it go at all, with the exception of our more evolved and aware men, of course. We are not saying all men.

GF: The simple answer to that question would be yes, it's those traditional patriarchal religious cultural constructs that are framing the entire conversation, framing the entire culture. But it is very hard to change a culture while you're living in it and a lot of things happen in the process. I mean for example, it's risky to go against cultural expectations. You risk your relationships. You risk people saying bad things about you. You risk being held in contempt by other people. Gloria Steinem describes "women who look like us but they act like them." I think some of them are just co-opted because they get more rewards for being like their oppressors than by looking at the bright light of their own opportunities to thrive independently in this world. And until it becomes easier for them to do that, they are not likely to make that shift. So, I don't know where to lay the blame. I think it would be better to ask, "What would be the right thing to do here and how can we make there be more rewards for being free and equal and fair and just and how can we make more of that happen?"

KT: Right. Definitely stay positive rather than finger-pointing, but at the same time you have to shed light on the fact that, sometimes we call them handmaidens of the patriarchy or Stepford Wives. You see her, she's always standing next to her man who has just been caught in a brothel and she's wearing her pearls and her high heels and she's trying to smile and you know she just wants to kill him. (Laughs)

GF: Who would we be talking about now? (Laughing)

KT: They drag her out, as if her standing beside him makes it all right now. Our last guest, we were talking a little bit about how sometimes women are complicit in their own oppression. It's a complicated subject, you know. And a lot of the time it's economic. They're stuck in these situations, maybe not as much today as our mothers. Things are getting better for women, but we still don't receive equal pay for equal work. We only have 20% of women in leadership in academia, corporate America and religious institutions. We just don't see enough women out there taking the lead and being role models. And if you live in that bubble – I'll just say it – if you live in that Right Wing bubble, where I don't think women's leadership is encouraged quite as much, then it's harder because, like you say, you risk so much. You want to be like everyone around you and maybe they don't share your values. Am I totally off base, or …

GF: No. No. I don't think you're off base at all. I think that's absolutely right. We all want to be in a situation where the people around us think we're good. Where the people around us think we're worth being part of the culture, part of the society, where we get strokes for the behavior that we have, so it's hard. Right now, some of what we're seeing is exacerbated by the economic chaos and this feeling some men have that they are losing control in general, about their lives. What they see as women turning the world upside down, I see as finally setting it right.

KT: Right. It's hard to be the burr in your family's saddle.

GF: Yes, it is. (Laughing)

KT: Why isn't Mary getting married? Why isn't she having children? Why does she want to pursue the career and travel around the world or write books? How could she possibly be happy and satisfied? But we hear statistically, that women are actually doing better in society. There are more women graduating with degrees, and because of the economy – please correct me if I'm wrong, because I'd rather get it right – more women are the breadwinners now as men have lost their jobs because they've been outsourced, or they've been replaced by someone making less money, so in a way, have women benefited a little bit by the economy going haywire because now they're catapulted into a new role?

GF: You hit on a number of really important issues. I'll try to braid them back together and tell you that is what prompted me to write my latest book, *No Excuses: 9 Ways Women Can Change How We Think About Power*. I saw that doors are now open for women. Not only are the doors open, but women have many advantages. Women have a lot of power in our hands that we don't seem to realize that we have, and therefore, don't always use. As you mentioned, more women than men are graduating from college. We live in a society where brains, not brawn, are needed for new technologies. For most of the work that's done, we need more brains, not brawn. Women make companies more profitable. When companies have greater numbers of women on their upper management and boards of directors, they make more money. So the case is strong for bringing more women into top leadership – not to take over all leadership roles, but for there to be greater diversity around the decision-making table.

Women buy 80% of consumer goods. We have an enormous amount of power of the purse. We make most of the buying decisions in our families. And you mentioned that women are becoming the breadwinners. More women, of course, are contributing to the family income. While men are still the primary breadwinners in 60% or so of the families, women are sometimes out-earning their husbands. Up to 40%, I see different statistics, between 27 and 40% of households in which women are out-earning the men. So, much rapid social change. That always brings about a reaction that can be very conservative. But the main issue that I found when I was researching *No Excuses* is that, although the doors are open, we can no longer expect anyone to walk us through them but ourselves. And while there still is external bias to deal with, we have changed most of the laws, so we can't blame laws. We can certainly blame cultural pressures, but you can't pass laws about that. We have to take the initiative on our own to walk ourselves through the doors and to bring another woman with us when we do.

KT: So I gather from what you're saying, Gloria, we're not always walking through the doors. What's holding us back and/or what's holding us back from helping other women? Because you always hear, sometimes women are the hardest on other women. Rather than being supportive, I don't know if this is urban legend, but they make it harder for other women, rather than giving women a hand-up.

GF: That is the predominant cultural narrative. But Catalyst has been studying women in upper leadership and how women in corporations treat women for 40 years now. Their research is impeccable and they find that women do help women. It's not so much an urban legend as the media narrative specifically designed to make us not feel good about ourselves. That's one of the biggest things women struggle with and justifiably. We are often portrayed in the media with such negative characteristics – who would want to have them? To get to your question of what's the problem, and why aren't we walking through the doors: by looking at the research, talking with women all over the country, and to be perfectly honest, looking into my own heart and soul, thinking about what I had done in my own life, in my own career, I found we have an outdated definition of power, as the men have usually defined it. Having power over someone or something. And as women we have borne the brunt of the negative aspects of that power – we've been discriminated against, we have been abused, and raped and beaten, why would we want that kind of power? And so, women back off from it. But we can start thinking about power as a positive force, as basically like a hammer: you can break something apart, but you can also build something with it. So if we shift our definition of power, from the outdated idea of power *over*, to the more expansive idea of power *to*, then, when I talk to women, as I speak all over the country, I see faces start to relax. And women say, "Oh yeah, I want that, I want that kind of power."

KT: So you're saying we don't want to become that thing that has become such a thorn in our own side? So unconsciously we resist it?

GF: We resist it and we dance around it. It's a relationship. It's almost a spiritual relationship between ourselves, our images of ourselves, and this thing we think of as power out there, which is really an amorphous force. But if you think about it, the power *to* is what lets you make the world better for your family, yourself, the world.

KT: Yes, the power to do this or to do that.

GF: The power to innovate, the power to earn money for your family. So ultimately, power over is oppression. We don't want that. It's good that we don't want that. Power to is leadership. It's taking responsibility. It's being able to say, "I'm confident. I'm capable. I can go do this. This is my intention. I am going to embrace my power. I am going to walk with intention to achieve the goals I want to achieve in my own life." That to me is a healthy relationship with power.

KT: And I'm thinking it could be a good lesson for men as well. It would be a new dynamic for them in how they work in the world.

GF: It's a complete paradigm shift of how power has been thought of in the ages.

KT: I'm thinking too, I'm sure you're probably familiar with this: in the Scandinavian countries, they have "the 40% solution," where after their education has been paid for (by the State) these countries want to reap the benefit of that, so they have a requirement that corporate boards have 40% women in top tier staff. At first corporations baulked at the idea, but then a few years later, as you said before, they saw the benefit of the diversity of new ideas and how they benefited from it. Do you think there's much chance we will ever see that here in the United States? Or is that just one of those socialist, European notions (laughing) that will never go over in the United States?

GF: That's a really good question. My guess is we won't see quotas here in the United States, but if we make the business case for it, we'll see more and more women on boards of directors, and in the upper echelons of management. What is it that drives the American economy? The American political philosophy? It's all about the capitalistic way of looking at things. Even in that framework, what you see is it's really good for your company to have more women in those leadership positions. Change is not going to happen overnight. And there is some blowback right now, even in Europe, from what I've been reading, that corporation boards be constituted of 40% women, but you can't deny the data. And they can't deny the data. What women need to do is to get together as a team, as a network, as sisters. I call this Sister Courage. To reach out to someone else and have the courage to raise the issues and get together with people who feel like you do and present your case. And when you do that, just like when you're building a social movement, you can make change in the society and in the workplace. I think we should be going for 50%, never mind this 40%. (Laughing)

KT: I agree! I agree! You also said a moment ago, how the media spins things. There was an article that came out, I think, by Ruth Rosen, who talked about how the media took over the message of the feminists who were trying to create a movement for an equal society. A society for caring and sharing. But they spun it into this idea that women wanted to have it all. That we all had to be superwomen and if we didn't achieve that, then somehow feminism failed. But I think her position was the message got skewed. That wasn't what feminists were out to do, anyway. Women just wanted the choice of what they could do. Maybe you can help me here. Are you familiar with that article?

GF: Yes, I did read Ruth's article and it was excellent. It was a good response to a mis-framing of the issue and I think she pointed that out very eloquently. Who ever asked men if they could have it all? Nobody ever said to a man, "Can you have it all?" Because no one can have all of everything. But everyone can decide what "all" means a lot to them. I can decide, in my heart of hearts, what would make me feel fulfilled. In my career. With my family. In my social life. In my spiritual life. Those are the things I want to make decisions about myself and I need to be able to go and get them. I need to be able to earn them. "Can women have it all?" is just the wrong question. I have a friend, a brilliant writer, Linda Hirshman. She wrote a book called *Get to Work*, which caused a great deal of controversy, explaining to women that when people try to paint you as being bad for wanting to have it all, they're trying to get you out of the workplace. They are trying to have power over you so you don't have a chance to earn your keep. But you have to earn your keep because you can never depend on someone else to support you. You need to be able to earn your own money. You need to do that in order to thrive as a human being, not just to be able to pay your bills. You need to feel you're contributing to society.

KT: I wonder how many men and women realize that which lives below the surface there. And what I mean by that is, this idea that if society's women don't have the ability to support themselves, to be liberated, then you have them under your thumb. You have them where you want them, if you're that type. And then women aren't free. They have to acquiesce and do whatever it is society tells them good little girls do. And I wonder how many women are actually aware of that? Because there are so many women that seem to just buy in to this idea there is something wrong with being able to strive for those things. Look, I come from the South. You're taught to be nice, not to make waves. You're taught the best thing for a woman is to be a homemaker. To want other things, sometimes they still cock an eyebrow at you, like you want too much or you're not normal. Or who do you think you are? The way I look at it is, anyone that would encourage you to be less than you can be, or anyone who would not want you to be able to support yourself, it's almost as if it's a shortcoming in themselves because they don't feel like they can hold on to you if you grow. Does any of this make any sense?

GF: Well, yes, and I was smiling. I grew up in the South also so I know exactly what you're talking about and I know how engrained those traditional gender roles are, but that doesn't make it right that women have traditionally been shunted into low-paying jobs or put in the stay-at-home caregiver roles. The fact that an injustice has always existed does not mean that it should always exist. And the fact that women are gaining economic power certainly doesn't mean we want men to have less of it. What we mean is in a fairer world, what we're really looking for is an economy where everyone can thrive and contribute their best gifts. And that will ultimately be better for both men and women.

KT: I agree with you. And I think I have the words for what I was struggling to say a moment ago. There are some men in our society who would rather it not be that way because then they have more control. Whether we're talking about women's reproductive freedom or whether we're talking her economic freedom, they want to have their thumb on the woman so that, well, it almost gives men license not to be the best he can be, because if a woman is stuck with three kids pulling on her shirt, or she doesn't know how to balance the checkbook, or she can't go out and earn her own living, then she almost has to put up with anything. That's what I'm trying to say! And I think in a lot of places in this country, a lot of women still live like that.

GF: Yes, and there's a reason why the words "barefoot" and "pregnant" have been used together in common parlance, because those are the two basic things anybody needs to have power in his or her own life. You have to have control over your own body, your physical being, including our childbearing, and you have to be able to earn money or have enough money so that nobody can coerce you. That you can be independent. So that you can enter into relationships from a position of your own integrity, your own strength, and your own desire, as opposed to necessity for your survival.

KT: And not feel guilty for wanting to have the power to. There's nothing wrong with that and I think in some parts of the country, I think in some circles, women are made to feel like they're not a good Christian, or they're not a good woman, they're some liberal devil, if they want to have the power to. That they're not satisfied. They should be satisfied without having the power to.

GF: I say something like, "You made me feel blah, blah, blah ..." My husband will say, "I can't make you feel that way. Nobody can make you feel any way you don't wish to feel." That would be a part of my message. Which is, yes, things might happen that could make you feel a certain way, but it's ultimately your free will that determines if you will do that or not.

KT: Yes, don't buy into that manipulation, if that's what's going on.

GF: That's right. Exactly.

KT: So, Gloria, your book, *9 Ways Women Can Change How They Think about Power*, do you want to start giving some of these tips if we haven't touched on them already?

GF: The reason I wanted to give women very specific concrete tools and tips is because I think there are too many books that tell us what's wrong with us. Women can't, women don't, women shouldn't. I've been a practical activist all my life on the front lines, so I wanted not just to talk about why we have these issues, but to say, okay, so we have these issues, and here are some ways we can deal with them. I start with "Know Your History." Know your history and you can create the future of your choice. Women don't learn the history of the amazing women through the ages. The history books, by and large, have been written by men with men as the heroes and the protagonists. There have been many amazing women, so I think we should make women's history mandatory within all history classes, in elementary school and college.

KT: I hear you, sister! I believe that too!

GF: We need to tell those women's stories. If you know where you come from, then you have a better idea of where you might be able to go.

KT: That gives permission for women to stretch and grow and not be stuck in a little box that they grew up in.

GF: Yes. If you can't see it, then you can't be it. The second "power tool" is: "Define Your Own Terms." First, before someone else defines you. Who's the first person to raise their hand and say something in a meeting? If there are men and women, almost 80% of the time, it will be a man who will first start to talk. If you go to a lecture, who asks the first question? It's almost always a man. We are going to be defined. So if we don't say the first word, and define ourselves, somebody else is going to define us, and we might not like how they do it.

KT: That's like how feminism has gotten defined as this horrible thing.

GF: Exactly, and we shouldn't let that happen. It's exhausting sometimes to keep on getting out there and saying, this is who I am, this is where I stand, this is what I mean, and not do it in a defensive way. I tell this to women over and over and over again when I talk about communication skills to enable us to define our terms and get what we want. Use simple declarative sentences. Just say it and call it by name. State what you want. State who you are. There are seven other power tools; I don't know if you want to go through all of them.

KT: Let's do one or two more.

GF: Alright. Let me tell you one of my favorites. I love to talk about it in part because very often it's the one women recoil from the most: "Embrace Controversy." I believe that controversy is your friend. That if an issue is controversial it means it's important. It means that people are paying attention to you and that is the moment you have a platform. You can actually state your case. People are going to listen to you. Even if they disagree with you. Even if it causes conflict. And it's in that process of having that conflict that people have to think about and clarify their own values. I call it "the 7 Cs of Controversy." In that moment of conflict, of having to clarify their values, that change will happen. So, I teach women how to ride into the wave of controversy, use its energy to propel you forward instead of letting it frighten you and make you step back.

KT: So then, having said that, Gloria, do you think this controversy we've had for the last two years with Republicans going crazy trying to limit contraceptives and abortion, has it actually been a good thing?

GF: I think in the long run it is, and I say that because, remember I mentioned at the beginning of this show, I mentioned we go through these cycles. Well, I went through the same cycle about twenty years ago. And that's what happened. We stated our case and the majority of people overwhelmingly said it's not the government's business to tell people how many children to have, or how to decide when they're going to have children. So that's when we began a successful effort to get contraception covered by insurance plans. So today, they're having the same battle again. And I think it's because it's easy when you're not front and center in these debates, it's easy to step back and not keep being proactive. If you're being proactive, you're going to be pushed back. So, the simple answer to the question is, yes, it's very good there is this debate. It forces people to think about and clarify their values about issues. And you see women getting activated in a way they have not been activated for several years, and that's a good thing.

KT: But do you think it's going to be enough? I know women who are really worried that if things do not go Obama's way, or Democrats lose the White House and Senate, they're scared to death what legislation Republicans may pass moving forward in our country.

GF: You must take the fear and turn it into action. One of the things a young woman said – I learn so much from these young women I've had the chance to talk to – and one young woman put it this way: "Choose power over fear! Choose power over fear!"

KT: Yes!

GF: That's so smart. Yes, of course this is frightening, but don't let it frighten you. Use it as energy to take yourself forward and do what needs to be done. And what needs to be done is, instead of getting afraid of it and backing off, we need to be out there with ten times more legislation protecting women.

KT: Absolutely. Well, compared to twenty years ago, because I wasn't in it then, how do things compare now to then? Are more women activated? Are we being equally successful? Can you give listeners a barometer?

GF: There are a few different ways to look at it. This year, more women are running for Congress than ever before. That doesn't mean we're going to have 50% women in Congress, but it does tell you something. It says something about how activated women are. It takes a lot to go from, "I'm worried about what's happening in public policy" to, "I'm going to actually run for office." That's one barometer. Another barometer is we have seen people to be more willing to do some of the straightforward, front-line activism like carry a picket sign, go to town hall meetings and ask questions. This is important because those who are trying to keep progress from happening are always activated; they're zealous. The Progressive side – that has a hard time keeping its troops activated and motivated.

KT: Yes, I've said that many a time. We're just too "live and let live" – we don't have many zealots! (Laughing)

GF: Right. We're very tolerant. The whole point for us is we just want people to be able to live their lives and make their own decisions, but we can't afford not to be engaged. The economy is also forcing more people to have more egalitarian relationships and I think that makes a huge difference. Because if you have two people making the money, then you are eventually going to have two people participating in vacuuming, and in taking the kids to the dentist and all the things that routinely have to be done in a household. So, it subtly and slowly changes the power balance. That's more profound that it seems on the surface.

KT: Now if we could only get to the point where they are in Europe where men are expected to take six months off when they have a child. Both parents are expected to take off six months. Now there's some family values for ya! (Laughing)

GF: There's actually some valuing of families, isn't it? (Laughing)

KT: It's so crazy when you think about it. So many things. I just shake my head when I think of the perceptions of people in our country, so brainwashed and duped. So, any other tips you'd like to share with women, how they might start thinking about power? I wonder if we need more women in the media? I would like to see more women speaking to women's issues. I know Gloria Steinem and Jane Fonda tried to create that Women's Radio Network, but it fizzled. It seems like we need more women out there showing the way, especially women with Left and Progressive ideas.

GF: We definitely need more women in positions to decide what is a story and what isn't a story and how the story will be framed. We are seeing many more women's faces on the screen. We are seeing more women journalists. Women are actually the majority of journalism graduates now. More than in the majority in the newsroom, but they are very much in the minority in the people who lead the newsroom and the people who decide what the program is going to be. In the people who actually have the clout positions in media companies that decide what the whole narrative is going to be.

I'm delighted that you mentioned the Women's Media Center. You're right that Gloria and Jane and some other women tried to create a women's radio network that did not fly; however, the non-profit arm of that endeavor, which is called the Women's Media Center, is not only alive and well, but it's really thriving. One of the things that we do – I'm on the board – is what we call pitching a fit, so when there is sexism in the media, we go after it. We were a big force behind getting Don Imus off the air. We were a big force behind getting many of Rush Limbaugh's sponsors to bail out on him. We go after them even if they're Progressive. Ed Schultz said something that was quite sexist and we went after him. He apologized on the air. We have a campaign called Name It, Change It in collaboration with the Women's Campaign Fund and we're tracking political media, which is really the worst. We all remember how Hillary Clinton was treated. Her ankles, her voice, her laugh, her cleavage.

KT: I think the latest was how she wasn't wearing make-up.

GF: Yes. Or I cross my legs when she comes into the room. That sort of thing. It was pretty awful. So, we watch out for all those things and we take action. We organize people to take action and it works.

KT: What about the Fox News women? The Dr. Laura kind of women. Are they part of this news organization? Or are they separate and apart?

GF: That's a great question and I'm glad to clarify. No, I don't think they'd want to be caught within ten feet of the Women's Media Center. Women's Media Center will defend any woman. If Dr. Laura, if someone said a sexist remark about Dr. Laura, I'm sure we would leap to her defense, but, when it comes to the way she herself denigrates women, or denigrates women who want to be equal in this world, we certainly would not support that. It is a very Progressive organization.

KT: Gloria, it's been so much fun talking to you. I wonder if there is anything you want to share with listeners I have not thought to ask?

GF: I'd love to tell people I'd love to carry on the conversation further with them if they're interested and we can do that by them either coming to my website, GloriaFeldt.com, or social media. My blog is called Heartfeldt. I love to have people come and tell me what they think about what I write or suggest things to me. I can be found on social media @Gloria Feldt on Twitter. I'm on Facebook and LinkedIn as Gloria Feldt too, and I value the interchange with people. I'd love to know if people have read *No Excuses*, what they think, if they have another power tool to add to the list, so we can share it with other women.

I also invite anyone interested in knowing more about my new organization, Take The Lead, to visit www.taketheleadwomen.com and find us on social media: @takeleadwomen on Twitter, and Take The Lead Women on Facebook and LinkedIn. Together we are going to get women to leadership parity by 2025.

KT: Okay! Well, thank you so very much for your time. I really appreciate it and it makes me feel better knowing you're out there!

GF: Likewise. Likewise. By the way, I was looking at your website and I was looking at some of the things that you talk about and I wanted to let you know that my next book is going to have a lot to do with Lilith. So, she is my Goddess of choice. I've been photographed in my Lilith persona. So we'll have to talk about that sometime in the future.

KT: Most definitely! Thank you for that little tidbit. I appreciate knowing about that and I look forward to it.

Part IV

Rebirthing the Sacred Feminine
Sacred Activism

All truth passes through three stages. First, it is ridiculed. Second, it is violently opposed. Third, it is accepted as being self-evident.
– Arthur Schopenhauer

Chapter 32

My Prayer: Let Women Be Priests*

by Fr. Roy Bourgeois

After serving as a Roman Catholic priest for forty years, I was expelled from the priesthood in November 2013 because of my public support for the ordination of women.

Catholic priests say that the call to be a priest comes from God. As a young priest, I began to ask myself and my fellow priests: "Who are we, as men, to say that our call from God is authentic, but God's call to women is not?" Isn't our all-powerful God, who created the cosmos, capable of empowering a woman to be a priest?

Let's face it. The problem is not with God, but with an all-male clerical culture that views women as lesser than men. Though I am not optimistic, I pray that the newly elected Pope Francis will rethink this antiquated and unholy doctrine.

I am 74 years old. I first felt God calling me to be a priest when I was serving in the Navy in Vietnam. I was accepted into the Maryknoll Fathers and Brothers in New York and was ordained in 1972. After working with the poor of Bolivia for five years, I returned to the United States. In my years of ministry, I met many devout Catholic women who told me about their calling to the priesthood.

Their eagerness to serve God began to keep me awake at night. As Catholics, we are taught that men and women are created equal: "There is neither male or female. In the Christ you are one" (Galatians 3:28).

While Christ did not ordain any priests himself, as the Catholic scholar Garry Wills has pointed out in a controversial new book, the last two popes, John Paul II and Benedict XVI,

299

stressed that the all-male priesthood is "our tradition" and that men and women are equal, but have different roles.

Their reasons for barring women from ordination bring back memories of my childhood in Louisiana. For twelve years I attended segregated schools and worshipped in a Catholic church that reserved the last five pews for blacks. We justified our prejudice by saying this was "our tradition" and that we were "separate but equal." During all those years, I cannot remember one white person – not a teacher, parent, priest or student (myself included) – who dared to say, "There is a problem here, and it's called racism."

Where there is injustice, silence is complicity. What I have witnessed is a grave injustice against women, my church and our God, who called both men and women to be priests. I could not be silent. Sexism, like racism, is a sin. And no matter how hard we may try to justify discrimination against others, in the end, it is not the way of a loving God who created everyone of equal worth and dignity.

In sermons and talks, starting in the last decade, I called for the ordination of women. I even participated in the ordination of one. This poked the beehive of church patriarchy. In the fall of 2008, I received a letter from the Vatican stating that I was "causing grave scandal" in the Church and that I had thirty days to recant my public support for the ordination of women or I would be excommunicated.

Last month, in announcing his resignation, Pope Benedict said he made his decision after examining his conscience before God. In a similar fashion, in November 2008, I wrote the Vatican saying that human conscience is sacred because it always urges us to do what is right and what is just. And after examining my conscience before God, I could not repudiate my beliefs.

Four years went by, and I did not get a response from the Vatican. Though I had formally been excommunicated, I remained a priest with my Maryknoll Order and went about my ministry calling for gender equality in the Catholic Church. But last November, I received a telephone call from Maryknoll headquarters informing me that they had received an official letter from the Vatican. The letter said that I had been expelled from the priesthood and the Maryknoll community.

This phone call was one of the most difficult and painful moments of my life. But I have come to realize that what I have gone through is but a glimpse of what women in the Church and in society have experienced for centuries.

A *New York Times/CBS* poll this month reported that 70% of Catholics in the United States believe that Pope Francis should allow women to be priests. In the midst of my sorrow and sadness, I am filled with hope, because I know that one day women in my church will be ordained – just as those segregated schools and churches in Louisiana are now integrated.

I have but one simple request for our new pope. I respectfully ask that he announce to the 1.2 billion Catholics around the world: "For many years we have been praying for God to send us more vocations to the priesthood. Our prayers have been answered. Our loving God, who created us equal, is calling women to be priests in our Church. Let us welcome them and give thanks to God."

* *Article previously published in* The New York Times, *March 20, 2013*

About Roy Bourgeois …

Roy Bourgeois was born in Lutcher, Louisiana in 1938. He graduated from the University of Louisiana with a degree in Geology, then spent four years in the military. He received the Purple Heart in Vietnam. From the military, Roy entered the Maryknoll Order and was ordained a Catholic priest in 1972. He worked with the poor in Bolivia for five years, where he was arrested for his work in human rights and forced to leave the country.

Back in the US Roy became an outspoken critic of US foreign policy in Latin America. In 1990 he founded the School of Americas (SOA) Watch. Roy has spent over four years in federal prisons for his nonviolent protests against the SOA. In 1995, he produced a documentary film about the School of Americas called *School of Assassins*, which received an Academy Award Nomination. In 1997, he received the Pax Christi USA Teacher of Peace Award. In 2010, Roy was nominated for the Nobel Peace Prize.

In 2012, after serving as a Roman Catholic priest for forty years, Roy was expelled from the priesthood because of his public support for the ordination of women. Roy continues his work for peace, justice and equality and travels extensively, giving talks at universities, churches and groups around the US and abroad. He is the author of *My Journey from Silence to Solidarity*.

For more information contact: SOA Watch, PO Box 3330, Columbus, GA 31903

Websites:

www.roybourgeoisjourney.org

www.soaw.org

Chapter 33

Sexist God-talk:
Reforming Christian Language

by Jeanette Blonigen Clancy

I like what Shug in *The Color Purple* by Alice Walker tells Celie, a victim of incest: "Whenever you try to pray and man plop himself on the other end of it, tell him to get lost."

She explains to Celie that God in traditional churches is a white man's god. "God ain't a he or a she, but a It."

While the US military and other sectors are finally held more accountable for sexual misconduct, religion is still let off the hook for its key role in causing the worldwide abuse of females – sexist God-talk. Clergy no longer commit sexual assaults with impunity, but their God-talk continues to train minds in gender abuse, whether or not that is intended. As a Catholic who remains in the Church, I write to provoke greater awareness of its sexism and thus help to minimize sexism in the wider culture.

"God the Father," which dominates Christian language, reduces the Source/Creator of all reality to a male idol in the sky. His image arose from Yahweh in the Hebrew Scriptures, a set of books revered by the two largest religions in the world, Christianity and Islam. This God-image unavoidably trains people to imagine women inferior to men. It describes male power as natural, normal, proper, and right, making female power seem unnatural, abnormal, improper, and wrong. In this way the Christian "Lord" along with the ubiquitous drumbeat of "HeHimHis" promotes male domination and therefore gender abuse.

I consider sexist God-talk to be the most serious sin against society perpetrated by the institutional Church. In its scope and long-term damage, it is even more dangerous than clerical sex abuse because the latter developed as a consequence of worshipping a Supreme Being imagined exclusively male. Compounding the damage is the Christian tradition's sin emphasis, the conditioned belief that this all-powerful individual looks for and punishes transgressions "against Him." Indirectly, but effectively, the dominant male god invoked in churches endorses violence against women and other vulnerable people.

It should be obvious that the exclusively male image of God contributes to systemic and casual acceptance of women as subordinate and submissive, answerable to men who set the rules and make decisions. The imagined god directs females to assume a subservient attitude, as comes through clearly in Ephesians 5:22–23, which used to be a favorite reading at weddings: "Wives should be submissive to their husbands as if to the Lord because the husband is head of the wife, just as Christ is head of his body the church as well as its savior" (NAB).

The attitude appears more poignantly in the statement of the victim who said sincerely, ". . . if the wife is truly disobedient, then of course her husband has to beat her" (quoted in *Half the Sky* by Nicholas Kristof and Sheryl WuDunn). This mindset encourages husbands to bully their wives, men and adolescent boys to sexually assault women and girls without feeling guilty, and pimps to profit by selling females. It is impossible to deny the connection between worship of the male God image and worldwide abuse of females. Theologian Mary Daly said it best: "If God is male, then male is God."

In fact, the male god promotes all types of inequality by establishing hierarchy and domination as the essential, even sacred, structure of the universe. Steadily, incessantly, God-He talk in churches drips into minds, insidiously planting inequality and domination as the primary frame of human relationship, of all relationships – humans with each other, with Divine Source, with animals, with the earth. And, significantly, it provides the frame for clericalism, which motivates bishops to protect, not the victims of sexual abuse, but their own clerical, institutional status and privilege.

"Lord" and "Father" are not the worst. It is the pronouns "HeHimHis" that do the most damage by dripping into our minds without notice. Being the least explicit, they are the most difficult to challenge. Their steady, sly entry into our thoughts and imaginations, without our conscious awareness, plants the belief that male power is natural, normal, proper, and right. Male power is accepted; female power is not. Women who dare to take charge get labels like "Bitch."

Women politicians and business leaders are held to a standard different from male politicians. We have all – women and men – suffered deep psychological damage from language that reduces the unfathomable Mystery of All Reality to a humanlike individual of a certain gender. The Western world certainly contributed to global misconceptions with this God image. How powerfully our minds have been conditioned shows in the statement of a theologian who was trying to correct the mistaken perception. He tripped over it instead when he wrote, "God is not male; He is a spirit."

Catholicism actually forbids reverence for female images of the Divine, which would subvert the domination of the male god. Every reference to Divinity is kept strictly masculine – by Vatican decree and a dead tradition incapable of adapting to new insights. As a consequence, we are directed into idolatry – worship of an idol, a particular, imagined deity. We are commanded by Rome to ignore what we know and to identify the highest value of all existence, the author of gender, as exclusively male.

The effect of sexist God-talk is illustrated by what happened after I wrote this opinion in the *St. Cloud Times* in Minnesota. A woman reader protested and insisted that God "is a father, not a mother." For her, "God the Father" had become a definition of the Indefinable. She did not realize that "God" cannot be limited to any particular description. "Father" is only one image alongside thousands of diverse images in sacred literature, including female images in the Bible. A Catholic religious sister, on the other hand, showed her understanding that language shapes minds with this response to one of my blog posts: "It is indeed a male's world, a male's Bible, a male's theology and sexuality. Thanks for sharing your corrective insights."

Male bias rules so pervasively our theology and manner of speech that I observe well-meaning Christians wanting to, but incapable of cleaning up the sexist language. Here I offer suggestions for shrinking the power of "the Lord" and retraining our imaginations to accept the Divine Feminine. I found an appropriate vehicle for naming The Holy in new ways by participating in a vibrant movement – Roman Catholic Womenpriests (RCWP).

RCWP is a renewal movement in the Catholic Church that began in 2002 with the ordination of seven women in Germany on the Danube River. It arose during the long, oppressive papacy of John Paul II who reversed Vatican II reforms. One outgrowth of the Vatican Council was the expectation and widespread acceptance of women's ordination. John Paul stopped this momentum toward women priests by declaring in 1994 "that the Church has no authority whatsoever to confer priestly ordination on women and that this judgment is to be definitively held by all the Church's faithful."

Bishop Patricia Fresen, a Roman Catholic nun and Doctor of Theology, lived and taught theology in South Africa, where she witnessed its transformation by Nelson Mandela. As Mandela opened his country's eyes, and the world's eyes, to the racism of apartheid, she made the connection with sexism in the Church, an identical system of pervasive injustice. She illuminates the parallels between sexism and racism, and by extension, all oppressive systems: "Both racism and sexism give all power and privilege to one group of people to the exclusion of the other group. Both racism and sexism are horrendous systems of injustice."

While in Europe, Fresen learned about Catholic women priests and was profoundly stirred. Invited to be ordained, she responded with awed humility and consented to be ordained a Roman Catholic priest because, she said, "We learnt, in the apartheid years, that sometimes the best or even the only possible way to change an unjust law is to break it."

Then a male bishop persuaded her to be ordained a bishop by explaining that the RCWP movement needed women bishops to assure its continuation. Fresen joins others in the women's movement to teach us the connection between all systems of oppression.

RCWP has become the most effective challenge to sexism in the Catholic Church, as we can see from the Vatican's panicked retaliation against women's ordination under John Paul – defining it as one of the most grievous sins, excommunicating those who participate, and persecuting Catholic leaders who publicly support it. Its danger to the present power structure can be measured by the reactions it incites in Catholic officials. The excommunications, condemnations, and ludicrous arguments for male-only ordination amuse me because they speak so loudly about the movement's effectiveness. The RCWP movement motivates me to stay in the Church by providing a way to actively oppose its oppressive power structure.

I meet Christians who are not offended by God-talk loaded with lords and male pronouns. They think they're not affected, but I believe those least aware are most harmed. I invite them to imagine the effect on us of regularly praying to "the Lord." Could anyone imagine that it refers to a female? Could it bring a feeling of speaking to a wise, understanding, and compassionate grandma or mom? Many think "Father" is a nice image. But then, why not mix it with "Mother"? Like this:

God our Mother knows our needs. We are hidden in the secrecy of Her protection. She surrounds us constantly with Her love, Her wisdom and Her mercy. When troubles assail us, we turn to Holy Mother God.

If this sounds wrong, it signals conditioning to think God is male.

The Bible has a wealth of God-images that Christian churches never use: mother, midwife, homemaker, she-bear, mother eagle, sun, rock, fire, breath. Exclusive use of male images for God created an imagined deity in the sky and a thousands-of-years-old bias in our minds.

At our Womanpriest Masses, congregants hear evolved spiritual understandings from diverse religious traditions. We interfere with the imagined he-god by cleaning up the language. To replace "Blessed is He who comes in the name of the Lord," we say, "Blessed is One who comes in the name of God." The same can be done for all "He who" and "Lord" constructions. We say a creed adapted from one by Joan Chittester, OSB, beginning:

We believe in one God who made us all and infuses all of life with the sacred.

We believe in the multiple revelations of God, alive in every human heart.

We believe in Jesus Christ, who leads us to the fullness of humanity, to what we are meant to become ...

Our bishop invokes "our brother Jesus." The first time I heard it, relief and joy rose in me because I don't believe Jesus is God or that his death saved the world. I write the Intercessions for our Masses and strive to nudge our congregation toward larger understandings, for example,

For religions to transcend their doctrinal descriptions of spiritual reality and embrace Truth larger than we can imagine, we pray.

We sing a beautiful song written by Juliana Howard:

God our Mother, come to me.
Lift me up so tenderly.
Rock me, rock me, on your knee.
Mother, come to me.

We sing songs in honor of Sophia, the Greek word for WISDOM, who forms the model for the God-image Jesus Christ in the Gospel of John (according to the eminent theologian Raymond Brown). WISDOM literature appears in the books of Proverbs, Sirach, Wisdom, and Baruch. She speaks in long discourses in a voice similar to Jesus' voice:

The person who finds me finds life. (Prov. 8:35)
I have been from everlasting, in the beginning, before the world began. (Prov. 8:23)

More ways to disrupt the god of Christian imagination come from Sister Lucy Edelbeck, OP, who makes greeting cards:

WOMAN said, This is my body. This is my blood.
May God smile/ May SHE bless you.

Sister Mary Lou emailed this meditative response to a writing of mine: "I find it fascinating that our Beloved Source is NO THING, and ALL IN ALL, as well as VOID and FULLNESS OF BEING." Such appreciation of true Transcendence comes from awareness of sexist God-talk. Those of us still in the Christian tradition can reform it by taking every opportunity to subvert the he-god's control of the Christian imagination.

Let's clean up our God-talk and help to overturn immoral power structures around the globe.

About Jeanette Blonigen Clancy ...

Jeanette Blonigen Clancy speaks and writes as a Christian urging fellow Christians to expand their horizon. Despite being steeped in Catholic culture from grade school to grad school to the present, she does not believe Jesus is God or the savior of the world. In her books, articles, letters, talks, and blog, she vigorously critiques religious beliefs that clash with contemporary awareness, and she focuses on the psychological damage done by the patriarchy on both women and men.

She is the author of *Albany: The Heart of Minnesota* (1991); *Nestled Between Lakes and Wooded Hills: The Centennial History of the Avon Area* (2000); *God Is Not Three Guys in the Sky: Cherishing Christianity without Its Exclusive Claims* (2007); and the essay "Taming Testosterone" in the anthology *The Rule of Mars: Readings on the Origins, History and Impact of Patriarchy* (2005). For quotations from Jeanette's writings, see *She Lives! Wisdom Works in the World* by Jann Aldredge-Clanton.

Website: http://godisnot3guys.com

Blog: http://godisnot3guyscom-jeanette.blogspot.com

Chapter 34

Cosmic Christ and the New Humanity

by Matthew Fox

So much is pressing in on us from so many sides today. As I say, we are in the dark night of our species. Rabbi Heschel used to say we shouldn't just talk about the dark night of the soul but the dark night of society. But I think our whole species today is in a dark night, and a dark night as the mystics teach. This is not a bad place to be. It's an uncomfortable place to be, but it is a school of wisdom. We have to learn something here at this time in history, profound for our species, if our species is to survive and if we are to allow other species to continue to flourish as well.

So we're talking about a new humanity, and what might this begin to look like? Where are the seeds all around us to grow us at this time? Well, Thomas Berry puts it this way, and I think this is very, what should I say, encouraging, almost optimistic, at a time such as we live in today. He says "the dark periods of history are the creative periods." Let me say it again: "The dark periods of history are the creative periods; for these are the times when new ideas, arts, and institutions can be brought into being at the most basic level." So in other words, this cusp of the dark night of the soul, of the via negativa, is where also, the doors are opening up for all kinds of creativity across the board – in religion, in politics, in economics, in education, in journalism and media.

In other words, a time like ours is a time to go deep and to redirect the basic principles by which we've been living on this planet, by which we've been doing religion and so much else at this time. So I find that very encouraging, really, that a dark time like this is also an opening to a breakthrough. And that's what I think my Christ Path Seminar is about.

So we've been gifted, our generation, with the culmination of this quest for the historical Jesus, and it's very, very useful information. But it's not enough. The historical Jesus is only one of the wings on which the Christian tradition flies. The other wing is that of the Cosmic Christ and mysticism. And that wing has been especially undervalued for centuries. As Theodore Roszak says, the Enlightenment held mysticism up for ridicule as the worst offense against science and reason. So mystics have felt, what should I say, peculiar – they had to hide in the closet – for centuries in our churches, and so forth. But now is the time to bring this other dimension forward, and for lots of reasons.

Now, the key, I think, to this resurrection at this time is to recover the mystical dimension to our lives and to our communities, to the Christ path. The mystical tradition is calling us wherever we go.

Now then, I want to turn to the subject of mysticism. And of course, in the Western tradition, the archetype of mysticism is the Cosmic Christ. That's the archetype, it's the metaphor, it's the succinct way of talking about mysticism. And remember that the mystic is the prelude to the prophet. The prophet is the mystic in action.

But now, what are some of the understandings of mysticism? First of all, I want to remind you that we'll never have a perfect definition of mysticism because the left brain does definitions and the right brain is mystical, it's intuitive. And so it doesn't totally add up, so there's no one definition.

Dr. Howard Thurman, one of the great mystics of North America, who was the spiritual genius behind the civil rights movement, points out the multiple experiences of unity. That's mysticism: multiple experiences of unity. Mysticism is our unitive experiences – when you feel one with being, one with others, one with yourself, one with God. But notice, multiple experiences of unity. This isn't something that happens once in your lifetime. Meister Eckhart says for the person who is awake, breakthrough does not happen once a year, once a month, once a week or once a day, but many times every day. That's the promise of the mystic, which is all of us.

If you're going to renew religion, you've got to return to experience. Buddha experienced something under the Bodhi tree; Muhammad experienced something with the creating of the Quran; Isaiah, Jeremiah, all the prophets experienced what they were preaching about, and of course Jesus too. And that's what mysticism is. It's about experience. As the Psalmist says, taste and see that God is good. You've got to taste – no one can taste for you. No Pope can taste for you, no preacher can taste for you. They can awaken, but you've got to do it.

Now, Teilhard de Chardin, who of course was a scientist, a Jesuit, a mystic, and a poet, he came up with the name the Cosmic Christ – he was the second person to use it. Now, he died in 1955, so this is fifty years old at least. And the Cosmic Christ, then, is about the divine Presence, the divine Image found in every being in the universe – in every whale, in every tree, in every forest, every lion, tiger, polar bear, human, galaxy, supernova, planet, and atom. It's a macrocosm and it's a microcosm. And it is a reminder of the sacredness of all being.

Now, I wrote a book on the Cosmic Christ twenty-five years ago this year. And I once was lecturing, and a woman came up afterwards and she said, "I just loved your book on the Cosmic Christ – it changed my life for sure." She said, "I loved it so much I've read it twice. I just have one question."

I said, "What's that?"

She said, "What's the Cosmic Christ?"

That's a humble moment for an author, you know. But actually I've had a long time to think about that exchange, and I realized actually it's a compliment – that I didn't put the Cosmic Christ in a definition, in a box. I kept it in the area of experience. And so you have to tell me what your experience of the Cosmic

Christ [is], you have to paint it for me, dance it for me, sing it for me, make poetry for me.

I had a dream years ago that's been absolutely primal in my whole life since. And there was one clear sentence in the dream, and it said this: "There is nothing wrong with the human species today except one thing." Wow, is that good news – just one thing is wrong with us. "You have forgotten the sense of the sacred." That's what the dream said. And that's what the Cosmic Christ is all about: it's about bringing back the sense of the sacred, the holiness that is in all things.

Now you know what the Cosmic Christ is: it's the holiness in all being. And once you know this, everything changes, and your energy comes back, our energy comes back.

Mary Oliver says there is only one question – how to love the world. The mystic is a lover, folks. That's as simple a definition as you can get. The mystic in you is the lover in you. And we live in an anthropocentric culture that talks about falling in love and finding a mate, you know, until death do you part. But folks, there's a lot more to fall in love with than your mate. We fall in love with wildflowers, we fall in love with poetry, we fall in love with music, we fall in love with forests, with tigers, with animals, with beings of all kinds. We fall in love with friends and ideas. And, you know, this world is a banquet of lovability! And we're starving, and we stuff ourselves with more booze and more addictions to television and more football and more this and more that. Now, I like all these things – I like football. But there's a limit to it. And we have to go through these processes of purification of our love, and that too is part of the, a very big part of the via negativa, of the dark night.

Now, in winding up this opening meditation on "Our New Humanity," I want to talk kind of concretely about those who are in communities, whether those communities be parishes, whether these communities be Base communities that you're starting up, or whether you're just waiting for an inspiration about what really will be your connection, whether the community be your family or extended family. I just want to ask the question: What is a parish? What is a caring community? What does a community do for us and we for the community?

I try to distill, and I'm saying there are two things involved in any healthy community. And that is, it turns out lovers – it turns out mystics, the mystic in every person. That's what a healthy community in the spirit of the Christ path is doing. And secondly, it turns out prophets – that is to say, spiritual warriors. The mystic says yes, the prophet says no. The prophet, as Rabbi Heschel says, interferes with that which is interfering with the glory, the sacredness of life – that which is crucifying the Christ all over again.

And we have to get over this thing that Jesus died on the cross. Rainforests are dying on the cross, polar bears are dying on the cross. You know, let's get into 2012. All the sins of the world did not happen at the hands of the Roman Empire 2,000 years ago. There's a lot happening at the hands of the Wall Street empire, the American empire, and other empires of our day. And it's all part of burning down denial to see this appropriately.

And one more point: Thomas Aquinas said – and he had a pre-modern consciousness, you see, which is closer to indigenous consciousness than modern consciousness – he said Revelation comes in two volumes: the Bible and nature. So much of modern religion, modern Christianity, has been all Bible-oriented because, of course, the modern era began with the invention of the printing press. The Bible was printed, which was great, disseminated great stuff. But it's so text-oriented. We must get back to this pre-modern consciousness that nature itself is revealing the divine to us on a daily basis. And this is the Wisdom tradition of Israel, which is the tradition of Jesus. All the scholars today agree he comes from that tradition. It's not the tradition of the biblical book – it's the tradition of the sacredness of nature.

And I say we have to exegete – that means to study hard – not just the Bible book but nature itself. And for that we need scientists. Scientists are the exegetes of nature. But it's not enough to study just nature – we have to study human nature, psychology. We have to exegete human nature. Thirdly, we have to exegete human culture – art. I called on Mary Oliver today to teach us who the Cosmic Christ really is. We have to call on our artists, our filmmakers, our poets, our dramatists, our painters and the rest, and our musicians, to assist us to exegete the revelation that human nature is and human culture is.

It is this broad opening of our hearts to the sacredness of this journey, this 13.6-billion-year journey, that is staring us in the face, and that is inviting us with joy, with promise, with hope, to start over – to start over. And that's what I hope we can do together in our time together here in this program, the Christ Path Seminar.

About Matthew Fox ...

Matthew Fox is a spiritual theologian, an Episcopal priest and an activist. As a spiritual theologian he has written 32 books that have been translated into over 40 languages. Among them are *Original Blessing, The Coming of the Cosmic Christ, A Spirituality Named Compassion, The Reinvention of Work, The Hidden Spirituality of Men, Christian Mystics* and *The Pope's War*. He has contributed much to the rediscovery of Hildegard of Bingen, Meister Eckhart and Thomas Aquinas as pre-modern mystics and prophets. Fox holds a doctorate in the history and theology of spirituality from the Institut Catholique de Paris. The founder of the University of Creation Spirituality in California, he conducts dozens of workshops each year and is a visiting scholar at the Academy for the Love of Learning.

Website: www.MatthewFox.org

Chapter 35

The Gaia Project:
Renewal of Ancient Mysteries

by Carl A.P. Ruck

The ancient testimony about the religious experience offered to thousands of pilgrims in the sanctuary of the Goddess in the tiny village of Elefsina (Eleusis) some ten miles west of the great city of Athens is unanimous. The Homeric Hymn to Demeter declares that it was essential to the art of living:

> Whoever among men who walk the earth has seen these Mysteries is blessed, but whoever is uninitiated and has not received his share of the rite, he will not have the same lot as the others, once he is dead and dwells in the mold where the sun goes down.

The rite was performed annually for 2,000 years, beginning in the mid-second millennium BCE, in roughly the same place, modified and enlarged over the course of time to accommodate the ever-growing number of participants. Construction of the sanctuary obliterated the archaeological record of the earlier occupation of the site, but it is probable that it was sacred from Neolithic times, if not before. The rite as practiced through the Classical and Roman periods represents a transition from female dominance to an accommodation with patriarchal traditions.

In the sixth century BCE, it passed under Athenian control and became the defining influence that produced the mentality that characterized the Classical Age, which became the fountainhead of ensuing European civilization. Almost everyone of importance, as well as the common man and woman, foreigner and Greek alike of every status in society, sought out the initiation at least once in a lifetime. In the Roman period, the orator and philosopher Cicero declared it the greatest gift of Athens to the world, the essential impetus for humankind's elevation from savagery, imparting the power not only to live with joy, but also to die with better hope.

The paradigm uniting life and death was the seed implanted into the ground, entrusted to the darkness of the earth, in the expectation that it would return and sprout, without which there could be no life here in the realm above. What the initiates experienced was a journey of the spirit to a reality in a parallel dimension, establishing pathways of communication and rights of friendly reciprocal visitation, so that life was nourished by the accord or testament that defined the terms for humankind's relationship to Gaia. It was more than a mere metaphor. The initiates were offered the opportunity to identify themselves with the cycles of nature at the deepest level of their existence.

I was a member of a team in the 1970s that sought to uncover what actually happened in the sanctuary, for the initiates were sworn to secrecy and the event was termed a mystery. I revisited the topic in the 1990s and summarized our findings and subsequent research. When I asked my colleague, the Swiss chemist Albert Hofmann, shortly before his death at the age of 102 to provide a comment, even if only a sentence, in view of his frailty, he wrote: "Only a new Eleusis could help mankind to survive the threatening catastrophe in Nature and human society and bring a new period of happiness."

Elefsina is a place particularly blessed by Nature, a fertile plain bounded by mountain ranges surrounding the acropolis. The initiation hall was carved from the rock face of its southern slope, an architectural similitude of a subterranean cavern, and marked as sacred by its alignment to the depression between the twin peaks called the "Horns" (*Kerata*) that terminate the mountain to the west. Such alignment is typical of other Minoan and Pelasgian religious sites and identified the sanctuary by a sexual metaphor as the entrance, nestled between the breasts and spread legs of the Goddess, to the secrets that lay within her body. It was here in the surrounding plain that barley, the grain plant that was the staff of life, first sprouted. The place was further blessed topographically by the island of Salamis that lies nearby along its shore, providing a superlative nearly land-locked shelter for ships in its bay. Most people know of it from the account of the Battle of Salamis, when the Athenian admiral in charge of the allied fleet used his knowledge of the lay of the land to his advantage against the vastly superior forces of the invading Persian King Xerxes.

Eleusis was named like Elysium, a mirror of the paradisiacal fields (*Les champs Élysées*) that received the dead upon their arrival in the otherworld. It was sacred to the Goddess and her daughter, the two holy females, the "Mother" and the "Maiden," who could be ascribed names, after the patriarchal revision that established the Mystery, as Demeter and Persephone, although more sacredly, they were just the two nameless goddesses (*tó theó*), interchangeable as mother produced daughter and daughter in turn became mother. The male essential for their replication was the personification of the joyous shout of the initiates as they walked in procession to the place of arrival, *Iacchus* – a pun upon the deity of the ecstatic possession necessary to access the mystery, Dionysus/Bacchus, the god of wine and intoxicants. He was identical here with Hades, the lord of the netherworld, named as the "unseen one," which was also the name for the invisible realm to which the living disappeared for their arrival.

A third female shadowed the personae of two goddesses, the post-menopausal nursing mother, who went by the dread name of Hecate, the patroness of witchcraft, but all three roles were interchangeable, since the mother could become the wet-nurse of the daughter's child, and it was this third that joined the two holy ladies into a triumphant trinity. The mystery of the seed reborn was personified as the son born from the holy trinity, which had the mystery title of *Brimo*, the terrible queenship. He was their child, named after them – according to matriarchal custom – as *Brimos*, but he had another less frightful name befitting the benevolence of this trinity as the "triple warrior," *Triptolemos*. It was he who was entrusted with the art of living and he planted the first crop in the surrounding *Rarian* fields. He was the pacified antithesis to the toxic analogues of his parentage, life born from death. The initiates on the night of the great Mystery rematerialized in the cavernous hall of the sanctuary, after their spiritual journey, at the moment of his miraculous birth. They experienced themselves reborn, like him, a child conceived and born from death. The valence of death became positive through personal experience, and the lord Hades was recognized as a handsome youth of "good counsel" (*Eubouleus*) and as the source of prosperity (*Ploutos*) in both this real realm and the next.

These blessings and the prosperity of the Eleusinian plain were also an invitation to abuse its natural gifts after the desecration of the sanctuary and the supplanting of its religion by the modern world. It is today a microcosm for the destruction that has spread around the planet – the catastrophe that looms, threatening continued human existence. The bay of Salamis is clogged with tankers waiting to offload their cargo of crude oil to the mainland refineries that belch an air-polluting stench. The plain has dried into a desert that supports little agriculture. In addition to the refineries, two other industries process material wealth ravished from the earth, a cement factory and a foundry for iron. The symbolism could not be more obvious.

Few people now visit the sanctuary, or know of the ancient Mystery. Elefsina is not in the register of places recognized as a world heritage site, even though it was the center of a religion practiced for two millennia. The inadequate museum dates from the nineteenth century, and several of its treasures have been substituted with replicas. An effort is underway to improve the situation. The superhighway to Corinth now skirts the site, and the progressive local governments have worked to restore the village, with the streets around the sanctuary converted into pedestrian malls. The shore is planted with parklands and the sea is again clean enough for swimming. A large area of ruined and abandoned nineteenth-century factories adjacent to the sanctuary and below the present museum has been converted into a center for workshops and galleries for the display of art and theatrical performances.

We espouse this motto for the endeavor: "The Future Starts Here." As the place most desecrated for its abuse of Gaia, we propose that Elefsina become the nucleus and world center for humankind's renegotiation of its compact with its planet Earth. To this end, we are seeking recognition of the village and the archaeological remains as a world heritage site and the soliciting of funding from international and Greek donors to build a new museum complex, incorporating the area and some of the abandoned industrial ruins that now comprise the art center. The symbolism is simple. We do not propose to restore a defunct religion or to reverse the course of time, but to begin anew with a new contract with Gaia. To this end, the existing refineries, foundry, and cement factory cannot be removed, since they would merely have to reappear elsewhere. As in antiquity, we depend on the bounty of Gaia for prosperity.

The museum complex would be multifunctional. One of its tasks would be to investigate ways of mitigating the deleterious effects of exploiting natural resources. Industrial constructions are actually works of extraordinary complexity and ingenuity. At the new Elefsina, they will learn to operate cleanly, and surrounded by parklands they can be seen as monuments, gigantic sculptural testimony, functioning efficiently and beautiful, as their modern designers conceived them. An analogue is the way that the Mexican city of Monterrey proudly incorporates its disused factories from the nineteenth century into its cultural identity as works of art.

In addition to furthering research into the past and the study of the Eleusinian Mystery through seminars and conferences, the museum complex will look to the future. Among the sponsored activities will be investigations into rediscovering a personal commitment to Gaia through techniques of meditation, spiritual exercise, alternative medicine, and artist workshops. The center would also support research into environmental remediation and new sources of energy and safe methods of tapping the planet's gifts.

Eventually we hope to see agriculture return to the Rarian plain, and make the museum a destination of pilgrimage again for the modern world.

About Carl A.P. Ruck ...

Carl A.P. Ruck is Professor of Classics at Boston University, and an authority on the ecstatic rituals of the god Dionysus. With the ethno-mycologist R. Gordon Wasson and Albert Hofmann, he identified the secret psychoactive ingredient in the visionary potion that was drunk by the initiates at the Eleusinian Mystery. In *Persephone's Quest: Entheogens and the Origins of Religion*, he proclaimed the centrality of psychoactive sacraments at the very beginnings of religion, employing the neologism "entheogen" to free the topic from the pejorative connotations for words like drug or hallucinogen.

Chapter 36

Gaian Interconnectivity and the Future of Public Myth

by Professor Andrew Gurevich

If we surrendered to earth's intelligence we could rise up rooted, like trees.

Instead we entangle ourselves in knots of our own making and struggle, lonely and confused. So like children, we begin again.

– Rainer Maria Rilke

I remember our time together quite fondly, Karen. *Voices of the Sacred Feminine* was the very first radio interview I'd ever done and, my goodness, did we cover a lot of ground! Essentially, I had two primary points to make. And I feel like we covered them well as we weaved an empathetic web of Gaian interconnectivity and quantum entanglements!

First, I wanted to discuss how new findings in neuropsychology, evolutionary biology, hemispheric science and consciousness studies are revealing that the "Goddess" can be understood as an ancient, neuro-spiritual "technology." The personification of the synergistic union of the brain's creative and critical faculties, she emerges when we put our logic in service of our intuition. This research suggests that the Goddess represents the reunification of the sensibilities; the visceral, interconnected, energetic web that is the source of thought itself. Our wisdom body, manifest.

For millennia the "founding fathers" of Western philosophy, theology and science have insisted on maintaining an epistemological wall between mind and body, between rationality and emotion. But this separation is essentially arbitrary and ultimately limiting to us as a species. This split in the sensibilities (and the resulting domination of left-hemispheric thinking) would eventually produce a culture hindered by the false dichotomy established between our reason and our passion. Forced to choose between intellect and instinct, the "Goddess" rescinds to the background and people lose their essential empathic connection to one another. Society now becomes bent on raping, pilfering and dismembering itself in a cannibalistic frenzy of corruption and greed.

As inheritors of this unsustainable, murderous paradigm, we have added the horrors of predatory capitalism and industrialism to this ongoing sacrificial violence. The world's elites now define themselves as possessing the moral authority to subdue the earth and use its resources as they see fit. Partnership is replaced by ownership. Consumption trumps cooperation. Instead of living within the cycles of the natural world, as a contingent part of the web of life, humankind sets itself apart from and above it. Our authority is now codified through subjugation. We serve "God" in this model by imprisoning the Sacred Feminine, making "Her" indefinitely submissive to male authority, coercion, use and abuse. We do this by turning her gardens into prisons, her cycles into shackles. She is ours to consume. The spiritual sadism of this patriarchy seeks to control the Sacred Feminine through subduing Her primary manifestation: the natural world. And the systems of thought we devised to help us understand our place in the Cosmos now obscure and separate us from it.

Our dominant spiritual traditions stem from this left-hemispheric "hallucination" which separates us from our mythic home and amounts to a collective "cancer" on the body of our actual home. Instead of celebrating and preserving sacred space, we find ourselves destroying, defiling and disregarding it. Rather than developing sustainable and responsible models for human habitation, our sociopolitical institutions have become ensnared in a counter-intuitive struggle to condemn and choke off those very models. The Earth has become the scapegoat for our multi-generational guilt and insatiable greed. Our primary transgression: forgetting our connection and responsibility to it. Ironically, with the mytho-historical choice to subjugate the Sacred Feminine we have relinquished any control we may have once had within the material and spiritual worlds, even as we sought to master them. To live within the Great Mystery was to live fully, to live dynamically. Life was not seen as banishment from Paradise but rather immersion in it. In the beginning, the world was God (and Goddess). And we worshipped accordingly.

The research in consciousness studies, neuropsychology and hemispheric studies is suggesting that for our society to survive and reinvent itself in new and meaningful ways, it must somehow quickly and completely alter its perspective and rethink the social institutions and beliefs that have brought us to the brink of collapse. We must immediately shift into a right-hemisphere dominant perspective and define our culture along the lines of empathy and compassion instead of narcissism and competition or we will not survive. A return to the embodied Image of the Goddess might be the only thing capable of initiating such a monumental paradigm shift. As the manifestation of the right hemisphere's creative faculties, she does not need to be officially recognized in rules and decrees. Her "laws" are not written in books, official mottos and legal documents but visible in the changing of the seasons, the pathways of the constellations and, it turns out, in the neurological "soft wiring" of our species itself. When the hemispheres of the brain are unified (but with the slight advantage given to the right), our intellect, emotion and instinct all work together to connect us to the world and each other in meaningful, benevolent ways.

As the archetypal embodiment of this process, the Goddess represents the very highest goals to which our species can aspire. She is Lady Beatrice who beckons Dante into the pure, white light of transformational radiance and love. She is the Lady of the Lake in Arthurian legend: symbol of regenerative power, natural morality and archaic spiritual wisdom. Faust, tortured by the meaningless existential Void of Western philosophy, finds sanity and peace, if only momentarily, in the image of Margarete. She embodies, for Faust, the "eternal feminine" (*das Ewig-weibliche*) that "draws on us" to aspire towards our highest selves. She is Scheherazade, the "city-freer" or "world-freer" of *One Thousand and One Nights*, who coaxes the murderous, jealous king back from the brink of madness by weaving a healing web of narrative connectivity.

Always and forever we aspire. And the aspiration takes root and grows in mother's body and is then born from the swollen belly of her living Cosmos. The Goddess represents the limitless potentiality of our individual and collective minds. As such, she has traditionally taken many forms but remains the same primary principle. A symbol of the circle of life and the fusion of the whole, she represents life and death, light and darkness, the union of opposites. In any of the traditions in which she appears, including the American one, she is the symbol of life, change and regeneration.

To "worship" the Goddess, then, would be to understand that you are valuable to your community not because of what you have, but because of what you do with what you have to make the world a better place. The Goddess, politically speaking, beckons us to acknowledge and protect the "Commons" and to expand them to include education, healthcare, safe food, clean water and sustainable economic opportunity for all. When we stop taking more than we need, we will have more for those in need. Goddess "worship," it must be stressed, is an ancient technology meant to trigger the empathic drives of our collective right hemispheres. This is not about joining a new religion or passing new laws. It does not cost a lot of money or require anybody to change worldviews or political affiliations. Goddess consciousness is about recognizing that life is precious and sacred and that by increasing the dignity and freedom of all living things, we increase our own. The Goddess is the symbol of our highest responsibility to one another. Through understanding eyes, she is that purest image of our own potential to evolve from *Homo sapiens* (the knowing creature) to *Homo empathicus* (the empathic creature). She allows us to see ourselves in the Other and, thus, to embrace it.

The second point I came on your show to discuss had to do with the Paleolithic wall art in the Chauvet Cave in southern France and what it has to teach us about the past (and possible future) of public myth. Many scholars feel that the religious beliefs of the Paleolithic have been dormant for millennia; irrecoverable from the mists of a preliterate, "pre-historical" void. But the images in caves like Chauvet provide a valuable window into the spiritual wisdom of our ancestors. Their religious identity remains visible in the changing of the seasons, the interconnected biodiversity of ecosystems, and the embodied image of the feminized, vegetative world. The paintings in the cave re-present a living testimony to the creative power of Mother Earth. The cave is a shrine, a place of worship, a sacred space in the "womb" of the Great Mother; set up for her adoration, seasonal ceremonies and mystical rites. There are many clues within the cave and in the surrounding region that point to the essence of this "first" religion; one based on identification and cooperation with the natural world. To see them clearly, however, we must look with the right kind of eyes.

In the Chauvet Cave, the Sacred Feminine emerges as the embodiment of the creative energy that gives rise to the great menagerie of living, manifested forms. Numerous anthropological studies suggest that ancestor worship would have been a central theme as the earliest concepts of religion developed among Paleolithic cultures. In the quest for the ultimate "source" of life (perhaps the core of all theological thought), it stands to reason that the clan would look back to its own origins for the mythological framework in which to understand the origins of all life. In these Upper Paleolithic societies, where the mother may have been regarded as the sole parent of the family, ancestor worship was thus the basis of sacred ritual. The recognition of that "First" woman as the creator of all human life, of all life in general, may have been formulated in this very capacity at the Chauvet shrine. The wall art establishes a sacred space for the veneration and worship of that "First" Mother: the Creatrix of the living world. Indeed, the several Venus statues found throughout the region of the Chauvet Cave are the most tangible physical evidence that the societies of the Upper Paleolithic understood the special mythological significance of women in early clan society. This is so, simply because although not all women are mothers, every human comes from a mother. In a matrilineal society that venerates ancestors as sacred, "She" is the source, the mysterious life-giving spirit of all the living.

The Chauvet Cave shrine, therefore, is more than just an artistic and archaeological curiosity. The cave contains vital information for citizens of the modern world. It is significant because it suggests that for tens of thousands of years, our ancestors venerated a "deity" who personified the Great Goddess. These ancient cultures were animistic, acknowledging the existence of spirit in all things, but they also recognized the feminine principle as primary for life, spirituality and consciousness. She represented abundance, fertility, and new life. She was the ground of our mythological being. As such, it seems that before women became possessions of the modern, warring patriarchal mythologies, they were possessors of the divine light and creative energy. The inventors of agriculture, pottery and weaving, women represented the highest potential of human cooperation and achievement. A balance that has been lost in the guise of scientific, economic and philosophical "progress."

When I spoke about the cave at the recent conference of the

Society for the Anthropology of Consciousness, a woman came up to me and introduced herself as an artist and art historian who had actually been in the caves. She had sketched the wall art, standing no more than five feet away, and felt the transformative spiritual energy I was writing and speaking about. She told me that she stood weeping uncontrollably in front of the art but never quite understood why. What I said about the cave had resonated with her and explained her intense emotional reaction to the art in the caves. What I said was this: The art comes from a time when we were recognizably human. Any notion of it being the product of "primitive" man is dispelled by the elegance, grace, skill and clear mythological intention of this stunningly complex wall art. These people are us. However, they are "us" from a time when we still were "us." Thirty-two thousand years ago, we were not Christians, Jews, Muslims or Hindus. We were not Americans or Canadians or Germans or French. We were not Republicans, Democrats or Independents. We were simply human. In this modern world we are all born into such ironclad, concrete specificity. Religious labels, class distinctions, political affiliations, ethnicity and nationality differentiate us from one another before we even develop a sense of self. And before we have a chance to explore our innate sense of connection to one another and to the rest of the living world.

The Chauvet Cave precedes all of that. It is a direct window into a time when we had more in common with one another than not. The woman at the conference said that this was exactly what made her cry. Standing in front of the art she said to herself, "This is Me. This is us." I think this has direct implications into what you were asking me about how to reach out in love to people like fundamentalist Christians or the Koch Bros. We spend so much time arguing with one another about our differences that we have really lost sight of what connects us all. The power of the Chauvet Cave (and of archaic Goddess-consciousness in general) is that it comes from a time when we had not yet lost that essential connection to one another and to the natural world. One can feel this when viewing the art. This is right hemispheric activity, of which the Goddess is the highest manifestation.

So I think we can start there with these "Tea Party types and Republicans." We can try to engage them in conversations about that which we all share. It won't be easy but I think we can hold the space and just keep bringing it back around to the things we all have in common. Our true, shared human inheritance. This is the essence of what I call "Gaian Interconnectivity" and a prescription to trigger right hemispheric states of empathy, compassion and deep, transformative peace. This is why I study the caves. I have devoted my life to trying to understand our earliest mythological symbols and interpreting them in ways that are faithful to the original context while also providing a framework for them to have meaning in the modern world. Getting a Christian to "worship the Goddess" might be a tough sell but getting them to focus on that which is shared by all living things may not be. Especially if we can engage their emotions through non-linguistic, visible symbols of connectivity, balance, equanimity and peacefulness. We can, in other words, get them into the Goddess's camp without them even knowing it. And once they experience these states of transformative wisdom, the wisdom of the body, they may well be forever changed by it.

The Goddess of Chauvet calls us all home. Through her we are able to fire the deep inner peace circuitry of our collective Gaian mind: the clearest way to save ourselves from certain extinction. To save the species, we must kill the Ego. And reunite the hemispheres in pursuit of our shared mythological inheritance.

About Andrew Gurevich ...

Professor Andrew Gurevich lives with his wife and two children in Portland, Oregon. He teaches Writing, Religion, Literature and Philosophy at Mt. Hood Community College. Gurevich's work integrates his training in literature, philosophy and theology to explore the ancient mythological structures that underscore our modern social systems and philosophical paradigms. His desire to discover and connect with the Sacred Feminine began early in life due to a troubled relationship with his own mother and has led him to research the Goddess archetype in the earliest human religious traditions dating back some 800,000 years. His work has appeared in *Popular Archaeology*, *The Ecologist*, *The Voice*, *Reality Sandwich*, *The Mago Blog*, *Evolver.net*, *Current*, and in the books *The Afterlife Survey* and *Mother Earth Book*.

He is a regular speaker at academic conferences, community lectures and on radio programs such as Dr. Karen Tate's *Voices of the Sacred Feminine*, Haseena Patel's *Leave No Girl Behind*, and Charles Shaw's *Random Chuck Droid* podcast. He has written and lectured about the deep psychology of the climate change denial movement; epigenetics, neuropsychology and religious symbolism; Goddess mythology in the United States and in "Old Europe"; and the resurgence of the Sacred Feminine in the mystical traditions of Judaism, Christianity and Islam. He is currently writing a book about the Native American myth of the Spider Woman and her mythological and cultural implications for modern society. His work incorporates the latest findings in consciousness studies, neuropsychology, hemispheric science and cultural anthropology to explore the ancient "technologies" of our collective wisdom traditions and how these technologies have been used to create personal and communal identity.

Chapter 37

Earth, Spirit and Action:
Letting the Wildness In

Transcript of interview with Starhawk

Interview:

KT= Karen Tate
ST = Starhawk

Tonight I am excited to have returning to the show, Starhawk. She is the author of twelve books on Goddess religion, earth-based spirituality and activism, including *The Spiral Dance, The Fifth Sacred Thing, The Earth Path* and *The Empowerment Manual: A Guide for Collaborative Groups*, on power, process and group dynamics. Her newest book is a picture book for children called *The Last Wild Witch*. She is currently working with Yerba Buena Films on a feature production of her novel, *The Fifth Sacred Thing*, http://fifthsacredthing.com/ and working on a sequel.

Her books have been translated into Spanish, French, German, Danish, Dutch, Italian, Portuguese, Polish, Greek, Japanese, and even Burmese. Her essays are reprinted across the world and have been included in numerous anthologies. Her writing is influential and has been quoted by hundreds of other authors, turning up in magazines, trade and academic press, and even inspirational calendars. Her books are often found in college curriculums.

She is perhaps best known as an articulate pioneer in the revival of earth-based spirituality and goddess religions. She's the co-founder of Reclaiming, an activist branch of modern Pagan religion. She continues to work closely with the Reclaiming community.

A committed activist for global justice and the environment, Starhawk also teaches Earth Activist Trainings: courses in permaculture and regenerative design with a focus on organizing and activism, and a grounding in earth-based spirituality. You can find out more at her respective websites: www.earthactivisttraining.org and www.starhawk.org or at her blog found at www.starhawksblog.org

Interview starts:

KT: Starhawk, my honored guest, thank you for your patience and welcome back to the show!

I thought I would start with some of the questions that have been emailed in. People want to know, what you think is your biggest accomplishment throughout your decades of work.

ST: I would say my biggest accomplishment is that other people have taken on so much of my work. "Reclaiming", which is a group I work with, creates rituals, does witch camps; there are so many people teaching, writing, so much creativity, that I have been able to pass on the skills and insights so that other people can take pieces of the work and make it their own.

KT: So you've created an awesome legacy. Starhawk, some of these questions are political; I guess you could probably expect that because of your activism. Riane Eisler has said publicly that Goddess is a Democrat, considering a two-party system. If Goddess had a political affiliation, would you agree that the concerns of Democrats, they seem to be aligned a bit more with Mother Earth, Lady Libertas, social justice of Kali. Would you agree with her? Or is that too far afield?

ST: I wouldn't identify the Goddess with any political party. But I would identify Her with a set of values and principles, with taking care of people and recognizing our interdependence. I don't know if you and the listeners are familiar with George Lakoff. He is a linguist and wonderful writer about the whole political scene. And about our underlying metaphors that stretch our understanding in politics. And he talks about these two overarching frames through which we view the political world. One of which he calls the "Strict Father frame" which tends to be held up by the Republicans and the Right Wings, and those that are even further Right than the Republicans, if such a thing is possible. And that's the Patriarchal view ... the world is like a family, and needs a strict Father to keep them in line. You've got to have discipline in order to survive in a tough world. And if you get given too much you are being coddled and it will make you weak.

And the other "frame" is what he calls the "Nurturing Parent frame." The country is like a family and the job of a parent is to really nurture and empower their children, and to protect them, but to also give them the means to express themselves and develop themselves.

And that's the framework the Goddess stands behind; it's the idea that "Yes, we have to nurture each other, we have to take care of one another, we are all in this together, we are not separate." And the more that we understand that, the more that we build our politics and our programs and our policies around that, then the more fair, just, abundant and beautiful world we can have.

KT: Well, I certainly agree with you there. One of our other listeners said that during the past presidential election, folks like Gloria Steinem came out and gave their opinion against Sarah Palin, even though so many women seem to be getting behind her. They fear that she may actually end up in government leadership in the future. Do you have any comments about that?

ST: Well, just because somebody happens to have female genitalia doesn't mean that they actually stand for the values of nurturing and caring and helping the next generation. And, unfortunately, I don't think Sarah Palin does a very good job of representing real power and real nurturing values.

There was a time in the women's movement when everything seemed very simple. "Women were good, men were bad." It's not that simple. If anyone doubts that, take a look at Condoleezza Rice or Margaret Thatcher. It's about the values that we hold. It's not about what's dangling between your legs.

KT: Why do you think so many women jumped on her [Sarah Palin's] bandwagon?

ST: I don't know any that jumped on her bandwagon.

KT: You saw the crowds she drew and she continues to draw them. There were women defending her with their lives. I couldn't understand it. I don't know if you have given it any thought. I was wondering if you had any ideas about that. Could they relate to her because she was a "soccer mom" or she was like one of them?

ST: I think a lot of women are conditioned to not necessarily look at what our best interests are, or who is representing our best interests. And unfortunately, politics in this country is so much about image and so little about substance. There may have been women who saw her and thought, she is cool, she's got those cute glasses.

KT: And she's got such a sexy wink, right? (Laugh)

ST: But I have to say to me her appeal was not there.

KT: Okay. Another reader writes in and says she wants to thank you for all the consciousness you raise for the Sacred Feminine. And in her opinion, some of the most important work for our time. Her question is about engaging in conversation with fundamentalist Christians. She says, "Recently online, there was a mother asking for advice on her son who is having trouble reading. She stated that she reads to him every night and is reading Harry Potter books to him. In the column, the folks said to her, 'Well, I see you attend church. You might want to check with them about the Spiritual aspects of young children reading Harry Potter and books like the Sorcerer's Stone. Yes there is a fight between good and evil, but the main idea is to use magic, which is not relying upon God's power. Harry Potter literally teaches children how to actively cast spells. And witchcraft is like rebellion to God. And after all he IS jealous.'"

So to get to the actual question it is: "Would you, Starhawk, engage in conversation with this woman, and if so what would you say?"

ST: I would engage in conversation with just about anybody, but sometimes you have to think some conversations are just going to be useless. If someone is coming from that perspective you are probably not going to change their mind about something.

For me, I love the Harry Potter books. I think they are great for kids because they awaken the imagination. And they awaken a sense of fantasy, a sense of courage, you know, how you face obstacles. The books are about friendship and how you bond together in friendship.

If you don't want your kids reading books like that, there are always the Elsie Dinsmore books. Maybe we should encourage all the little Christian children to read the Elsie Dinsmore books and then we might get a lot more recruits. (Laugh)

I actually just wrote a book for children called *The Last Wild Witch*. It's published by "Mother Tongue Inc" (the wonderful women that publish the We'Moon Calendar). It is a picture book for children. The reason that I wrote it was that many years ago, I got mad that there were all these negative images of Witches out there, and very few things that were positive images of Witches.

I think Harry Potter does a wonderful job of having a magical world, which kids love. And the characters are very rich in there, because they are both positive and negative. All the characters are very dimensional. Very few of them are all good. And as the books go on, even the characters that seem all wise and all good, at a certain point you start to see their underside, their shadow side, their human side. As Harry grows and gets older he gets into that developmental stage where we all do see that our parents and those wonderful figures also do have feet of clay.

I think it's a really brilliant service that she (J.K. Rowling) has done for kids.

KT: Okay. Do you want to tell us a little bit more about your new book?

ST: It's called *The Last Wild Witch* and it's about a perfect world, a perfect town in a perfect world where there is a rule for everything and a right way and a wrong way to do everything. Nobody ever breaks the rules, except once in a while. Because, at the edge of the magic town is the last wild forest. And there, lives the last wild Witch. She spends her time brewing her magic brews, singing her magic songs, and every now and then when the wind is in the right direction, some of that wildness gets inside everybody.

And then, the kids don't stand in straight lines, and they don't obey the rules. And they want to stay outside and not sit inside and do their lessons.

So the parents and the adults decide that they need to do something. And they decide to go into the forest and chop it down and get rid of the wildness and get rid of the witch. The children manage to find a way to stop them. Not only to stop them, but to open the adults up to some of the wildness so that, by the end, the Witch and the town are reconciled. And the Last Wild Witch comes into the town, and the wildness and "civilized" co-exist in a whole new way. It's really better for everybody.

KT: What age group did you write this for?

ST: It's targeted for 6–9 year olds. But it can be read to much younger children, and I keep hearing from a lot of adults that THEY like it.

KT: You can get it on Amazon or any of the usual places?

ST: You can go to www.starhawk.org and get links to an online bookstore, you can get it through Amazon.com. There are some bookstores that are carrying it, you can ask your bookstore to carry it. They can also go to Mother Tongue Inc and get information on how to order it.

KT: And that way it supports these Pagan organizations rather than Amazon.

ST: Yes. I use an online distribution company called Hundred Fires. That's where my website links. I encourage people to buy books from their independent bookstore. Many of them struggle to stay alive and stay in business.

KT: This sounds like a wonderful Solstice gift.

ST: It's a great gift to give to your Pagan kids and a great gift to give to the children of your fundamentalist cousins. Probably that woman who doesn't like Harry Potter won't like this book at all.

KT: I have Catholic relatives in Louisiana who think I'm going to burn in Hell. I think that would be a perfect Christmas gift to send to them. (Laughing)

Well, Starhawk, one of our other listeners wrote in and asks "Are you familiar with the popular TV series *True Blood*? What do you think about how they made the character of the Witch turn out to be the evil one?"

ST: I just heard about that but I haven't seen it. I am a secret fan of Buffy however and love how they have a Witch who is actually a good Witch and is part of the team of good. At one point when Buffy got sucked into a demonic computer program, they brought in a "Techno-Pagan" to get her out.

KT: I have to admit *True Blood* was a really good show, but I have to agree with this listener. The vampires are good and evil, but they have done a number on the Witch. It's unfortunate.

Starhawk, of all your works, do you have a favorite book? Is one of your projects your pet?

ST: I would say, probably, *The Fifth Sacred Thing* would be the one that I would pick if I had to pick just one.

KT: From an author's point of view was it harder to write fiction?

ST: It's not so much that it's harder but it's a very different process. The reason I haven't written as much fiction is because it takes concentration and space and lack of distraction to create that other world and enter into it. I haven't had a lot of uninterrupted time since writing *The Fifth Sacred Thing* and *Walking to Mercury*. But I am currently writing a sequel to *The Fifth Sacred Thing*.

KT: When we first talked about you being on the show, one of the topics we discussed was called "Earth, Spirit, and Action." Do you want to talk more about that?

ST: For me, earth-based spirituality has always been linked with political action and environmental action. And I think right now we are in this moment of crisis around climate change, and we are gearing up for talks in Copenhagen in December, at a time where the world urgently needs to make major shifts in little things like our economy, technology, energy systems, transportation systems, production systems, food production systems, and we need to make those shifts right now. We don't have the luxury of endless time, of putting things off, the delays, all the obstructions the Republicans and corporations are trying to put against this urgent need to make this tremendous shift. To me, that's a spiritual question, it's not just a physical or practical question. It's a question of "Are we capable of really understanding that there are things that go beyond our immediate profit and our immediate convenience?" The basic life support systems that sustain the earth and sustain the planet have to be respected and have to be the centerpiece of what we do and the decisions that we make. It's not a little afterthought, where we decide we will take care of the earth if it doesn't inconvenience us too much.

To me that is the great spiritual crisis of this age. Pagan and Goddess worshippers need to be active and involved and at the forefront of helping that shift to occur.

KT: Are there any particular groups or areas that you would say to Pagans and Goddess advocates: "If you don't have your own pet project or pet organization this would be a good one to volunteer, or send money, or do whatever you can do for it"?

ST: One of the organizations I like a lot is called the "Transition Town Movement." It started in Britain and it's now come to

North America as well. It is centered around people organizing their home communities to make a plan for how we are going to move to an energy descent economy, how we are going to use the resources we have right now to create the resources that we need, in order to make this shift. People can look at that and look at some of the things that I do. I teach Earth Activist Training, which is permaculture design.

Permaculture is a whole global movement of ecological design based on the understanding that human beings can actually learn to create systems that meet our needs and actually heal and regenerate the ecosystems around us. If we start by observing nature, looking at nature, working in the way that nature works, and letting nature be our guide and model. So looking for permaculture courses in your area, looking at what kind of actions and demonstrations will be happening this December around the climate change conferences, looking at the tremendous local initiatives going on and positive things going on right now. Figure out where your heart is around all this and get involved in helping create this new world that we need to build.

KT: What do you think the problem is? Are our leaders not convinced? Or are they just not saying how dire the circumstances are because they are in the pockets of corporations? What would you say to that?

ST: I think the corporations have a huge influence. Denial is a big factor. We have all grown up with a cultural story... a story of progress. A story that says, "We have now transcended nature. Now we no longer have to worry about the things that our ancestors had to worry about. We no longer have to be bound by nature's constraints."

To really grasp climate change, we have to counter that story. We have to understand that actually we ARE bound by nature's constraints, just as much as our ancient ancestors were when they were running around with the mammoths in the caves.

We are nature. We cannot separate ourselves from the natural world. It's that story, that desire, to get out from the material world and not have to deal with any limits on our desires or consumption or our ability to exploit the world around us. That is what is holding us back from making the changes that we need to make.

KT: Would it be going too far to say that the greed that Capitalism breeds, that the greed in Capitalism is holding us back as well?

ST: Capitalism in a sense gives us false promise. It says you can have an economy that's endlessly expanding in a finite world. You can't. Not if that expansion is about extraction and exploitation and using up resources. In a finite world, there are limits to the resources we've got. There are limits to what we can take, there are limits to growth, and if we don't understand those limits and we over-run the carrying capacity of our world, we can't necessarily bounce back from that.

KT: So would you say environmentalism is maybe the biggest challenge that Pagans face today? Or is it just ONE of the challenges, because certainly having people understand who Pagans really are continues to be an issue. Do the challenges to Pagans come from within their ranks? From outside their ranks? Is it mostly environmentalism? All of the above?

ST: I would say it's "All of the above." Certainly the environment is a huge challenge on every level right now to all of us. Just because somebody is a Pagan doesn't necessarily mean that they are much of an environmentalist. Unfortunately I know plenty of Pagans that are not all that conscious about turning off their lights or driving their cars or growing their food, or whatever. Just like, I'm sure we all know Christians that are not living up to the ideals in their religion, or Jews, or anybody else. I'd say we face multiple challenges but to me the big overriding one is: "What's going to happen to this beautiful Earth that we love?"

Are we going to be able to preserve enough of the biodiversity and the wonder and the beauty of this planet that our children and our great grandchildren will know something of a world similar to the one that we have known? Or are we looking at a really horrific and grim future that's going to result in hundreds of millions of deaths, massive worldwide hunger and thirst and starvation, immense loss of biodiversity, all those things that we know are coming down with climate change? That to me is the big question.

KT: So really it's a human challenge; it's not even just a Pagan challenge.

A question came in from a listener: How do you think Barack Obama is doing – are you disappointed?

ST: I would say in some ways I'm disappointed. I was disappointed that my friend Van Jones who was one of his advisors around Green Jobs, that he didn't stand up and defend him when he was attacked by Glenn Beck and the Right Wing and let him be hounded out of office. In other ways, the virulence of the opposition is so strong, you have to give him credit for hanging in there and attempting to do the things that he is attempting to do. Mostly I think we need to look at ourselves and say, "Hey, there's that story about Roosevelt when he took office and the Unions came in and said 'This is what we want.' And Roosevelt said, 'I want that too; make me do it.'"

We need to be out there involved, out in the streets protesting sometimes, calling our representatives, really active and engaged. It's up to us to do it and to create this social movement and the pressure that's going to allow him to do these things and what he wants to do.

KT: What's your take on why Progressives or Liberals, the Left, why are we so much more passive than the virulent Right that just seems to steamroll over the Left?

ST: George Lakoff has good insights. He says the Left has false expectations. People aren't moved by debates about policy and reason that are dry and intellectual and divorced from emotion. And he gives a lot of data in his most recent book *The Political Mind*. Real reason is emotional, it's not just intellectual. You could read his work from a feminist perspective and say, "Yeah, we have been saying that all along."

Real reason and intuition and emotions and all those things are intertwined and you can't completely separate them. The Right Wing has been much better at recognizing that and appealing to the emotions. They understand that the power of repetition, the message is repeated over and over again, and it sticks and it creates structures in the mind that become fixed. We could learn to do that ourselves. But we have to be willing to look at how we think, how we speak, how do we convey a message that speaks to people at a deeper level than just intellectual.

KT: Do you see real change happening, considering the years you have been at this? Should we have hope that change is really afoot and the Sacred Feminine is being rebirthed into our world?

ST: I think we should have hope. And not just hope but determination and will to say the values of caring and nurturing, the values that the Goddess represents, are being rebirthed and make sure that happens. We shouldn't be passive about it; we can be engaged in creating the change. I think if we do that, then we have tremendous hope. I have hope because I do have my own deep spiritual connection to the Goddess. I don't believe the Goddess is stupid or suicidal. I believe she evolved human beings for a purpose, to be her healing hands and loving heart. We may be growing in to the job.

But I also believe that as we make the decisions to turn our culture around, then we have tremendous allies in the natural world that we can draw on, that will be awakened, that will be available, that will help us with the work of healing. Some of those are as simple as soil bacteria, or fungi, or worms, the simplest humblest things under our feet. Once we start to look and appreciate those things, they have tremendous powers to break down toxins, to build living healthy soil, to sequester carbon out of the atmosphere. So I am very hopeful.

KT: I'm sure you are familiar with the Findhorn Institute. Is that part of what you are talking about as well?

ST: I'm talking about something even less esoteric than Devas, nature spirits, although I do believe we can work with those beings. But I'm talking about actual soil bacteria; there's nothing more magical than these ancient creatures which were the first forms of life, which have tremendous abilities to affect the basic biochemistry of the planet. They created the atmosphere we breathe. They figured out how to photosynthesize. How to take energy from sunlight and use it to break apart carbon dioxide and water and re-combine them into food... sugars, starches, carbohydrates. That is a tremendous miracle. It's a miracle that science has explored and there are so many people that are now doing exciting work, people like Dr. Elaine Ingham in Oregon who brews up compost teas that restore the living healthy biology to the soil. Or Paul Stamets, author of *Mycellium Running*, who lives in Washington who has been doing amazing work with mushrooms and their ability to break down toxins. There are organic gardeners and farmers that know the secrets of how you build living soil and how you restore dead soil to health. All of those things are aspects of the Goddess.

KT: During the course of the work you have been doing all of this time, were there any important turning points that stick out in your mind that maybe you can say, "Things are really getting better"? Or "We are going to experience that paradigm shift"?

ST: I had a wonderful experience a couple of years ago. I was down in Big Sur taking a permaculture workshop and I went outside and there were giant birds that looked like great giant vultures but they were different somehow. It turned out that they were the California Condor, which went to the very brink of extinction.

There was a breeding program and I remember one of my very first points of awareness about ecology was hearing about the attempts to save the condor, thirty years ago.

And now they have enough that they have been able to release a number of them back into the wild. And there they were, flying around Big Sur.

And to me, that's kind of an emblem of the fact that there is hope. There is the potential sometimes to save some of the things we thought were lost. I believe once we make the shift, there are great powers of healing that exist in the world that are waiting and eager to work with us.

KT: Do you put any stock into the 2012 hoopla or do you think that maybe the end is really going to be the beginning of the Sacred Feminine?

ST: I'm old enough that I have been through a number of these things. There was the Age of Aquarius, the Harmonic Convergence, Y2K, there's 2012; I think it does represent the shifting of a cycle, but it doesn't mean the world is going to end. Or that there will be some kind of giant cataclysm that we will necessarily see or know at the moment. There are lots of shifts that happen much more subtly. I am hopeful that we will make that shift. We are faced with making so many changes on major levels. Hopefully some of that 2012 energy will help us do that.

KT: Who were your mentors?

ST: My mother was one of my mentors. She was a psychotherapist. She was an expert in loss and grief. My father died when I was 5 years old and left her as a single mom to raise me and my younger brother. She would talk to me a lot about her clients and about her ideas, even when I was very young. I think that for me was very formative of how I see the world. I grew up from the beginning with this idea that people did things for mysterious emotional reasons that weren't always evident on the surface.

And if you didn't understand why somebody did something, you might be able to delve deeper into their history or into their reservoirs of pain. And maybe then you would understand why they were behaving the way they were behaving.

And of course there were other wonderful women at the beginning, especially around feminist spirituality. People like Merlin Stone, Z Budapest, we mentored each other, kind of grew up together. A lot of us didn't have elders; we were having to re-invent the tradition as we went along. We just had our 30th Anniversary Spiral Dance ritual, and a couple of my old friends, Bonnie Barnett who helped write some of the music for our ritual, came up from LA. My friend Susan Stern, who did the Goddess invocation at the very first Spiral Dance, my friend Kevyn Lutton who macraméd the Goddess costumes, we all went out to tea and it was wonderful to think back on the coven that we had together many years ago. In a sense we mentored each other.

We would create a ritual, and then we would go back and talk about what worked and what didn't work. And what we intended, and why we thought it might have worked or not.

That was how we created a lot of what we do now.

KT: You were really trailblazing new ground. What are you working on now? AND, what would be one of the most important insights you would like to leave our listeners with?

ST: I'm working on the Earth Activist Trainings, which are Permaculture Courses that combine a grounding in earth-based spirituality with a full permaculture design certificate course. And also a focus on organizing and activism.

You can get information by going to www.starhawk.org or www.earthactivisttraining.org

That's one of my main focuses. And another one of the focuses is Copenhagen and activism around what's going to happen with climate change. I'm always writing. I write a lot of different kinds of things. I have a blog of my own and you can find it at www.starhawksblog.org. It's called "Dirt Worship."

But my major project is bringing *The Fifth Sacred Thing* to the screen and writing the sequel. I'm passionate about doing that because the novel shows us a positive vision of the future and there are very few hopeful visions out there.

I also write for a *Washington Post* News Week blog on Religion called "On Faith."

KT: We have a caller for Starhawk.

Caller: My question is about how to create awareness in suburban middle-class community? People are just completely out of touch with everything that you are talking about, which seems so familiar to me. And it seems like such a small pot of people who have this sense of awareness.

ST: I think the Transition Town folks have some good ideas on how to begin. Rob Hopkins, who founded the movement, has a book called *The Transition Handbook*. He talks about starting events in your neighborhood, doing things like "movie night," pot lucks, ways to get people involved; there are a lot of wonderful resources around as far as movies and videos to show people, including one called *The End of Suburbia*.

Often people are willing to do something if it seems social and fun like a party. Whereas they normally might not be willing to come to something that's a political meeting or "How would you like to do a Pagan ritual?" Think about what are the issues in your area and how can you connect around them to meet the different kinds of needs or the concerns that people have.

Organizing around emergency preparation response is also another road to people's awareness. Get people together and tell them to get our neighborhood prepared (for emergencies). "Let's not wait for it to happen."

That can be a way to get into talking about things like where you are going to get your food if the current system goes down. Or how you are going to take care of one another if something happens and you don't have access to the usual resources that you usually have access to.

Maybe you would also like to celebrate some of the stuff that is going on in your neighborhood.

There is a wonderful group in Portland, Oregon called "City Repair." They actually organize neighborhoods to create gathering places out of intersections, and do public art projects. They also get people involved in community gardening. There are a lot of different ways where we can meet people where they are.

There are common things that everybody needs, like food, rather than expecting people to come and meet us where we think they ought to be.

Caller: Those are wonderful ideas. And you talked about coming to a Pagan ritual. I actually do things like that, I teach Sunday School at a Unitarian Universalist congregation. I have the opportunity to do Pagan rituals with kids. It's wonderful, and I am also a school teacher in a public school and I do environmental units. I teach the Gaia hypothesis to kids. It's all wonderful, but the moment I say something, one of my neighbors will say to me, "You know, you are starting to sound like a Pagan." And I say, "I am a Pagan." And they are terrified.

I'm thinking, knowing where I come from, knowing how I think and knowing who I am, how could a word (Pagan) be so alienating, how could a word make you seem so subversive?

ST: I'm going to recommend to you George Lakoff's book *The Political Mind*.

He talks about that, and when I read that book, I understood it. He talks about how things get linked in the mind and they make neural patterns. You get a set of ideas, like Pagan, evil, whatever, and it's like a pathway that's there, already constructed.

And the only way to take it apart is to actually make it visible. And then to create some alternative linkages and pathways, and reinforce them by repeating them over and over again.

When I read that, I thought, "That would mean we were intuitively right to call ourselves Witches rather than use a more acceptable word."

The word "Witch" has power. If we don't examine it and counter its negative associations, if we don't go through that process with it, then it's like a stick to beat you with.

It's an aspect of deep cultural association of women with evil, and women's power with evil. And an association of danger with any form of knowledge that's not approved of by the authorities. There are a million linkages in there, and if we do go through that process of taking them apart, and looking at them and creating new and different linkages they remain unquestioned and unconscious, but they still affect us. If we do examine the word and create new associations, it becomes a way of addressing all of those assumptions, on a very deep level.

So it's work and one of the things to remember is that these kinds of changes don't happen instantly or immediately. They take time and they take repetition. I often hear people say, "I don't want to work with her" or "I don't like him." And you ask, "Have you given her this feedback?" "Have you told him what he's doing that you don't like?"

They say, "I gave her feedback and she didn't listen." "He hasn't changed; he still is doing the same things!"

Giving people feedback once won't make them change. If you decide you want to stop smoking or something, how often do you immediately succeed in making that change?

You usually don't; it takes a long time, a lot of repetition, falling back and forth, before you get those new patterns set.

And the same is true when we give personal feedback, and even more when we try to make political changes or shift cultural ideas or assumptions linked to words like "Witch" or "Pagan." People respond with shock, the second time with less shock, the third, fourth or fifth time they are getting used to it. By the twentieth time they might have realized they are a Pagan and by the twenty-fifth time they swear they always were a Pagan.

KT: (Thanks the caller for calling in)

Starhawk, anything we haven't covered that you want to make sure we say to our listeners before we have to say goodnight?

ST: I want to encourage all the callers and listeners to find a way to establish your own relationship and your own connection with nature, to give yourself some time each day to be in nature, even if nature is just your back yard or an empty lot. Watch, learn and observe, connect with the natural world, because that is what feeds us as well as what we are most called to protect. And as we do that, then we develop the understanding and learn the language that we need to communicate back to nature.

And remember to draw on the help and those allies that are there waiting for us to do that healing work.

KT: Starhawk, it's been a delight. We went from one end of the spectrum to the other with our questions but it has been insightful and informative. It helps people have a better barometer check for what Goddess ideals are, and what it means to be a Pagan, and a political Pagan.

Thank you very much for your time and for taking part in the series.

Chapter 38

Goddess Icon Spirit Banners: Ambassadors of the Divine Feminine

by Lydia Ruyle

Art and the Ancient Mothers call me on a journey. I am a 78-year-old artist/scholar pursuing Goddess research for decades with my mind, body and spirit. I create icons. Each image was created and revered at some time in human history. Since 1995, the icons have become Goddess Spirit Banners, sacred images of the divine feminine from the many cultures of the world.

How did I find the Goddess? SHE called me and I listened. SHE told me to see, touch, learn, laugh, cry and share with art, stories and sacred places of Mother Earth. SHE continues to support my work. I do my part by eating well, exercising and keeping on keeping on. Two major bodies of art, Crop Circle Banners and Goddess Icon Spirit Banners, have manifested since I was 60!

The first Goddess Icon Spirit Banners in the series were for an exhibition in 1995 at the Celsus Library in Ephesus, Turkey where they flew for the month of July spreading their energies. Since then, the banners have blossomed from eighteen to 300 today. I take the banners to sacred sites to empower, teach and share their stories in Australia, New Zealand, China, Cambodia, Japan, South Korea, France, Germany, Hungary, Romania, Bulgaria, Greece, Malta, Finland, England, Iceland, Italy, the Czech Republic, Poland, Switzerland, Mexico, Canada, Peru, Costa Rica, Brazil, Argentina, Colombia, Russia, Turkey, Ghana, South Africa, India, Nepal, Tibet, Bhutan, Hawaii and the mainland US.

The Goddess Banners transform space and time. They make it

possible to communicate one on one with the divine feminine in her infinite manifestations. Hanging in the Celsus Library, they re-membered the Goddess, stirring the energies and sending them out into the world. They also absorb the energies from each sacred place they visit and share that energy as they travel.

The banner designs reflect the cultural image-making traditions of time and place in the world and in art history. The banners are portable, lightweight and can be shipped easily. Made of rip-stop nylon, the colors are bright and strong. Most are 36 inches wide by 72 inches long. Two are circular like wind socks. The banners may be hung with light coming through them or on a wall with light reflected from them. They also can hang from poles and be carried in processions. At Machu Picchu we anchored them with tent stakes.

How do I choose the images? They literally find me. When I get an invitation for an exhibition, I research the images of the feminine divine in a culture, then create banners of the images. My artistic eye sees the visual and spiritual connections.

How do I create the banners? First I draw the image. Next I blow it up and have it transferred to rip-stop nylon. Then I design the background. Louise Keirnes, my vexillographer, then sews the figure and the background, creating a banner. Louise has sewn ALL my Goddess Banners since 1995. She is 85 years old. Finally I paint the image using acrylic fabric paints. Recently, I've been using paints that reflect light, thus enhancing the image.

Which one is my favorite? The one I am working on now. She has my full creative attention and energy. The creative process is like the birth process: inspiration, gestation, effort, manifestation, then letting go and letting be. Idea, i-dea, means "from the Goddess."

How long does it take to create a banner? It just depends. Some happen quickly, others take years. I create and paint the banners in my home studio which is made of rammed earth. I literally live and create in Mother Earth on my grandparents' land in Greeley, Colorado where I am surrounded by art and images of the feminine divine. I also create on my travels. Some of the early banners were painted in a small kitchen on a golf course and others in studios in Italy and Chicago.

The "girls," as I affectionately call them, are multimillion-mile travelers, Ambassadors of the Divine Feminine with infinite stories and detours. They hang in conferences, libraries, galleries, studios, offices, kindergartens, art centers, universities, town halls, a golf club, woman's prison, a musical production and a funeral celebration. I also create Goddess Prayer Flags which are 18" x 18" smaller versions of the banners. I leave them at sacred sites to empower the divine feminine images and herstories.

Sometimes the girls travel alone; other times I accompany them. Since 1993, over 300 pilgrims have joined me and "the girls" in Britain, Turkey, France, Germany, Greece, Italy, Sicily, Malta, the Czech Republic, Russia, Mexico, Peru, Hawaii and southwestern US. On the journeys, we sing, dance, play and learn about the Goddess from very special wise women and each other. The journeys are soul journeys. They are about finding the divine feminine within and without in the culture of the particular pilgrimage.

My book *Goddess Icons: Spirit Banners of the Divine Feminine* grew out of the many exhibition catalogues I created and Xeroxed. Now PDFs on my magical Mac keep a record of my images and the internet makes it possible for the girls to be in approximately twenty exhibitions around the globe each year. Keeping track of their journeys is a full-time job.

As an artist, I've learned that finding the creative spirit within changes the paradigm without. The great advances of humankind have occurred through creativity and imagination. The creative is the place where no one else has been. You get there by choosing to explore, by hard work, by taking risks and not quite knowing what you're doing. What you will discover will be yourself. The journey is full of experiences and surprises, as you learn from both your demons as well as your angels along the path. So, choose a path with heart and as Joseph Campbell says, Follow Your Bliss!

Equally inspirational is Leonardo da Vinci who said: "Learning is the only thing the mind never exhausts, never fears, never regrets." And learning and wisdom are feminine in many world cultures.

I believe we are here to learn and education is the best hope we have for the human race and the planet. Human experience, written, spoken and recorded in artifacts, art and architecture links human beings in time and space. Education is how we pass humankind's accumulated knowledge on to future generations. Knowledge develops the foundation for human ethics and values. In our technological computer world, it is even more important for us to learn from and understand history, for history/herstory is ourselves. In studying it, we discover ourselves.

Equally important is our spiritual journey. We are spiritual beings on a human path to learn wisdom and compassion through the choices we make each day. In case you haven't figured it out yet, YOU are in charge of those choices. Along the way may you laugh, sing, dance and paint, walk in love and beauty, trust the knowledge that comes through the body, speak the truth about conflict and pain, practice great generosity, take only what you need and think about the consequences of your actions for the next seven generations.

"You must be the change you wish to see in the world." said Mahatma Gandhi. It's good advice which I've followed for eight decades with persistence, practice, patience, and hard work.

The Ancient Mothers called me to weave a web to bring about a greater consciousness of the divine in each human and nature, to recognize the oneness of ALL. In my teaching, travels, and exhibitions, I meet thousands of people interested in the Divine

Feminine. The ALL for me is the Goddess with a Billion Faces, Places and Names.

We are ALL one.

About Lydia Ruyle ...

Lydia Ruyle is an artist, author, scholar emerita of the Visual Arts faculty of the University of Northern Colorado in Greeley, Colorado where The Lydia Ruyle Room of Women's Art was dedicated in 2010. She was given a Lifetime Achievement Award by UNC in 2013. Ruyle has a Bachelor of Arts from the University of Colorado at Boulder, a Master of Arts from UNC and has studied with Syracuse University in Italy, France, Spain, and with the Art Institute of Chicago in Indonesia. She works regularly at Santa Reparata International School of Art in Florence, Italy and Columbia College Center for Book and Paper in Chicago. Her research into sacred images of women has taken her around the globe.

Thirty years ago, Ruyle began collecting images of women from art history while teaching at UNC. She used the images in her art, and in 1987 *Better Homes & Goddesses* was born for National Women's History Month. For twenty years, she led women's pilgrimage journeys to sacred places. Ruyle creates and exhibits her art, does workshops and is a speaker at conferences throughout the US and internationally. Since 1995, her Goddess Icon Spirit Banners, which made their debut at the Celsus Library at Ephesus, Turkey, have flown in forty countries, spreading their divine feminine energies. Her work is included in over thirty books. *Goddess Icons: Spirit Banners of the Divine Feminine* was published in 2002 and *Turkey Goddess Icons: Spirit Banners of the Divine Feminine* was published in Istanbul in 2005. *Goddess Icons: Spirit Banners of the Americas* will be published in 2014.

Chapter 39

The Natural Spiritual Authority of Woman

by Vajra Ma

I was 35 years old before the idea of a Mother Creator was introduced to me. It was a concept which seemed strange to me at first, but once I had stepped through the veil of my conditioning, it made much more sense than its widespread and accepted reversal, that of a male-birthing-all creation. And, once given the Rosetta Stone by Mary Daly and many other feminist authors to decipher the reversal which had demonized the Great Mother, I proceeded to reverse the reversal in my own understanding, my own consciousness, my own awareness. I opened Pandora's Box! True to the Great Reversal,[1] this box was not filled with curses, dangers and evils, as threatened in the patriarchal distortion of Pandora's original story, but abundant with the rich and varied gifts of a loving Mother Creator. Pandora literally means "giver of all gifts." The Pandora's Box that opened for me was rich with the legacy of Woman's Natural Spiritual Authority.

"With Woman's ... what!?"

If that is what you are thinking, then you, as I once did, along with a majority of the human race, don't know that Woman once held the spiritual authority in the world, let alone that we came by it "naturally."

Like most average Westerners, I grew up in a world where the Tree of Knowledge in the Garden of Eden was forbidden. Along with it, the ancient symbols of the Great Mother's serpentine life-force rising through the human body, the Tree of Life, had been reversed into symbols of evil. Especially the female body which is the Tree of Life *par excellence,* which literally represents "carnal knowledge," was equated with the source of everything that ails humanity. This demonization of Woman extends far beyond Western Judeo-Christian cultures into Islamic, Hindu, Buddhist and many other cultures, and globally into all systems based on them and supported by them.

The fact is that in evolution and in history, women are the creators of humanity. This goes beyond the mere physical but encompasses the cultural, artistic, and, most of all, the spiritual. It is only in the past 6,000 or so years of recent humanity, that myth and propaganda has attempted to turn this upside down and backwards.

I had been walking the path of modern Goddess spirituality, a movement that began in the late 1960s, for nearly twenty years before this particular string of words came to my mind: *"woman's natural spiritual authority."* Though women's spiritual authority is a re-claiming that is central to the modern Goddess and women's spirituality movement, I had never read or heard this exact string of words before. It came to me as I was preparing a presentation for The Goddess Temple of Orange County, founded by Ava Park. Years earlier, I had encountered feminist author Vicki Noble's term "female spiritual authority" and probably tucked it away in a corner of my mind. But the word "natural" had not been connected to the context of spiritual authority. And when that connection happened, it suddenly catalyzed a cascade of realizations that reverberated in my body and has continued to multiply and expand even as I write this thought.

Women can draw strength and confidence knowing that the dynamics of Woman's natural spiritual authority are based in nature, in reality, and that they are universal to Woman regardless of belief systems and societal constructs. Thus the word "natural." Neither reality nor human experience provide for a dichotomy between the physical and the spiritual, between natural vs divine. In fact, far from being separate, it is from the nature of the female body, which encompasses Woman's power to create life, that a matrix of inseparable emotional, physical, mental and spiritual dynamics unfolds, naturally and spherically. This is the basis of Woman's Natural Spiritual Authority.

And herein lies its tremendous power to "save the world." There is nothing to invent or construct. We merely need to wake up to reality. The rest will follow.

Woman as the Creator of humanity is a natural extension of Woman's relational power in birthing, protecting, sustaining, teaching and guiding her children. And of humanity, Woman's children. Men can participate in this Motherhood as well by opening and connecting to all around them in a direct, sensate way, unfiltered by dogma or conditioning and by recognizing that this connection is more easily accessed by women. They can be part of this by revering and respecting women in their holistic sensual awareness.

No one questions a woman's authority and responsibility to physically nurture the child she has birthed. Then why question her authority to guide her child spiritually beyond conditioning it to conform to androcentric spiritual authority, an unnatural authority that was appropriated and assumed by patriarchy through the institutions of nuclear family, marriage, and the male ownership and dominion over life and life resources.

In reality, there is no unnatural authority. In reality, authority is inextricably linked to that which we have authored, that is, created. To *author* means to *create*.[2] But the word "authority" has been divorced from its creative root and truncated into dominance and an impersonal "power over," as in "the author-ities" who have the "power" to take something away from us or coerce us into doing something we don't want to do. Without originating, without creating, i.e. without authorship, there can be no authority, but only dominance and control.

Natural authority, on the other hand, is an inherent part of life-giving, of authorship, rather than an artificial, abstract imposition on the freedom of others. The best pattern for authority in nature is its fundamental manifestation in mother and offspring as an integral part of the experience of life. Mothers lead their baby, cub, kid, calf or foal through the early, formative processes of life.

For good reason, one of the oldest epiphanies of the Goddess is the lioness. She is an incomparable mother, protector and provider. The lioness who creates her cubs is supremely responsible to them. She protects, guides, warns and sets limits. And these limits, warnings, and guidelines are not arbitrary or artificial. They are not separated from reality, and not self-serving for the insular benefit of the lioness. Instead, they arise in direct, intelligent relationship to reality. The lioness mother provides food, leads them to water, teaches them how to hunt and guards against predators, and knows when to hide or run for safety or to stand and fight. The mother exercises authority over her offspring not in an ego-fest of domination, but on their behalf, *in service to them*, in natural interrelationship with them. The babies know this and their response to her authority is the very thing that enables them to survive and mature into adulthood.

The same is true for a woman and child and her responsibility to care for that child, including the responsibility for the additional human dimensions of emotional, mental and spiritual maturation. This is natural, and there is nothing as natural as this. As such, woman has authority over that child, a natural authority born of her responsibility for the life of that child.

This is natural authority arising from direct connection to Source. Far from being self-indulgent and self-serving, it is, however, self-referenced and speaks from a knowing of the inner Source and the fundamental interrelatedness between all of us. Thus, it has no impulse to dominate. Natural authority is relational and self-referenced at the same time. It is a contextual matrix of relationships, not a vertical hierarchy of dominance and coercion. Authority cannot be separated out, and to attempt to do so results in something dead, like a hand amputated from an arm, like the artificial, unnatural authority as it operates in today's world, a dismembered "authority."

There is no such word as "patrix," and that is for a good reason. Woman, womb, life, and the cosmos are the only plausible and legitimate references for using the word "matrix." Matrix is defined as *a situation or surrounding substance within which something originates, develops, or is contained, the womb*.[3]

Woman's natural spiritual authority is based in this reality. The nature of woman, including her body, her womb, her psyche, female modes of functioning, the entirety of these facts is interrelated in a matrix. And it is this very non-linear nature, the "lineage from within," the *Hidden Stream*,[4] which is at the core of Natural Spiritual Authority.

Natural authority is inseparable from reverence for life. From love. The quintessential embodiment of this reality is Motherhood – with a capital M. This encompasses both the highly personal experience of being a mother and the transpersonal experience of the supreme spiritual principle of love intrinsic to Motherhood. Without the one there could not be the other. Woman's Motherhood is nested in the vaster underlying love and Motherhood of Earth and the cosmic womb.

Far from operating as limiting essentialism or biological determinism, this context of Motherhood places Woman as central in the expansive matrix of natural and therefore undeniable powers. The fear of these undeniable powers explains why patriarchy has vilified and demonized the female body, and flesh in general.

Natural spiritual authority trusts and relies upon the knowing about life and about protecting life which is often denigrated as "mere instinct" rather than acknowledged in its true scope. Woman must again step into that natural spiritual authority – take that responsibility and take that risk – because, ultimately, there is no survivable alternative.

About Vajra Ma …

Vajra Ma teaches outside the codification of established traditions and doctrines. She has designed and facilitated women's ritual since 1986 and has integrated Goddess knowledge and feminist spirituality with experiential body wisdom (the conscious awareness of subtle body energies) to forge Woman Mysteries of the Ancient Future Sisterhood, a modern mystery school and Priestess lineage based in the devotional moving meditation she originated, The Tantric Dance of Feminine Power®: The Womb-Sourced Yoga of Feminine Wisdom. The Tantric Dance of Feminine Power evolved through decades of Vajra Ma's personal work from the innate power and wisdom of woman's body. It is the source work for many "tantric dance of" derivatives. She has developed demanding priestess training programs in her Woman Mysteries priestess lineage.

Aside from her own books, the student guide *The Tantric Dance of Feminine Power* and *From a Hidden Stream: The Natural Spiritual Authority of Woman*, Vajra Ma is featured in *Daughters of the Goddess*, an anthology of women's spiritual work in America and in *The Heart of the Sun: An Anthology in Exaltation of Sekhmet*. Her work has been the subject of scholarly papers presented at national conferences on religion.

Vajra Ma holds ministerial credential through the Temple of Diana, Madison, Wisconsin and has an extensive background in dance and vocal studies and theatre arts. She teaches with warmth, humor and a bedrock compassion. She resides in Sunny Valley, Oregon with her husband Wolfgang Nebmaier. She is a devout worshipper of chocolate.

Website: GreatGoddess.org

Chapter 40

In Service to the Divine Feminine

by Ven. Rev. Patrick McCollum

My work today in the world is guided by the voice of the Mother, and I, in each waking breath, am filled with Her Love. She serves as my guiding light and I am forever grateful for the amazing journey that She has taken me on and the unique places and incredible opportunities I get to participate in while in Her Service.

My first encounter with the Goddess happened when I was 15 years old. I was riding my motorcycle to my girlfriend's house when a drunk driver hit me. I was pronounced dead for five to six minutes, but in that time I was conscious of myself and had what is now called a near-death experience. In that experience, I went through a tunnel of light and saw the Goddess for the first time.

"What is it that you want from me?" I asked in her presence.

"I want you to serve me," she said, and so I agreed to do so.

Nothing in my life has been the same since that profound moment, and from that day on I have listened to what she tells me and I do it. It's that simple. And so here is my story:

My journey in connection to The Goddess led me to become a Wiccan Priest. The story of that initiation can be read about in my book, *Courting the Lady*, available at courtingthelady.com. It also led me on a path to work as a chaplain inside the nation's prison system where I began to see the huge amount of discrimination that is leveled against minority faiths and those of different races and cultures.

Through the Goddess's guidance I have been working for about seventeen years in the prisons on issues of religious freedom and minority faith rights. I have fought and won almost

2,000 separate discrimination cases during this work, not only in the prisons, but also in housing discrimination, women's rights, and employment. During these last seventeen years I have also successfully established minority faith alliances between Pagans, Hindus, Buddhists, Native Americans and other minority faith groups so that we could work together to shift the consciousness of our country toward pluralism and acceptance of the other. As a result, I am now regarded as one of the foremost experts on the topic of minority faith rights in our government institutions. Another aspect of my work toward advancing minority rights in prisons came about after I saw a movie called *Field of Dreams*. In the movie, a man builds a baseball field with the belief that if he builds it, all of the best baseball players in the country will come and play there. As I watched the movie, the Goddess's voice rang in my head. She said, "Build the field and they will all come!"

This instruction came as a powerful revelation to me. For years I had been battling discrimination issues in the prisons one by one, but what I wanted to do was to change the entire system all at once. But to do that, I would have to find a way to shift the consciousness of every administrator of every prison system in the United States. So I created the National Correctional Chaplaincy Directors Association (NCCDA), my "Ball Field," and invited the heads of every prison religion program in the United States to attend and join, and to my amazement, they all came! I partnered my association with the American Academy of Religion to bring religious scholars in to educate government chaplains so that they gain an accurate understanding of the beauty of each spiritual tradition. The work of the NCCDA has expanded now to include chaplains who work in hospitals and in our military which also have issues with discrimination. Now the NCCDA is in its tenth year, and it has been highly successful in advancing minority faith rights in prisons all across the country.

It was very painful for me to see how much discrimination

and lack of human kindness there was in our correctional facilities and government systems, and I realized that they were but a microcosm of the problems reflected in our larger world. My longing to create a path that heals this gaping wound motivated me to expand and take action on a larger scale. Using the *Field of Dreams* analogy, I decided to create a much larger worldwide playing field ... One which would teach a new guiding narrative for our planet. I realized that to bring peace to the world, I would need to create a new global story in which everyone fits in and everyone belongs, and one which everyone, no matter what their religion, race, or culture, would be comfortable buying into.

And so I went to work.

In October 2010, I was honored with an invitation to give a keynote speech in Parliament at The World Forum of Spiritual Culture in Astana, Kazakhstan. The venue included political and spiritual leaders from around the world. How I got invited, and everything that followed after, is nothing short of a miracle, but with the Goddess as my guide, I guess I should have expected it. The full speech can be read on the blog on my website, www.patrickmccollum.org. This speech was my first attempt to roll out my new planetary story, one that unites us all as family rather than dividing us. And it is a story not only of our own human connections to one another, but also a story that ties together all of creation and our interconnectedness and interdependence to survive.

My message in Kazakhstan created a resonance that touched many political and spiritual leaders at the time and ultimately ended up sending me on a three-year adventure that has been, and continues to be truly extraordinary.

Since my speech in Kazakhstan, I have shared my story and vision around the world. I have been initiated in and recognized by many spiritual traditions and gained the respect of many influential people. In India, I am known by many as the Venerable Shide Gyarpo, which means simply, the King of Peace.

This name was originally given to me by Rinpoche Lama Gangchen at Borobudur on the Island of Java, but it seems to have carried on to other places. There are many Hindus who now recognize me as a Pagan Hindu Saint, and I have been gifted with the name "Babaji," meaning "Revered Father." To Native Americans, whom I have made many connections with and for whom I have fought numerous battles for equality, I am known as "He Who Speaks With the Mother."

I have also been invited to many major world events as both a respected speaker and spiritual leader, representing The Goddess and world peace. Among the most recent was the Maha Kumbh Mela in 2013. The Kumbh Mela was a month-long event, and the 2013 Maha Kumbh Mela was the largest gathering of human beings in the history of our planet. An estimated 100 million people physically attended!

The event itself was dedicated to the three most sacred rivers and three sacred Goddesses of Hinduism: Yamuna, Saraswati, and Ganga. At the center of their intersection is a swirling vortex that creates a small island called the Sangam. This island is considered by Hindus to be the most sacred spot on Earth.

The Hindu traditions believe that bathing in the river during the Kumbh, after a group of chosen Saints have blessed and bathed in it, imparts a sacred energy that cleans up one's karma. What turned out to be an incredible privilege for me as a Priest of the Goddess at the Kumbh was that I was invited to do the opening blessing for the 100 million people. Following that, many significant world-changing things happened, and I played an integral part in many of those changes.

Here were some of those events:

I had the honor of being the distinguished speaker opposite the world-renowned environmentalist, feminist, and author, Vandana Shiva. This was a huge event packed with officials and press and I was the opening speaker. I addressed the audience on the part the Divine Feminine plays in nature, and called upon the men and women of the world to connect with that part of themselves in their work to preserve nature and our planet.

In particular, I called upon women to join together and use their power to create a shift in world consciousness and also reminded them that it is they who give birth to us all and who lay the first foundations for our children's behavior. I stressed that by exemplifying behavior that supports our planet and shows a reverence for those who inhabit it, women can change the course of the exploitation of our resources and help their children see their neighbors not as other, but instead as family.

Vandana Shiva and I now have a pact to work together for the rights of the environment and the rights of women around the world.

As a person connected to the Mother and our planet, I am especially concerned about the Earth itself and our treatment of it. Nature affects everyone and everything all over the entire planet. During the Kumbh Mela I was walking with a renowned Hindu Saint known as Swami Chidanand Saraswati. The Ganges before us was highly polluted and we were both very disturbed that such a sacred place could be the site of such irresponsible human behavior. As a result, Swamiji and I decided to go out on the Sangam dressed in our best spiritual attire, and pick up the trash in front of the millions of pilgrims present. We made huge piles of it all along the waterfront as we worked.

Typically in India, revered spiritual leaders would never do menial labor like this, and especially not something requiring direct contact with filth and trash. Such a thing is virtually unheard of. To see two highly respected holy men dressed in their traditional spiritual attire, raking cans and bottles and plastic out of piles of muck dripping with filth was a scene beyond their imagination. Pilgrims pointed at us and leaned out over their boats to get a better look. Many took out cameras and shot photos to take home.

I began to seek out the worst of the piles close to the pilgrims, and intentionally mucked right in front of them. Then after sorting out the trash from the mire, I would rinse my hands in the water next to the trash and then bless myself on the forehead. Then I would point to the trash pile and beckon them to join me. At first they were hesitant, but after a bit one or two jumped off the boat and joined in. Soon hundreds and then thousands joined in. The whole shore ended up being cleaned up of trash for the first time in modern history, and I knew we had hit a nerve. Then CNN showed up and sent our photo and story around the world, and the campaign went viral! Sometimes one is in exactly the right time and the right place to plant a seed that will grow beyond imagination, and this was one of those times.

Swamiji, I and others began to publicly share our thoughts in our speeches and such from that point on. "This river is sacred. Our planet is sacred; it is created by the Great Mother. We are in the Presence of three Goddesses. We can't let this be this way. We must take action to clean up the trash."

Shortly thereafter, I led a march with 5,000 school children to clean up every sacred river and forest in the world. That project also went global!

While I was in India, I had personally observed several direct incidents of the blatant disregard for women often heard of. I was infuriated by this and wanted to do something to change this problem. Then opportunity once again presented itself. Two major spiritual leaders and I, concerned about the poor treatment and lowly status of women in India, picked 100 "untouchable" fisherman's daughters to be part of a televised ceremony at the Kumbh Mela. The young women were considered to be the lowest on the totem pole of the class system. We brought them into our camp with lots of fanfare and press, and then showered them with rose petals and declared them to be Goddesses in front of everyone. The crowds cheered and the faces of those young women as they were honored in such a powerful way will remain forever etched in my memory and that of their community. This was a profound moment of change, and I had the incredible honor to play a direct part in it. The government of India, moved by the response, has committed to make this an annual event.

I have pictures of this on my website and the look on the faces of these young women is so beautiful. This event served to launch the opening of the Divine Shakti Festival, the celebration of the Divine Feminine at the Kumbh Mela.

All of these acts of service have been quite spontaneous. Our single act of mucking trash in front of all of the pilgrims has gone viral across the world. One TV station said this is the most significant event toward saving our planet in modern history.

I am reminded that a part of my work in the world is to weave the different religions and cultures of the world into a giant fabric that is not only strong and beautiful, but also one that is so tightly woven, yet still flexible. I see diversity as sacred and critical to the survival of the whole. There isn't an "us" and "them" or an "enemy out there;" there is only "all of us in this together," united in the origin of creation, the Luminous Light of Beginning.

My Goddess tradition sees human diversity as sacred. Imagine a stained glass window in a lofty Gothic cathedral. There are many different and diverse shapes and beautiful colors in any window, but the same white light shines through them all. I see the individual panes and colors as being all of us, and the light that shines through as being what many call Divinity. Should one pane be broken, the beauty of the whole will be lost, and from my perspective that is important to remember. And lest we all forget, the channels of black lead holding the colors together are even more critical than the panes themselves; for it is they which represent the intersections of each kindred piece. Break or loosen any joint that holds them together, and the whole thing eventually comes undone.

So it is with humanity. We are all so different, and in our different ways, we each contribute to the beauty of the whole.

Once we begin to insist that people be only one certain way, or have only certain accepted beliefs and practices, we have lost the essence of truth.

I would like to invite you to join with me in my work. I would like to invite you to see yourself as an essential unique piece of the puzzle, with gifts and talents critical to bringing goodness into our world. You can start today by making peace with your brothers and sisters, your parents and your friends. Stand firm in your spiritual path. Walk boldly in answer to the question, "What would Love do?" There is nothing you can't do if you put your mind to it. And together, we are unstoppable.

About Patrick McCollum ...

The Ven. Rev. Patrick McCollum has walked the Sacred Path since 1965. An initiate and High Priest of one of the nation's earliest Wiccan circles, he has worked diligently to keep alive the mysteries and magic passed down through this oral tradition for centuries. His work exemplifies the Feminine Divine and is dedicated toward bringing her message to all.

Ven. Rev. McCollum is an internationally recognized spiritual leader whose work toward human rights, social justice, and equality for all religions and spiritual traditions, transcends cultural, religious, and political barriers. He is the 2010 recipient of the Mahatma Gandhi Award for the Advancement of Pluralism. He was also named as a World Inner Peace Ambassador by Thai Buddhists and was given the title Venerable.

Ven. Rev. Patrick McCollum served as an advisor for the United States Commission on Civil Rights, and his comments and insights were forwarded in a report to both Congress and the President of the United States.

Ven. Rev. Patrick McCollum also serves as Development Director for the United Nations NGO, Children of the Earth, and helps oversee youth leadership projects around the world. In addition, he serves as the Minority Faith Issues Chair, for the

American Correctional Chaplains Association, and as Founder and Co-Chair of the National Correctional Chaplaincy Directors Association. He is a Board Member for four other non-profits.

Lastly, in 2012, he founded The Patrick McCollum Foundation, a non-profit organization promoting a sacred planetary vision that respects religious diversity and advances progress toward equality, human rights, equality for women, and world peace.

Website: www.patrickmccollum.org

Part V

In Memory of Layne Redmond

We are always together in the place of blessings, flourishing on the bank of the calm mind, filled with our song of satisfied creation, radiant in the pulse of all that is, of all that ever was, of all that ever will be ....We begin again, to begin at the beginning, to end again, to end at the beginning ...We begin to begin, to begin at the beginning, to end, to begin, to begin at the ending ...

– Layne Redmond

In Memory of Layne Redmond

(August 19, 1952 to October 28, 2013)

Layne Redmond was interviewed on Voices of the Sacred Feminine Radio several times and with each conversation she inspired, informed and uplifted me and my listeners. She made that bright red cord of interconnection between past and present, ancient and contemporary priestesses burn bright. In the final days of her life we discussed having her contribute to this anthology but time got away from us. Layne passed away on Monday, October 28, 2013 and she will be greatly missed by us all. Fortunately, with the help of Trish De Groot of Golden Seed Productions and Miranda Rondeau, this inclusion was possible. It is my great honor to pay tribute to our beloved teacher, wayshower and foremother who enabled us to glimpse the lives of women and priestesses as she spent her life sharing her research into *When the Drummers Were Women*, the title of her famous book.

Chapter 41

Why the Frame Drum Was at the Core of Ancient Mediterranean Spiritual Rites

by Layne Redmond

The first sound we hear is the pulse of our mother's blood. We vibrate to this primordial pulse even before we have ears to hear. All the eggs a woman will ever have form in her ovaries when she is a four-month-old fetus. This means that the sacred egg that developed into the person you are now, formed in your mother's ovary when she was growing in the womb of her mother. Each of us, male and female, spent five months in the womb of our grandmother, rocking to the beat of her blood. And our mother spent five months rocking to the pulse of her grandmother's blood, and her mother pulsed to the beat of her grandmother's blood. Back through the pulse of all the mothers and all the grandmothers, through the beat of the blood that we all share, this sound returns us to the preconscious state, to the inner structure of the mind, to the power and the source of who and what we actually are: the pulsing unified field of all consciousness existing everywhere, within everything, beyond past, present, or future. The sound of the drum has represented this primordial pulse of creation since the beginning of human ritual.

It is an ancient thought that rhythmic sound is at the root of all creation, that the world is structured by sound, and that life is rhythm. In India the influence of rhythm and tuning on consciousness has been explored for thousands of years and is considered a form of yoga – Nada Yoga. The primary concept of nada yoga is that ultimate reality emanates from a primordial first sound, the pulse, which echoes the twentieth-century scientists' concept of the Big Bang that created the universe. The frequencies of this root vibration create our physical world. As human beings, we are also emanations of this vibration and subject to the laws of sound. This archetypal pulse of consciousness vibrates within us as the sound of our own heart beating.

Every human being on the planet took form to the primal pulse and this sound has the power to draw us back to our earliest stirrings of awareness. This is why drumming has been at the core of shamanistic, religious, and transformative rites since Paleolithic times. The power of rhythmic sound returns us to the pre-socialized, unconditioned, and balanced state of awareness we experienced in the womb.

Rhythmic sound generated by a master drummer can captivate and move the conscious mind out of the way. This enables the facilitator, the shaman, priest/priestess or healer to deliver healing, integrating messages directly to deeper, less conscious realms of the mind that influence behavior. When participants in the process are also moving, chanting, breathing, and/or drumming, the therapeutic aspects of the experience are greatly magnified.

These kinds of spiritual and therapeutic rhythmic practices synchronize not only our minds and bodies, but also the two hemispheres of the brain. In a state of hemispheric synchronization, the capacities of both the left and the right brains function simultaneously. The mind becomes more concentrated, synthesizing information much more rapidly than normal. The conscious and unconscious levels of the mind communicate and integrate more easily. Emotions are easier to understand and transform. Insight quickens and creative intuition flourishes, giving us the ability to visualize and manifest ideas quickly. Rhythmic breathing and movement encourages alpha waves to become dominant in the brain, allowing muscle tension to be reduced. This predominance of alpha brain waves also creates the release of endorphins – potent brain chemicals that help us cope with pain and are part of the mechanism for dealing with and eliminating fear and anxiety. As stress fades, a more beneficial state of peaceful awareness can manifest. Scientists believe that hemispheric synchronization may be the neurological basis of transcendent states of consciousness and emotional feelings of spirituality.

These are some of the reasons that the frame drum was at the core of the ancient religious traditions and that women were so identified with this drum. Symbols, like the lotus, that represent creation, birth, or the womb, were often painted on the frame drum or the drums were painted red – the color of blood, the color of life. The frame drum, represented in the hands of the goddess or her priestess, illustrated her power to create the universe with one stroke on her drum – with one big beat of her primordial heart – everything vibrated into existence.

About Layne Redmond …
In the words of student Miranda Rondeau*…

Layne was diagnosed with cancer in June 2013 and given one to two months to live – and she lived these last few months to the fullest. She said it was the best days of her life. She was cremated October 31, 2013 and people globally gathered to honor and send her off with music and song.

She lived her last days with courage, grace, and determination to finish her film and the new edition of her book, *When the Drummers Were Women*, which has inspired thousands of women and men, and taught many to drum over the last twenty years. She has changed many lives along the way and opened a path for many women to drum, to create sacred ritual space and follow their dreams. She has left a legacy of resources for generations to come. She has written books, recorded many music projects, written articles, created instructional material on CD, DVD and YouTube, designed her own line of signature series drums with REMO, produced films, and has researched and collected thousands of images of women frame drummers, recovering their spiritual historic significance. She was known as a Master frame drummer, teacher, author, historian, educator, mythologist, composer, recording artist, filmmaker, world traveler, yogini and Bee Priestess. She will be greatly missed. We are in deep gratitude for the path she has paved for so many along the way.

Layne, may your flight home be full of peace, love and light. May you always be in the hearts of all those who have been touched by you.

Website: www.layneredmond.com

Conclusion

by Rev. Dr. Karen Tate

We have to take responsibility for our own education. We must have the courage to rethink and challenge everything we've been taught at our dinner table, from the pulpit and in the educational institutions we attended, because patriarchy has infiltrated every aspect of our inner and outer lives. It is truly incredible what we have accepted as normal for so long.

Sadly, "bible ecology" has given men license to destroy the planet and exploit women and workers across the globe. Species are going extinct every day and Mother Earth continues to be assaulted, poisoned, and fracked. The Bible, along with other patriarchal religions, is used to justify violence, racism, homophobia and the income inequality so many are suffering from. For far too long we have accepted domination, discrimination, abuse and exploitation without challenge.

It is imperative both genders seek and find the seeds that might blossom into a *new normal,* and our Mother has always been there giving us the clues. Answers can be found in ideals of the Sacred Feminine, within the mythology of some goddesses, and Divine Feminine archetypes or role models. It is vital we give ourselves permission to re-evaluate patriarchy's influence and also reinterpret what patriarchy may demonize or marginalize because it challenges the rich and powerful or the ruling class and status quo. We must resist fear-based rhetoric as we determine for ourselves what is socially, morally and legally acceptable.

Yes, our Mother has always been there, sometimes in the shadows, other times in the bright light, pointing the way. Why don't we plant those seeds she offers and see what fruit might blossom? What has been swept beneath the rug and hidden from us may actually better serve the most of us and create a more sustainable world, alongside the Sacred Masculine, in true partnership.

And this is exactly what my wonderful guests have been doing over the years, pointing to the light and shadows cast by our Mother. I'm so proud to have the opportunity to provide a platform for these passionate and dedicated wayshowers who have shared their wisdom on Voices of the Sacred Feminine Radio, some of which has punctuated their message in this book. All these women and men, inspired by ideals of the Sacred Feminine, are offering us new ways to negotiate our inner and outer landscape – and we must use all the tools from Her sacred tool kit to save ourselves and our beloved Gaia.

As we will it, so shall it be.
As we will it, so shall it be.
As we will it, so shall it be.

About Rev. Dr. Karen Tate

Having discovered the Feminine Face of God and what that means for women, men and the species of Mother Earth, Karen became an emissary of the Sacred Feminine, combining spirituality, feminism and women's empowerment to offer the world a real alternative to the domination and oppression of patriarchy – the rule of men and the authoritarian father.

As an independent scholar, speaker, radio show host, published author, sacred tour leader and social justice activist, Karen's work for three decades has been inspired by her interests and passion for travel, comparative religions, ancient cultures, women's herstory and the resurging interest in the rise of the Feminine Consciousness. Her voice combines feminism, spirituality and uplifting women, all of which inter-mingle within her projects resulting in her being named one of the Top Thirteen Most Influential Women in Goddess Spirituality and a Wisdom Keeper of the Goddess Spirituality Movement.

Her first book, *Sacred Places of Goddess: 108 Destinations*, has garnered prestigious endorsements, while her second book, *Walking an Ancient Path: Rebirthing Goddess on Planet Earth*, was a finalist in the National Best Books of 2008 Awards. Her newest book, *Goddess Calling: Inspirational Messages and Meditations of Sacred Feminine Liberation Thealogy*, out in the spring of 2014, is already getting rave reviews from her mentors and peers.

Tate's work has been highlighted in the *Los Angeles Times*, *Seattle Times* and other major newspapers. She is interviewed regularly by the media and has hosted her own internet radio show for the last nine years, Voices of the Sacred Feminine Radio, considered a treasure trove of insight and wisdom for our time. Her work has segued into writing, producing and consulting on projects which bring the ideals and awareness of the Sacred Feminine into the mainstream world through television and film. She can be seen in the new documentary, *Femme: Women Healing the World*, produced by Emmanuel Itier of Wonderland Entertainment and actress Sharon Stone.

Karen has been married to husband, Roy, who she describes as *the wind beneath her wings* for the last 30 years and she credits him for his love and support behind the scenes enabling her to be so active in all phases of her work.

Website: www.karentate.com

Voices of the Sacred Feminine Radio –

http://www.blogtalkradio.com/voicesofthesacredfeminine

Contact Karen at: ancientcultures@ca.rr.com

References

Introduction – by Rev. Dr. Karen Tate

http://thegreenfuse.org/ecofem.htm makes reference to the four pillars of patriarchy.

Chapter 2 – Lady Liberty: Goddess of Freedom by Selena Fox

An earlier version of this article appeared in *CIRCLE Magazine*.

Aldington, Richard & Ames, Delano, translators (1968). *New Larousse Encyclopedia of Mythology*. New York: Prometheus Press, page 216.

Capitol Visitor Center:
http://www.visitthecapitol.gov/sites/default/files/documents/content/brochure/2650/statue-freedomen.pdf

Connery, Sam. "Taking Liberties with an American Goddess," in July 1996 issue of *Smithsonian Magazine*. Washington, DC: Smithsonian Institution.

Cox, William A. (1927). "The Goddess of Freedom How Lofty She."

Dale-Green, Patricia (1963). *Cult of the Cat*. New York: Weathervane Books, page 47.

Encyclopedia Mythica. "Libertas." Online at
http://www/pantheon.org/.

Fox, Selena (1988). *Goddess Communion Rituals and Meditations*. Barneveld, WI: Circle Publications, pages 9–10.

Fox, Selena. "Freedom with Lady Liberty," in Spring 1991 issue of *CIRCLE Magazine*. Barneveld, WI: Circle Publications, page 7.

Fryd, Vivien Green. "Political Compromise in Public Art: Thomas Crawford's Statue of Freedom." Online at:
http://www.people.virginia.edu/~tsawyer/DRBR/fryd/fryd.html

Green City Network. "Tiananmen Memorial." Online at:

http://www.greencity.com/tianemem.htm

Immigration website. "The Statue of Liberty History & Creation." http://library.thinkquest.org/20619/Stsym.html

Levins, Hoag. "The New Jersey State Seal." http://www.levins.com/ik9.html

Monaghan, Patricia (1997). *The New Book of Goddesses & Heroines*. St. Paul, MN: Llewellyn, pages 124–125, 195.

National Park Service (USA). "Statue of Liberty History." http://www.nps.gov/stli/index.htm

New York State Senate. "State Seal." http://www.nysenate.gov/state-seal

Owens, Michael R. H. "Lady Liberty: The Changing Face of Freedom." Online at: http://xroads.virginia.edu/~CAP/LIBERTY/lady_frm.html

Paine, Thomas. "Liberty Tree." http://greatseal.com/liberty/libertytree.html

Scullard, H. H. (1981). *Festivals and Ceremonies of the Roman Republic*. Ithaca, NY: Cornell University Press, pages 101–102, 197.

Simpson, D. P. (1960). Cassell's New Latin Dictionary. New York: Funk & Wagnalls, page 344.

Statue of Liberty–Ellis Island Foundation, Inc. http://statueofliberty.org/Statue_History.html

Zimmerman, J. E. (1971). *Dictionary of Classical Mythology*. New York: Bantam, page 288.

Chapter 3 – Persephone Returns: Worshipping the Divine Mother and Daughter by Rev. Shirley Ann Ranck, PhD

1. Spretnak, Charlene. *Lost Goddesses of Early Greece*. Boston: Beacon Press, 1981.

Chapter 5 – Sekhmet: Powerful Woman by Candace C. Kant, PhD

1. Anne Key and Candace C. Kant. "Sekhmet The Incomparable

One: Ancient Goddess of Egypt." In *Heart of the Sun: An Anthology in Exaltation of Sekhmet*, edited by Candace C. Kant and Anne Key. Las Vegas, NV: Goddess Ink, Ltd., 2011. Pp. 7–8.

2. "Many Names of Sekhmet." In *Heart of the Sun: An Anthology in Exaltation of Sekhmet*, edited by Candace C. Kant and Anne Key. Las Vegas, NV: Goddess Ink, Ltd., 2011. Pp. 32–36.

3. Roynan Steres. "Daughter of the Sun." In *Heart of the Sun: An Anthology in Exaltation of Sekhmet* edited by Candace C. Kant and Anne Key. Las Vegas, NV: Goddess Ink, Ltd., 2011. P. 13.

4. Candace C. Kant. "Sekhmet's Charge." In *Heart of the Sun: An Anthology in Exaltation of Sekhmet*, edited by Candace C. Kant and Anne Key. Las Vegas, NV: Goddess Ink, Ltd., 2011. Pp. 83–84.

Chapter 10 – Motherhood and Power by Barbara G. Walker

Excerpted from *Man Made God* by Barbara G. Walker. Stellar House, 2010.

Chapter 14 – Honoring Goddesses Reawakens Women-Honoring Multiculturalism by Elizabeth Fisher

1. *Rise Up and Call Her Name: A Woman-honoring Journey into Global Earth-based Spiritualities*, a course written and edited by the author of this article, was published by the Unitarian Universalist Women's Federation in 1995 and reissued in 2007. This thirteen-session curriculum explores the qualities and meaning of a variety of female deities from around the world. Taken by thousands of groups and individuals, this journey is both inspiring and life changing.

2. Laura Amazzone, *Goddess Durga and Sacred Female Power* (Hamilton Books: 2010).

3. Marija Gimbutas, *The Civilization of the Goddess: The World of Old Europe* (San Francisco: HarperSanFrancisco, 1991).

4. Christine Downing, *The Goddess: Mythological Images of the Feminine* (New York, NY: Crossroad Publishing Co., 1981).

Chapter 15 – Healing, Freedom and Transformation through the Sacred Feminine by Jann Aldredge-Clanton

1. Jann Aldredge-Clanton, *Breaking Free: The Story of a Feminist Baptist Minister* (Austin, TX: Eakin Press, 2002).

2. Jann Aldredge-Clanton, *In Whose Image?: God and Gender* (New York: Crossroad, 1990); revised and expanded edition (Crossroad, 2001). *In Search of the Christ-Sophia: An Inclusive Christology for Liberating Christians* (Mystic, CT: Twenty-Third Publications, 1995; Austin, TX: Eakin Press, 2004).

3. Jann Aldredge-Clanton, *Praying with Christ-Sophia: Services for Healing and Renewal* (Mystic, CT: Twenty-Third Publications, 1996; Eugene, OR: Wipf & Stock, 2007).

4. Jann Aldredge-Clanton, *Inclusive Hymns for Liberating Christians* (Austin, TX: Eakin Press, 2006), and *Inclusive Hymns for Liberation, Peace, and Justice* (Austin, TX: Eakin Press, 2011).

5. Jann Aldredge-Clanton, *Seeking Wisdom: Inclusive Blessings and Prayers for Public Occasions* (Eugene, OR: Wipf & Stock, 2010).

6. Jann Aldredge-Clanton, *Changing Church: Stories of Liberating Ministers* (Eugene, OR: Cascade Books, 2011), and http://www.jannaldredgeclanton.com/blog/.

7. *Changing Church*, p. 340.

8. *Hokmah* is the word for "Wisdom" in the Hebrew Scriptures.

9. *Ruah* is the Hebrew word for "Spirit" in the book of Genesis and elsewhere in the Hebrew Scriptures.

10. See my book *In Whose Image?: God and Gender* for a detailed account of female divine names and images in the Hebrew and Christian Scriptures and in Christian history.

11. Amnesty International, "Broken Bodies, Shattered Minds: Torture and Ill Treatment of Women" (2001).

12. United Nations General Assembly, "In-Depth Study on All Forms of Violence against Women: Report of the Secretary General, 2006," A/61/122/Add.1.6 (July 2006).

13. The United Nations Population Fund, The State of World Population 2000 report, "Lives Together, Worlds Apart: Men and Women in a Time of Change" (2000).

14. Nicholas D. Kristof and Sheryl WuDunn, *Half the Sky: Turning Oppression into Opportunity for Women Worldwide* (New York: Knopf, 2009), p. xvii.

15. Louise Arbour, United Nations High Commissioner for Human Rights, "International Women's Day: Laws and 'Low Intensity' Discrimination against Women" (March 8, 2008).

Chapter 18 – Why Would a Man Search for the Goddess? by Tim Ward

1. Dorothy Dinnerstein, *The Mermaid and the Minotaur*, p. 88.

2. Carl Jung, "Marriage as a Psychological Relationship," *The Development of Personality*, CW 17, par.338.

3. *Gilgamesh* (Penguin Mentor edition), p. 43.

Chapter 20 – Goddesses, Dildos and Jesus by Dr. David C.A. Hillman

1. Hesiod, *Theogony* 1–8. Hesiod (2007). Hesiod: Volume I, *Theogony. Works and Days. Testimonia*. Translated by G.W. Most (Cambridge: Harvard University Press).

2. *Orphic Hymn to Athena*, 32.7. Athanassakis, A.N. & Wolkow, B.M. (eds.) (2013). *The Orphic Hymns* (Baltimore: Johns Hopkins University Press).

3. Aeschylus, *Prometheus Bound* 794. Aeschylus (2009). Aeschylus, I, *Persians. Seven against Thebes. Suppliants. Prometheus Bound. Testimonia*. Translated by Alan H. Sommerstein (Cambridge: Harvard University Press.).

4. *Homeric Hymns* 108. Homeric Hymns (2003). *Homeric Hymns. Homeric Apocrypha. Lives of Homer*. Translated by M.L. West

(Cambridge: Harvard University Press)

5. Augustine, *De Civitate Dei Contra Paganos* 7.24. Augustine (1963). Augustine: *City of God*, Volume II, Books 4–7. Translated by W.M. Green (Cambridge: Harvard University Press).

6. *nec virginitas adimatur*, 7.24. Augustine (1963). Augustine: *City of God*, Volume II, Books 4–7. Translated by W.M. Green (Cambridge: Harvard University Press)

7. Ovid, *Fasti* 4:151–4. Ovid (1963). *Ovid: Fasti*. Translated by G.P. Gould & J.G. Frazer (Cambridge: Harvard University Press).

8. *De Civ. Dei* 7.24. Augustine (1963). Augustine: *City of God*, Volume II, Books 4–7. Translated by W.M. Green (Cambridge: Harvard University Press)

9. Smithers and Burton trans. *Priapeia* 24. Burton, Sir Richard & Smithers, L.C. (1995). *Priapeia* (Hertfordshire: Wordsworth Classic Erotica).

10. Juvenal, *Satires* 6:314–19. Juvenal (2004). *Juvenal and Persius*. Translated by S.M. Braund (Cambridge: Harvard University Press.).

11. Prudentius, *Peristephanon* 13.21–26. Prudentius (1953). Prudentius: *Against Symmachus* 2. *Crowns of Martyrdom. Scenes from History. Epilogue.* Translated by H.J. Thomson (Cambridge: Harvard University Press).

12. Prudentius, *Peristephanon* 13.57–8. Prudentius (1953). Prudentius: *Against Symmachus* 2. *Crowns of Martyrdom. Scenes from History. Epilogue.* Translated by H.J. Thomson (Cambridge: Harvard University Press).

13. Prudentius, *Symmachus* 1.115. Prudentius (1949). *Prudentius*, Volume 1. Translated by H.J. Thomson (Cambridge: Harvard University Press).

14. Libanius, *Oration* 24. Libanius. (1963). *Libanius: Selected Orations*, Volume I, Julianic Orations Books 4–7. Translated by A.F. Norman (Cambridge: Harvard University Press).

15. Mark 14:51–52. New American Standard Bible (2002) (Grand Rapids: The Zondervan Corporation).
16. Mark 14:3. New American Standard Bible (2002) (Grand Rapids: The Zondervan Corporation).

Chapter 24 – The Advent of Patriarchy
by Cristina Biaggi, PhD

* From her book, *The Rule of Mars: Readings on the Origins, History and Impact of Patriarchy*

The Rule of Mars: Readings on the Origins, History and Impact of Patriarchy includes contributions from archaeologists, anthropologists, poets, and academics representing different countries and belonging to the major races of humankind. Biaggi enlisted contributions by designing a questionnaire which she sent to her mailing lists prompting recipients to undertake three tasks:

1 – A historical examination of the origins of patriarchy, when and where it occurred, the events that precipitated it and how it expanded.

2 – An examination of the role patriarchy plays in our contemporary world situation.

3 – An examination of why patriarchy emerged as a cultural paradigm.

In conclusion, her book is divided into five sections:

- Origins of Patriarchy, examines how and when and why one gender managed to be dominant over the other.
- Ramifications of Patriarchy, includes papers that have a more philosophical bent and/or examine the contemporary impact of patriarchy.
- Philosophical Perspectives, includes opinion pieces founded in fact instead of personal opinion.
- The Personal is Political, includes papers that are more personal, feelings about patriarchy rather than thoughts about patriarchy.
- Pathways for Change, includes papers that look to the

future and the possibility of change.

Chapter 25 – The Essence of Good Business: Companies That Care by Riane Eisler

* This article is adapted from Riane Eisler, *The Real Wealth of Nations: Creating a Caring Economics* (San Francisco: Berrett-Koehler, 2007, 2008). Copyright 2013.

Burud, Sandra, and Marie Tumolo, *Leveraging the New Human Capital*. Mountain View, Calif: Davies-Black, 2004.

FSB/WINNING WORKPLACES, Best Bosses 2004: Distinguished Finalists. Retrieved from http://www.winningworkplaces.org/bestbossesaward/previouswin_2004_fnl.php

The Retention Dilemma. Hay Group, 2001. Retrieved from www.haygroup.com/library/index.asp

Santa Barbara United Way survey, 2000. Retrieved from http://www.unitedwaysb.org/worklife.html

Circadian survey, 2003. Retrieved from http://www.circadian.com/media/Release-03Aug12.html

Life's Work: Generational Attitudes toward Work and Life Integration. Radcliffe Institute for Advanced Study, 2000. Retrieved from www.Radcliffe.edu/research/pubpol/lifeswork.pdf

The Most Important Work-Life Related Studies. Work and Family Connection, 2005.

Bright Horizons Child Care Trends, 2002. Retrieved from http://www.childcareinhealthcare.org/employer-sponsored-child-care.php

http://www. familiesandwork.org/

Chapter 26 – Antidote to Terrorism by Jean Shinoda Bolen, MD

1.   Eisler, Riane. *The Chalice and the Blade* (San Francisco: Harper & Row, 1967).

2. Bolen, Jean Shinoda. *Urgent Message from Mother* (Boston: Conari Press, 2005).

3. Bolen, Jean Shinoda. *The Millionth Circle* (Berkeley: Conari Press, Boston: Redwheel/Weiser, 1999).

4. Sheldrake, Rupert. *A New Science of Life* (Los Angeles: Tarcher, 1981).

5. Gladwell, Malcolm, *The Tipping Point* (Boston: Little Brown, 2000, 2002)

6. Tannen, Deborah. *You Just Don't Understand Me: Women and Men in Conversation* (New York: Ballantine, 1990).

7. Taylor, S.E., Klein, L.C., Lewis, B.P., Gruenewalt, T.L., Gurung, R.A.R., & Updegraff, J.A. "Female Responses to Stress: Tend and Befriend, Not Fight or Flight," *Psychological Review*, 107(3), (2000).

Chapter 27 – Making the Case: Women, Pagans and Those Valuing Religious Freedom Should Vote Democratic by Gus diZerega

1. http://www.washingtonpost.com/blogs/she-the-people/wp/2012/10/24/is-mourdocks-comment-more-extreme-than-akins/

2. http://www.huffingtonpost.com/2013/10/11/ted-cruz-birth-control_n_4084857.html

3. http://rhrealitycheck.org/article/2011/10/13/house-passes-hr-358-the-let-women-die-act-of-2011/

4. http://www.thedailybeast.com/articles/2012/02/09/the-contraception-fight.html

5. http://healthland.time.com/2012/10/05/study-free-birth-control-significantly-cuts-abortion-rates/

6. http://videocafe.crooksandliars.com/heather/rep-cliff-stearns-admits-he-believes-women

7. http://www.huffingtonpost.com/tobias-barrington-wolff/virginia-ultrasound-bill_b_1278832.html

8. http://www.huffingtonpost.com/2012/03/27/republican-lies-

womens-bodies_n_1374027.html

9. http://obsidianwings.blogs.com/obsidian_wings/2006/06/
   the_hpv_vaccine.html

10. http://www.alternet.org/story/37485/why_the_religious_
    right_fights_cancer_prevention

11. http://www.washingtonpost.com/wp-srv/national/daily/
    oct99/abortion9.htm

12. Jean Reith Schroedel, *Is the Fetus a Person? A Comparison of the
    Policies across Fifty States* (Ithaca, NY: Cornell University
    Press, 2000).

13. Harvey C. Mansfield. *Manliness* (New Haven: Yale University
    Press, 2006. 66.

14. Michael Ledeen, *Machiavelli on Modern Leadership: Why
    Machiavelli's Iron Rules Are as Timely and Important Today as
    Five Centuries Ago* (Truman Talley Books (St. Martin's Press),
    1999). 89–90.

15. http://www.ethicsdaily.com/southern-baptist-scholar-links-
    spouse-abuse-to-wives-refusal-to-submit-to-their-husbands-
    cms-12832

16. http://www.npr.org/templates/story/story.php?storyId=
    120746516

17. http://www.truth-out.org/buzzflash/commentary/item/
    16581-fundamentalists-derail-more-important-messages

18. http://thehill.com/blogs/ballot-box/senate-races/263761-nrsc-
    chairman-cornyn-defends-mourdock-after-abortion-
    comments

19. http://www.truthdig.com/report/item/the_radical_christian
    _right_and_the_war_on_government_20131006

20. http://www.valleynewslive.com/story/19900791/senator-
    says-%20bishop-crossed-the-line-between-religion-politics

Chapter 30 – Gifting and Peace by Genevieve Vaughan

1. Mann, Barbara Alice (2000). *Iroquois Women: The Gantowisas*.
   New York, Peter Lang.

2. Waring, Marilyn (1999) [1979] *Counting for Nothing: What men value and what women are worth.* Toronto, University of Toronto Press.

Chapter 39 – The Natural Spiritual Authority of Woman by Vajra Ma

1. Mary Daly's term.
2. *American Heritage Dictionary,* Second College Edition, 1982.
3. *American Heritage Dictionary,* Second College Edition, 1982
4. Refers to *From a Hidden Stream: The Natural Spiritual Authority of Woman* [A Primer for the Future of Humanity] by this author. Available from her website, www.GreatGoddess.org

Chapter 41 – Why the Frame Drum Was at the Core of Ancient Mediterranean Spiritual Rites by Layne Redmond

*Miranda Rondeau has been a long-standing student and support to Layne Redmond since 1994. A singer, musician, Remo frame drum artist and teacher, Miranda chants in a devotional language of her own. She facilitates Vocal Play shops, Frame Drum Workshops and Music Sound Bath Journeys. She also initiated the online presence of Women Frame Drumming via social media. http://www.facebook.com/MirandaRondeauMusic and http://www.facebook.com/WomenFrameDrumming

CHANGE
MAKERS
BOOKS

Changemakers publishes books for individuals committed to transforming their lives and transforming the world. Our readers seek to become positive, powerful agents of change. Changemakers books inform, inspire, and provide practical wisdom and skills to empower us to create the next chapter of humanity's future.

Please visit our website at www.changemakers-books.com